Not With My Life I Don't

Preventing Your Suicide and That of Others

D0061315

Howard Rosenthal, Ed.D.

 ACCELERATED DEVELOPMENT INC.
Publishers
Muncie　　　　　Indiana

𝒩ot With My Life 𝒥 Don't

Preventing Your Suicide and That of Others

1 2 3 4 5 6 7 8 9 10

Printed in the United States of America

Technical Development: Virginia Cooper
Tanya Dalton
Delores Kellogg
Marguerite Mader
Sheila Sheward

Library of Congress Cataloging in Publication Data

Rosenthal, Howard, 1952-
    Not with my life I don't.

    Summary: Discusses the causes of suicide and how
it may be prevented. Also examines suicidal behavior
and how a person's will may be used to save his or
her life.
    1. Suicide—United States—Juvenile literature.
2. Suicide—Prevention—United States—Juvenile
literature. 3. Teenagers—United States—Suicidal
behavior—Juvenile literature. 4. Self-help
techniques—Juvenile literature. [1. Suicide.
2. Suicide—Prevention] I. Title.
HV6548.U5R67   1988   362.2   88-70011
ISBN 0-915202-77-8

ACCELERATED DEVELOPMENT Inc., PUBLISHERS
3400 Kilgore Avenue, Muncie, IN 47304
(317) 284-7511

ACKNOWLEDGMENTS

This book stands by itself as a landmark in the field of suicidology because it marks the first comprehensive attempt at producing a self-help guide for self-destructive individuals as well as a handbook for helping others who may be prone to harm themselves. Due to its novel format, the advice and support I received from others was crucial. Nevertheless, I shall take responsibility for all the information contained herein.

Foremost, I would like to acknowledge with warm appreciation my wife Patricia, whose careful and faithful assistance was invaluable in every possible respect. Her input was priceless and literally made the ideas presented come alive. I also would like to thank my entire family for their continued support throughout the project.

I would be remiss if I did not mention the ardent work of Angela Randazzo, who helped compile the material.

The fine suggestions of Peggy Tyler and Nancy Thurman were instrumental and worthy of mention.

Thanks go to Anne Steinberg, who repeatedly emphasized that my ideas had merit and needed to appear in print.

In addition, my appreciation goes to the wonderful hotline volunteers at Life Crisis Services, Inc., in St. Louis, Missouri. They were, indeed, a prime source of inspiration.

I also am grateful to my wonderful typists, Molly Lu Vonland and Kathryn Workman.

And lastly, my publisher, Dr. Joseph Hollis, must be commended for making the information contained in these pages available to distressed individuals, their friends, and mental health workers.

TABLE OF CONTENTS

1

AN ARROGANT
STATEMENT BY
THE AUTHOR

Seemingly every time you gear up to read a self-improvement book nowadays, the author, in all his or her arrogance, flatly states that the work contains the most important material you will ever read. Those with a flair for diplomacy, would merely call this a gross exaggeration. I simply prefer to call it a lie.

Truthfully now, books on *Tuning Your Toyota* or *Cooking Cantonese* variety can hardly be considered life or death matters. (Though we certainly need more books of this sort, and I am sure I would be the first on my block to purchase and read such titles!)

Having exposed the old worn out cliche "this is the most important book you will ever read" for what it really is (a gross exaggeration at best) I am going to say forthrightly that this book genuinely is the most important one you may ever come across. Sound paradoxical? Not really.

You see, this is a self-help book about suicide. A terrible tragedy which does not have to happen. So, if you have ever thought about harming yourself, don't bother asking for whom was this book written; it was written for you. Here, in these very pages, you will find help for your unhappy state of mind and some sage advice if you have any suicidal friends, children, or students. If your problems are primarily of a psychological nature, you will see why suicide is never, ever the solution to your problems. Always a better solution exists—I'll stake my reputation on it.

Part of the reason I have been so straightforward in the first few paragraphs is to convince you of my sincerity and to let you know that I always will tell it like it is. I will explain precisely what you need to know in order to eliminate your troubled condition, and I promise I won't water it down, nor will I sugar coat it. I have written this book as if your life depended on it, because it could. When you finish this book you will probably furrow your brow, close the cover, toss it back on your dresser top and clamor: "You know, by golly, he's right. Not with my life I don't."

Since I personally hate to read long, drawn-out, irrelevant or boring tomes, I have vowed to keep this book very short, lively, and exciting to read. Perhaps you falsely believe nobody cares what happens to you. Well think about it, I care or I wouldn't have taken the time or energy to write this book. And you, well you care, or you wouldn't be reading this book. Together we can do it. I know so, because I have helped hundreds of other people just like yourself. Today, many of these people find that believing they ever contemplated taking their own lives as hard to comprehend.

What good is a perfectly tuned Toyota that purrs like a kitten or some mouth-watering Cantonese cuisine if you're not around to enjoy either? Is this the most important book you'll ever read? At least one arrogant author has the guts to say: "You bet it is!"

2

THE INFORMATION
NO ONE SHOULD
BE DYING TO KNOW

Over 700 pairs of eager eyes of all ages were glued to me as I slowly, yet, dramatically eased away from the walnut podium which graced the huge community lecture hall.

"The greatest secret in the human race," I told them, "is that the suicidal person doesn't really want to die."

The audience was completely taken aback. They were shocked, stunned, and downright surprised. You could hear a pin drop. No, actually, they were quieter than that. So quiet, you could hear an ant inching its way across the deep pile burgundy carpet which covered the floor of the lecture hall.

I didn't need the powers of a mind reader to know that the audience was wondering how a suicidal person could not want to die. Somehow that never quite makes sense to people.

I continued, "The human body innately wants to live. If you scrape your hand or foot, your body will immediately initiate a healing process. If you have a cold, the flu, or internal problems, your body will produce antibodies, and sometimes increase the white blood cell count to help fight the illness."

"Now, what would happen right this moment if I would begin holding my breath in an attempt to kill myself?" The crowd responded with a myriad of answers which collectively rumbled. "You're absolutely correct," I responded, raising my voice as I spoke, "I would pass out, and then, I would automatically begin breathing again. THE HUMAN BODY WANTS TO LIVE!"

I stood motionless as I slowly combed the rows of the lecture hall with an intense burning stare. "Some of the best evidence comes from suicide notes. Typical suicide note, folks:

Dear Mary,

I hate your guts. I'm going to jump off the Acme Bridge.

Love,
Bob"

A roar of laughter spreads throughout the crowd.

"Come on, people. The guy doesn't know whether he wants to wine or dine her with a steak dinner, or if he wants to take a flying leap off that darn bridge, and end it all."

(I often find it necessary to interject a healthy dose of humor into my lectures, since suicide is such an important, serious subject—so important, I can't afford to have people doze off, mentally balance their checkbook, or catch up on their weekly daydreams.)

Since I am blessed with the remarkable ability to ramble-on for hours on end, I decided to implement a little self-control and reinforce my point utilizing an actual example. People can plug into stories about people. They often succeed in making a point that endless theorizing fails to drive home.

"Every other Wednesday night, I run what is known in the trade as a survivors group. Does anybody in the audience know what a survivors group is?"

The crowd looked at me like a bunch of stoic Indians. Seems like nobody likes to speak up in such a large group of people and take a chance on being wrong. Actually, such self-defeating behavior stems from giving too much of Sam Hill about what others think of you, and that can cause some real problems, but more about that topic later.

"Come on now, I'm grading on audience participation. O.K., let me put it another way. Since nobody knows what a survivors group is, can somebody guess what it is?"

"Ah, that's a little better," I responded, as hand upon hand went up until the room looked like a picket fence factory.

"Yes, Sir. The gentleman in the third row with the royal blue sweater."

"Well, sounds like it would probably be a group for men and women who tried it and failed."

"No, that would make too much sense and nothing makes sense in the social sciences. Come to think of it, maybe that's why you have to go to school so long to study the field. Actually, the group you described would be branded a suicide attempters group. A survivors group consists of individuals who have lost a friend, relative, or loved one through suicide.

"During our last session of the group a young woman of 22 related the followig tale of woe. The woman's 19-year-old husband, Cliff,* felt things were piling up and he just couldn't take it any more. So into the garage went the family's Chevrolet station wagon, and down went the garage door. Incidentally, I'm told this is a very painful way to go despite what logic might tell us."

"Anyway, Cliff really wanted to get the job done so he flipped off the key for a moment, jumped out of the car, and grabbed a long line

---

*All the names and identifying details of the incidents depicted in this book have been carefully altered to protect the true identity of the actual individuals. Keep in mind, nevertheless, that all the stories are 100% true.

of plastic tubing he was utilizing for a construction project. He, then, carefully shoved the tube into the exhaust pipe and routed it into the front driver's window. Again, he fired the engine up. But, hey, this guy really wanted to get the job done. He spied their flexible garden hose and wedged it over the tubing he had already run through the window to provide an even more elaborate airtight seal such that even more carbon monoxide could invade his lungs. Up went the window again and the engine once more began churning. Before long, however, Cliff jumped out of the car to improve on his nearly foolproof plan. In order to initiate the coup de grace he threw a tarpaulin car cover over the vehicle and fired her up for the last time."

"I'm truly sorry to say, people, that this is not one of those lived-happily-ever-after stories. When the poor young woman returned home from work, she found her husband dead in the driver's seat...the ignition key off, Cliff leaning against the door... his hand on the door lock which was about three-fourths of the way up. At literally the last minute Cliff copped out. Even someone who seemingly wanted to die as vehemently as Cliff, really wanted to live. When he turned off the motor and went for the door lock, it was too late."

The audience became very silent. Once more I could hear our proverbial ant making his sojourn across the countryside of the lecture hall.

"You know, recently some research has been going on regarding NDE, which is the alphabet soup for Near Death Experience. A near death experience might be described as a situation in which the doctor may actually believe the patient is dead. Truly a brush with death of the highest sort. The amazing fact that shrouds NDEs is that persons who have undergone this phenomenon have less anxiety about death. Let me say that in another way: the person actually seems to fear death less than he or she did previously. Can anyone guess how such a finding would relate to suicide?" I was extremely careful to use the word "guess" this time around so I would get some audience response.

"Yes ma'am."

"Well, it just makes sense that such individuals would be more likely to kill themselves. Once the fear is gone there is a better chance you'll do it."

"Right, logically that seems to make sense, though research seems to show just the opposite. You see, here is the man or woman who comes so close to death that he or she can almost reach out and shake hands with their maker, and what happens is that the person begins to value life more. And with this new philosophical orientation comes change. Perhaps, he/she gets out of a high paying unfulfilling job and into a more humanistic form of employment. Maybe he/she becomes more accepting and less critical of the family. Appreciation of life increases and the tendency to take one's own life lessens."

A perplexed young woman in the front row squirms in her seat as she blushes a bit and sheepishly raises her right hand.

"Yes."

"Um, I guess I'm kind of lost. I was sent here by my high school paper to do an article on suicide and well . . . I don't understand. If most suicidal people don't wish to die why do they try to harm themselves?"

"A superb question indeed! You should go far in the field of journalism if you decide that's your cup of tea."

"The object of suicide is to stop thinking. The act of taking one's own life is intended to eliminate a catastrophic, horrendous, terrible mental pain which is seemingly worse than any physical pain one could endure."

I raised my voice in order to be certain this package of knowledge would reach out and grab each and everyone in the audience by the earlobes.

"When things pile up; when stress becomes overwhelming; when you look around and see no exit and thinking hurts; I mean, when it really truly is just too darn excruciatingly painful to think, that's when an individual toys with the idea of taking his or her own life."

"Let me tell you a little trade secret that may come as a bit of a shock to those of you who still find it less palatable to believe that the suicidal individuals don't necessarily want to die. I have noted in my clinical work with suicidal individuals undergoing counseling that such clients generally reveal an elaborate fantasy about how they will be saved."

I paused for at least 8 to 10 seconds which no doubt must have seemed like hours to this audience on the edge of their seats during such a hot and heavy lecture.

"Your job is to become fantasymakers . . . my job is to give you the tools."

3

BEYOND THE QUINCY COMPLEX

Suicide, what a subject. Never, have I seen a topic beset with so many mis-truths, half-truths, and downright lies as this one. Throughout this book I shall dispel the myths which come in all shapes and sizes—and replace them with some good old fashioned facts.

In this chapter, however, I want to zero in on numero uno. This is the head honcho, the big cheese, and the grand-daddy of all the myths which asserts that suicide isn't really much of a problem; it's just that we're talking about it a lot more these days.

I was once asked to speak with 300 law enforcement officers about the tragedy of suicide. The detective, who arranged for my speech, greeted me at the door of the hotel where the seminar was going to be held. He explained that a lot of the officers were wondering if the organization had chosen the topic merely because everybody else was having a suicide lecture this year or if it was genuinely a problem. "I guess I know the answer to that one now," he told me.

"Really, how so?" I inquired. He then went on to explain that very morning one of their fellow offices shot and killed his wife, teenage son, daughter, and then turned the gun on himself.

The data from the National Center for Health Statistics for the year 1984 indicated that 29,286 people committed suicide in America, making suicide the eighth leading cause of death. Homicide was twelfth. How sad to discover that, if an adult carries a weapon, he or she may be more apt to use it on himself or herself, than to use it for protection. Out of every 100,000 citizens, 12.4 die via their own hand.

Newspapers around the country have been billing teen suicide as an "epidemic" and rightly so I might add. Approximately 5,000 youths between the ages of 15 and 24 take their own lives each year. Suicide is the second leading cause of death in this age bracket. If the aforementioned stats didn't put a lump in your throat, then this one will. The Committee on Youth Suicide recently announced that one out of every ten teens will make a bonafide attempt by age 19. The bottom line is that every 18 minutes somebody in this country ends his or her own life and every 105 minutes it is a teenager.

When I share these statistics with concerned individuals, they will often let out a sigh of relief and comment that the only concession is that at least our senior citizens are exempt from this social malady. Actually, nothing could be further from the truth. Senior citizens commit suicide at a rate which is considerably higher than any other age group. Statistics for 1984 revealed an alarming 5,517 seniors found life too distressing to go on. Of those persons 65 and over 19.7 out of every 100,000 people decided to end it all in 1984. Compare that to the rate of 12.5 per 100,000 (as horrendous as that may be) which is the current rate for the 15 to 24 year olds. For each 1 hour and 36 minutes that ticks by an old person suicides, making this the thirteenth leading cause of death for citizens beyond the age of 65. But teenagers and senior citizens are not the only groups who succumb.

Suicide affects every age, race, color, and creed in our society. Every day approximately 74 whites, 5 blacks, and 6 non-whites prematurely end their own lives.

Now despite the reality that these statistics are high, the fact is that they are so low they are a lie. In fact, they are a blatant lie, because of what I like to refer to as the Quincy Complex after the well-known medical examiner of T.V. fame.

When Quincy—your local medical examiner or coroner— receives a case, he/she must classify it as suicidal, homicidal, accidental, or natural death. Easy enough, right? Well, not really.

You see, suicide is a verboten topic that we don't like to talk about; hence, many suicides are not coded as such. A client of mine recently mentioned that 12 years ago when his mother decided to end it all, his father, who was a well known business tycoon, contacted all the well known major media outlets and insisted they publicize the death as a heart attack, otherwise he would take legal action, as well as withdrawing valuable advertisement purchases he generally made from them. In fact, to this date, I am the only person outside the immediate family who knows it was a suicide.

Rather difficult to believe until you hear this next incident told to me by a very confused mother whose 19-year-old son took his own life with a hunting rifle he received for this birthday. Now, the fact that this young lad used a gun shouldn't surprise us, since firearms account for more suicides than all the other methods put together. In fact, firearms are used in 55% of all suicides. We live in a John Wayne, frontier mentality society, in which we believe guns will solve all our problems. Although I'm certainly not going to go off into a tangent or take a position on gun control, I feel it is necessary to point out that the suicide rate in homes I have worked with, which have guns—especially those in which they really know how to use them—is so high, it's almost embarrassing. Anyway, when the police came to the scene of the tragedy they carefully scanned the room in which the incident took place, then turned to the poor woman and said, "Still time to move a few things and make this one look like an accident, lady." I am pleased to say that nearly all the officers of the law I have dealt with are more helpful in cases involving suicide; nevertheless, I mention the incident in passing to illuminate the fact that many suicides never get recorded as such. In many cases, insurance considerations enter into the picture, companies not wishing to pay for self-induced death.

For many years coroners and medical examiners' jobs were made even more difficult by the popular belief that nearly all suicidal individuals left a note. Today, we know that, at best, 15 to 25% of the people who commit suicide give written documentation. Unfortunately, most suicide notes are mundane documents, which tell us precious little about the poor soul who found life too painful.

Often we ignore a profound social problem until it becomes overwhelming. I think you know what I'm talking about. We don't like to admit we have a societal problem, wrongly believing that, if we don't talk about it, it will dwindle and go away. In the 1960s we didn't have a drug problem, in the 70s we didn't have an alcoholism problem, and in the 80s we don't have a suicide problem. Except that somewhere, someplace, right this very moment, somebody is contemplating taking his or her own life. Again, in America someone takes his or her own life approximately once every eighteen minutes. You can stop it if you know what to look for. Unfortunately, precious few do. To identify these suicidal individuals you will need to be privy to some very specialized information. In the next chapter, I promise to deliver the goods.

4

MYTHBUSTERS AND THE SMOKE SIGNALS OF SUICIDE

Maybe I'm just a suspicious person by nature; curious, if you will. Perhaps my extensive training in the social sciences has caused me to forever question people's motives. Who knows? Anyway, when a mother calls me and asks for some pamphlets on suicide without an explanation, I suddenly become very inquisitive.

"If you could tell me a little more about your informational needs I could better pick out the appropriate literature," I explained.

"Well, you see, doctor, I was making my 16-year-old daughter's bed, and smack in the middle of the bed was her diary. Now, of course, I didn't really want to read it because that would be an invasion of her privacy." She paused for a much-needed breath of air and to give herself a chance to muster up enough courage to talk about such a scary subject.

I figured I could make things a bit easier by giving her a suitable opening. "But that's just how parents are . . . what did it say?"

She chuckled nervously. "Yes, yes, you're 100% correct. I did read it; I felt I had to. It said, 'This is not a diary but rather a book of feelings. If anybody picks up this book, I hope they will not read it, as that would be getting into my business. If, however, they read it after I commit suicide I hope they will realize how much pain I had been experiencing and how much I wanted help.'"

Do you see the ambivalence I mentioned earlier? Don't read this book, but if you do you'll know I'm crying out for help.

In cases such as this we throw the "um-hm" school of passive intervention and treatment out the window, for a moment, and we do something! In a nice way I said, "Hey, lady, we're past the pamphlet stage. Let's do something!" I called the school and found that this poor child was contemplating an attempt that very day with a stiletto gang war knife.

Talking, writing, joking, threatening, or obsessing about death and suicide are not normal. They are signs that something is wrong, indicators that action needs to be taken and pronto! Do most people think such behavior is normal? You bet they do.

A man in our suicide survivors group has a 17-year-old daughter who, unbeknownst to him, was incessantly talking and writing about suicide to her boyfriend before her death. At that time, the young lady was dating a guy her own age, who lived down the street. Fortunately, he was extremely perturbed about his girlfriend's actions and decided to seek guidance from his parents. Unfortunately, when he approached his parents with the dilemma, his mom laughed and said, "Oh, honey, don't worry about it, all 17-year-old girls talk that way."

Tell that to my survivor, who found out about his daughter's fixation with suicide and death six months after a 22-caliber bullet pierced her scalp. Teenagers often hide things from their parents and, thus, if the boyfriend's parents had taken this behavior a bit more seriously, there is a good chance this girl's life could have been saved.

Now please don't get me wrong, I'm certainly not blaming the boyfriend's parents. Only as of late has suicide come out of the closet. The whole intent of this book is to provide you with concrete information and give you a comprehensive course in emotional lifesaving. In fact, for years concerned citizens were told that those people who talk about suicide don't really do it. The truth is that many who talk go on to make attempts, or even more, sadly, get the job done.

I am forever getting calls from English teachers, who, surprisingly enough, are often the first ones to realize a child is in trouble. Their questions are always the same: "Do I take this paper seriously? All this talk about death and suicide. Isn't this just a phase kids go through? This was just a class essay or a short poem." The mythbusters, those wonderful researchers known as suicidologists, who investigate self-destructive behavior and have looked at literally thousands of cases involving suicide, tell us you should ALWAYS TAKE SUCH MESSAGES SERIOUSLY!

Here are some typical verbal or written statements individuals may make when they contemplate taking their own lives:

"You won't have to worry about me much longer."

"I wish I could go to sleep and never wake up again."

"I won't be bugging you much longer."

"Death seems so peaceful."

"Oh sure, I've been thinking about killing myself a lot lately."

"I'm going to a place where it's peaceful and where nobody fights anymore."

"One of these days you'll wake up and find me dead."

"The next time you see me I'll be asleep in a pine box."

"I'll commit suicide if she leaves me. It would hurt too much to go on living."

Another warning sign people often miss is the giving away of a prized possession. This could be a class ring a record collection, a cherished painting, or anything which has tremendous sentimental value.

Several months ago, I was contacted by a concerned mother whose 18-year-old son wrote a note in which he said a personal goodbye to all his friends as he was going to kill himself. Now this somewhat typical misinformed mother told me she wasn't worried (horrors!) since she knew, good and well, that those who talk about killing themselves never really do it. (Thank God from now on after reading this chapter you will know better!) What did worry her, however, was that at the end of the note he gives his best friend, Billy, his 1972 customized Mustang. This car was reportedly his pride and joy. A day never went by when her son didn't touch up a panel with a little more carnaba paste wax, fiddle with the custom 4-barrel racing carburetor, or readjust the timing until it was seemingly past perfection. Since I am a bit of a car nut myself, I could easily plug into such behavior, and I convinced this lady her son was sending out a written smoke signal indicating he was in serious trouble. Though this incident took place on Saturday, the youngster was up at school playing one last game of basketball— one of the few things he still enjoyed—before he would try to end it all. Rapid intervention stopped the attempt and helped this lad get back on the happiness track again.

The motive for this behavior is simply that the individual won't be around to use the prized possession anymore. Moreover, the assumption is that the individual will be remembered and, hopefully, in a positive light. I have personally noticed that the actual suicide attempt often occurs within close proximity to the gift-giving behavior. Sometimes, an attempt is made within the next 24 hours.

I once came across a newspaper article depicting the suicide of a 17-year-old high school football star. The story, surprisingly enough, appeared on the sports page. You see, suicide usually doesn't sell papers, and, thus, most accounts on the subject are hidden back on page 54 next to the classified ad for a basset hound in search of a home. Because this lad was a top notch athlete, however, the story appeared, and in great detail I might add, on the sports page. In the article, specifically stated was that the suicide came as a shock to all those who knew the young man; he "showed no signs." The article, nevertheless, stated the young man gave away his entire musical cassette tape collection, which took him years to compile, the night before he committed suicide. The smoke signals crying out for help are usually present. We only need to be more adept at reading them.

I once worked with the survivors of a very tragic combination suicide-homicide situation. The perpetrator of these acts of violence, against himself and others close to him, was described as nearly a perfect citizen. Everybody agreed this was one situation in which no warning signs has been given. About six months later, after I had delivered a public suicide prevention lecture, a very nervous young man approached me and told me that he "missed" an important sign: the man responsible for the tragedy had given him his finest suit coat the day before the incident, saying he wouldn't be needing it anymore.

Another clear cut sign to be cognizant of is risktaking or self-abusive behavior. Have you ever known a friend who behaved rationally until he got behind the wheel of a car and then turned into a daredevil maniac? Perhaps the person was flirting with death. Such persons are very self-abusive. If this idea seems less than palatable, an interesting statistic to know is that accidents are the leading cause of death for individuals 24 years of age and under. A tremendous number of such casualties are one-car accidents, ergo disguised suicides.

Often when I talk with parent groups about this phenomenon, I hear moms and pops say they find it difficult, if not downright impossible, to believe that their son or daughter is trying to end it all using the family's set of wheels. In a recent meeting where I was the facilitator, a woman raised her hand and tearfully explained that during her adolescent years she ran her car off the road on two separate occasions in an attempt to end it all. Another member of the group popped up and said, "Why Jane, I knew you when you were a teenager; you had everything going for you. I can't believe you really wanted to end it all. I was so jealous, you seemed to have had everything." In this respect I want to emphasize that human beings are like literary productions in that it is foolish to judge them by their covers. I have seen troubled individuals who seemingly possess endless material items and act as if they have the world in the palm of their hands. They smile at their neighbors, teachers, employers, relatives, friends, and even the family pet. These same unhappy individuals often display an aura of hopelessness and despair when not communicating directly with others. We are behooved then to become better people-readers and carefully watch the nonverbal behavior of our friends, children, parents, and spouses in situations void of interaction.

The tile of Karl A. Menninger's now famous 1938 classic *Man Against Himself* clearly captures the essence of risk-taking behavior. I have personally worked with clients who regularly burn themselves with cigarettes, or bite their own fingers to the point where it draws blood. Such behavior is actually a form of self-mutilation. Some of the most incredible cases I have ever worked with involve the act of pulling strands of hair from one's own head. Psychiatrists and psychologists have a twenty-five cent word for this behavior. They call it *Trichotillomania.* Trichotillomania, or for that matter, any form of self-abuse, can often stem from guilt and is really a form of punishment.

The amazing thing is that generally the guilt, hence the self-punishment, is unfounded and not warranted. I can remember working with a very attractive 13-year-old girl—attractive, that is, until she pulled off her scarf. She was completely bald. She had literally pulled nearly every strand of hair from her head. The young girl was unhappy and potentially suicidal. Gentle probing into her personality revealed that she felt personally responsible for her parents' divorce, which, needless to say, was the furthest thing from the truth. Such situations are never hopeless and with increased understanding and behavior changes, this youngster now sports a full head of hair, nice enough to be photographed for the cover of any hair stylist magazine.

Recently I came across a man who was throwing lit matches into a nearby gasoline can. Now that's what I call risk-taking behavior!

The so-called "sissy test" which is currently popular at the junior high or middle school level is another example of self-mutilating behavior. In case you are not familiar with the sissy test, it is performed with an ordinary pencil eraser. The individual vigorously rubs the eraser into his wrist or upper forearm area until blood is drawn.

I never cease to be amazed at how blind parents are in regard to their own children's behavior; then again, perhaps our teens are just being secretive. Time after time when I mention the sissy test to parents they will insist that the youngsters in their neighborhood don't engage in such self-defeating behaviors. "Go home and ask your kids," I tell them. Sure enough, the parents come back with something like: "My gosh, my son said half the class is doing it!" For those parents reading this book I will say, don't take my word for it, go home and ask your children.

Another variation of the tests is to rap another student on the back of the hand as hard as you can with a comb and then the other fellow smacks your hand back. The first person who weasels out and quits is branded a sissy, a wimp, or just plain chicken.

This is the 1980s equivalent—though, thank God, much safer—of the chicken races of the 1950s when two cars would come at each other head on at full speed and the first individual to turn away was labeled a chicken. I would instead label him a wise, sane individual!

The common practice of sticking a pin through one's cheek or any other form of self-punishment also would fall into this category.

Another well-known smoke signal that a suicide attempt may be near is a change in behavior which is out of character for that particular person. Recently, for example, I heard about a youngster who virtually lived for baseball; it usually permeated all his hopes and dreams. He was like a human computer when it came to recounting batting averages or other record book statistics, yet, when a relative offered him tickets to the World Series (which were almost impossible to come by), he turned them down for no apparent reason. Often, when something like this occurs, the person thinks to himself, "Why take the tickets, I won't be around to use them." In other instances, the person is simply so burdened by the stress in life that personal goals fall by the wayside.

An individual who requires only a few hours sleep each night begins taking naps throughout the day. On the other hand, a person who routinely sleeps nine hours a night will be unable to get more than a couple of hours of shut-eye.

I have observed people who live to eat rather than eat to live, suddenly say food doesn't taste so good to them anymore. "It's just too much of a chore to lift a knife and fork," they will tell you. The antithesis also can indicate that a person is in trouble. A person who is normally extremely cautious about his or her dietary habits suddenly starts eating like a horse and pigging out like no tomorrow will exist. And if someone doesn't pick up on the warning signs, there may not be a tomorrow. The father of psychoanalysis, Sigmund Freud, once asserted that dreams were the royal road to the unconscious; today we are discovering that dinner table manners may run a close second. Individuals who suffer from eating disorders have an incredibly high suicide rate.

Suicidals sometimes become quieter, withdrawn, and shun social activity. This is because their problems are so overwhelming that the mental task of solving them becomes nearly a full-time occupation. The don't have time for social interaction, nor do they crave it. Concentration dwindles and, at best, one's attention span is but a mere shadow of what it was during the time before the crisis.

Other sure-fire signs of danger are alcoholism or drug use. Now, I won't go so far as to suggest that such substances cause suicide, since that would be somewhat inaccurate. Some individuals who decide to end it all have never had a drink. I can, nevertheless, safely point out that many (if not most) individuals who decide to end it all are substance abusers. In fact, the Fifth Special Report to the U.S. Congress on Alcohol and Health in 1983 found that nearly 80% of the people who attempt suicide have been hitting the bottle or beer can at the time. Alcohol and drug abuse correlate very highly with suicide, as people turn to such substances for the same reason they turn to suicide: an inability to cope and handle the stress of day-to-day problems.

When I talk to teenagers nowadays about the problem of alcohol, I do my best to drive home the point that alcohol is a depressant. In other words, ingesting an excessive amount of alcohol will actually make you feel more unhappy and depressed. Unfortunately, in our society we glorify alcoholism. Heroes of the silver screen routinely propose a toast to somebody or something in order to celebrate while the heroine always seems to have joy juice around while engaging in romantic intrigue. It's all such nonsense. Yet, time after time, when I lecture to teens about the ills of alcoholism, I am reminded by them how "macho" drinking is. Because I've had this rationalization hurled at me repeatedly, I currently have an answer for them, which I think addresses the issue quite well.

I recommend that any youngster who believes this macho myth of alcoholism take a trip down to the wino section of his or her city. (A sad comment on our society is that most of us who live in a large or moderately populated town can easily find such a place.) I then suggest that the person take a look at one of the winos lying in the gutter. What you will generally find is a guy who is 24, yet he looks 74. His skin is wrinkled, his hair is totally gray, his breath smells like a liquor store, and we can't talk about his teeth because he doesn't have any! Next I point at random to a teenage girl sitting in the front row and I ask: "Is that the kind of macho guy you want to date?" The gal invariably shrieks something like "eww no!" I then waste no time in reminding them that the wino probably drinks more than all the guys in the audience put together.

I then remind them that white collar alcoholism—though more difficult to spot—runs even more rampant.

By now, I would imagine some adults reading this chapter have acquired a holier-than-thou attitude and are about ready to point out the superiority of their generation. Let me set the record straight by mentioning that some studies in this field indicate that alcohol may play a greater role in adult, than teen, suicide.

Drugs are an even greater problem. Ten years ago, when I worked with clients and would ask them if they were on drugs, they would say, "Me? No way, man I don't touch the stuff." Five years ago that stock line was changed to, "Well, once in a while, but I'm not taking anything now." Now, incredible as it may seem, people often show me the drugs. The sad part about all of this is that most individuals have had little training in medicine or pharmacology, and thus they have no idea what they are taking.

Not long ago, a 36-year-old insurance salesman flashed some pills in my face and said, "Look at these great downers." Those pills the man was making reference to were a brand of ordinary cold medicine one can purchase without a prescription over the counter at any drug store.

The most interesting case I ever encountered, however, involved an enthusiastic teenager who whipped out a packet of elongated tablets, winked at me, and said, "Hey, look at these great uppers."

"Uppers," I replied, "why that's Erythromycin, a wide spectrum antibiotic."

"Really, man? What type of high will that give me?"

"It will cure your pimples," I replied. "You could get the same effect from washing your face with a bacterial scrub, and it wouldn't upset your stomach, nor would it be as hard on your intestinal tract!"

Here comes the difficulty. A teenage girl decides she needs a little attention because things just aren't going as well as they should. So here is the scenario in the girl's head. This is what motivates her self-defeating behavior. She will begin by taking a few extra pills she received from the friendly neighborhood pusher or, just as likely, the family medicine cabinet.

Next she will be rushed to the local hospital emergency room. She is obviously unaware of the research which demonstrates that nurses often treat suicidal victims worse than any other type of patients. Rather than giving the individual the sympathy she feels she needs, the nurses will try to teach the patient a lesson. The nurse hence begins pumping the girl's stomach by shoving a tube, which is so large it rather resembles one of the city's water mains, down her throat. Some lesson!

Still, the girl contends that her mom will feel guilty and won't make her do so much around the house anymore. Dad, well, maybe he can see how badly she really wants that sleek new red Z-28 Camaro she has been drooling over. Perhaps he actually can afford to buy it for her after all. Her teachers too will take notice, and of course will feel sorry for her. In fact, from now on those grades of B will now magically be boosted to A's. And her boyfriend—this one I'm sure goes without saying—will come crawling to the hospital room on his hands and knees begging to come back to her. Why he won't even remember the name of the cute little blonde pompom girl he left her for last month.

Our hypothetical girl has made a mistake, however. She took a few too many pills or, perhaps, a fat-soluble drug, and thus cannot be saved. Now this youngster wants to live and everyone is powerless to save her. At literally the last minute our hypothetical teen changes her mind and wants to live, but it's too late.

If this story seems a bit far-fetched, let me assure you that I have seen it, as well as its adult counterpart, occur more than I care to remember. Now you can imagine how scared I get when parents, teachers, and teens themselves tell me that they want to deal only with persons who are truly suicidal and not the ones who are doing it just for attention. My answer is simply that if someone is dying for attention then that is precisely what they need-attention! As the aforementioned not atypical story demonstrated, we can't afford to make mistakes. Our job as helpers and concerned citizens is not just to try to stop suicide but to work toward circumventing attempts, which often can maim individuals for life.

Recently, I met with an elderly woman whose husband some-how braced an elephant gun such that it would eject a bullet in his mouth. Fourteen medical operations and half a face later, he explained to his wife he will always regret his split second decision. The ultimate irony was that the act was intended to put him out of his misery.

The mythbusters of suicide point out that suicide is basically a male phenomenon. Men commit suicide almost four times as often as women, while women attempt suicide almost three times as often as men. The explanation for this seems to be that men use more lethal weapons like firearms and, thus, get the job done in a higher percentage of cases. For years, women have been intent on looking good, spending hours on end fixing their hair and putting on their make-up. Hence, when they made attempts they often used methods which would not disfigure them badly such as sleeping medicines or razor blade slashes on their wrists. You might notice I said "made" rather than "make," because recently women have been becoming more like men, in the respect that they are using firearms much more than in the past. Let us hope that women's liberation has its limits. We don't really want women to be equal in every respect.

A social worker, who is a colleague of mine, told me of a women who made herself up like a fashion plate, put a cellophane bag over her head, and then turned a gun on herself. She wanted to be remembered as a good-looking woman.

While on the subject of attempts versus successes a note-worthy point is that (I hope you are sitting down for this one) about 150 to 200 teenage attempts occur, in society at large, for every actual success. Opportunity is not just knocking for us to save these kids, it is pounding to get in! I, thus, state flatly, we must be on the lookout for these signs. Of those persons who succeed, 40 to 80% in most age brackets have made a previous attempt. Small wonder behavioral scientists insist that a past attempt may be the strongest warning sign of all.

Lastly, I urge concerned citizens to watch closely for any behaviors which indicate that an individual has been making final arrangements. A person on the verge of suicide may make peace with enemies, settle his/her estate, or put money in grand-children's bank accounts. A teenager may complete a longstanding chore that parents have been bugging him/her about for years or clean out the locker at school.

Someone once humorously blurted out at a workshop I was conducting, "How would we know if you were suicidal? Since you know the signs so well, you probably could mask it and nobody would be wise to your motives."

"Well," I commented, "if I paid off my Mastercard, I would probably be contemplating an attempt. If I paid all seven of my Mastercards off, your best bet would be to phone for an ambulance."

I shall devote the next chapter to a warning sign that is so universal it seems to follow the suicidal around like a dark cloud hovering over a single individual on a sunny day. A smoke signal which, in a sense, encompasses all the rest. When we see such a sight on Saturday morning cartoons, it's a joke and everybody gets a good laugh out of it. When we see it in everyday life, it is deadly. Without any further ado, let us examine the sclerosis of suicide.

5

THE SCLEROSIS
OF SUICIDE

Depression is the kingpin of suicidal smoke signals. Psychiatrists have billed this affliction as the common cold of psychiatry. I call it the sclerosis of suicide. Though not everyone who is depressed commits suicide, nearly all the suicidal are, or have been, depressed. Fifteen percent of the people who suffer from a major depression go on and kill themselves.

The estimate is that at least 12% of the adult population will experience depression serious enough to warrant treatment. For years we have heard that children and teens don't get depressed. "It's the best time of their lives," people told us. In reality, the direct antithesis is true. It would be mighty difficult to conjure up an individual by the age of, say, 18, who has not felt depressed at some time during his or her life. An estimated 10% of the kids in this country suffer from some form of depression by age 12. And, as if the aforementioned facts were not enough, we now know that the scourge of clinical depression currently accounts for 75% of all psychiatric admissions.

Now what exactly is this strange animal we call depression? Basically, depression is the cognitive gyration of visualizing a glass of water which is half full and thinking it is half empty. It is tunnel vision and yet it is funnel vision. It is tunnel vision because no light seems to appear at the end of the tunnel, and it is funnel vision in the sense that your personal difficulties become the center of your entire universe. You don't care who wins the hockey game, which student is elected as your class president, or what the weather forecast is for the weekend. Depressed individuals often don't "thank God it's Friday" because they are too preoccupied with their private mental misfortune to know what the day of the week is. Such people feel emotionally down and at best extremely unhappy.

Here, in a nutshell, are the tell-tale signs of depression:

1. Poor appetite or increased appetite

2. Sleeping too little or too much

3. Loss of interest of lack of pleasure while performing activities

4. No energy or constant fatigue

5. Feelings of inappropriate guilt or worthlessness

6. Inability to concentrate or think effectively

7. Recurrent thoughts of suicide and death

8. Inability to walk or move as swiftly as normal. Moving or walking at an extremely rapid pace you can't control.

Sound familiar? They should; many of these symptoms sound frighteningly close to the smoke signals of suicide depicted in the previous chapter. To discover that depression and suicide go hand in hand comes as no small surprise.

Oh sure, from time to time everybody gets a case of the blues. Perhaps your bowling team loses the championship or you didn't get the promotion you were counting on. Maybe the term paper you slaved over for the longest three months of your life, which you just knew was going to be rewarded with an honors mark, is returned with a disappointing grade of "C" in the upper right corner of the title page.

Somehow, nevertheless, you seemed to survive these unpleasant situations. Of course, you were mildly upset, even crushed at the time, but you bounced back to normal a few days later.

Depression—at least the kind which can lead to trouble—occurs when you feel unhappy nearly every day for about two weeks or more and display several of the aforementioned symptoms. It's a condition which just lingers on and begins to interfere with your day-to-day activities. Depression holds no surprises for its victims. When things go well, you feel lousy and when things go badly, you feel likewise.

Now an amazing myth exists in relation to depression. When an individual becomes depressed he/she will sink lower and lower into a depressed state of mind until the person hits the so-called low point or nadir of depression. This is the period when the person feels the worst and is accomplishing little or nothing in life. Most people, including parents, teachers, and teen-agers, tend to believe that the danger of suicide begins to subside as the depression lifts. Actually, nothing could be farther from the truth. WHEN THE DEPRESSION BEGINS TO FADE AWAY, AND THINGS APPEAR TO GET BETTER, THE RISK OF SUICIDE CAN ACTUALLY BE AS HIGH IF NOT HIGHER THAN IT WAS DURING THE DEPTHS OF DEPRESSION. That is very important. I don't want you to forget it. The risk can remain extremely high for 60 to even 90 days after the improvement occurs.

I can't tell you how many clients who have lost a loved one through suicide tell me that the person's mood began to lift just before the suicide. "Everything started looking up for her, she was definitely doing better," they explain. A parent who was literally dumbfounded by her son's suicide said, "I don't understand it. He was becoming more content and less anxious. I was so impressed with his progress. It occurred just as life started going his way and he began making all the right changes."

The question of the hour thus becomes very obvious. Why, when life begins rolling out the red carpet and slowly reveals a bowl of cherries rather than a collection of prune pits, does the individual decide to throw in the towel? It is just so paradoxical because it seems one way and yet it is often the other.

Upon closer examination of this phenomenon I think you will find a certain sense of logic in this pattern such that it actually makes sense after all.

First, most acts of suicide are not purely the result of impulsive behavior. By this, I mean that most acts of violence directed toward the self are planned well in advance. Prior planning requires energy which the person may not possess while in the throes of depression. When an individual starts feeling better he/she can purchase bullets for the rifle, give away possessions, or make final arrangements.

Another reason is that when individuals begin to pull out of a depression their support systems often tend to fall by the wayside. Concerned others may wrongly assume that the person has snapped out of it and can now stand on his/her own two feet again. A number of research studies have actually demonstrated that patients released from psychiatric facilities may actually be more prone to harm themselves than before admission. Again, the support system—in this case provided by the warm, caring hospital staff—is eliminated.

People who have experienced severe depression sometimes feel they have been a burden to their family and friends. Thus, after they begin to do a tad better, they don't dare tell a soul when they start slipping back once more.

I'll tell you an amazing little secret: very commonly suicide prevention centers receive calls from persons on the brink of self-destruction who are in treatment and have not told their psychiatrist they are in trouble. "Dr. Frankenhelper is such a nice man," they will confide, "and I've made a lot of progress under him. I just don't want to hurt his feelings or disappoint him. I can't let him know I'm slipping back."

An additional aspect of this ironic dilemma is that once you have made a decision, any decision, even the one to do away with yourself, you feel less anxious. How often have you personally commented after making a tough decision that it was like having a giant weigh lifted off your shoulders? Simply put, most people feel better after making a tough decision with which they have been struggling for some time.

Behavioral scientists speak of a phenomenon known as "flight-to-health." This is literally a situation in which the helper is worried because the client gets well too quickly. This is the person who has been feeling absolutely horrendous and then without any apparent reason feels fantastic overnight. This indeed can be the most dreaded set of circumstances we can encounter. He/she has made the decision to put himself or herself out of anguish. The person suddenly acquired the necessary energy to carry out a plan of self-destruction and does.

The road to recovery is paved with setbacks, and this, of course, becomes a source of major concern for the person who begins to win the battle over depression. Unfortunately, however, an individual who encounters a setback or two may say to self that he/she never wants to experience such a horrendous mental pain again. Astute readers will recall that in Chapter 1 we established that the reduction of mental hurt is what motivates most suicides. Ending it all assures the individual freedom from the monster known as mental misery.

Lastly, let me cite the commonly overlooked fact that the initial steps in any self-improvement program are often the easiest. This is the direct antithesis of the self-help propaganda you may have heard which asserts that the toughest move in any self-improvement program is the first step. While this may in fact be true for some of the people some of the time, it certainly isn't true for all of the people all of the time. Imagine, for just a moment, that you are a 20-cigarette-a-day smoker who is intent on becoming a non-smoker. In order to implement your program of cessation you decide to smoke one cigarette less per day until you reach the magic figure of zero. Now if you are anything like most people, you will find it easy enough to smoke 18 or 19 cigarettes on the first couple of days. You won't notice any withdrawal symptoms or craving for nicotine. When you get below about 10, however, my guess is that you will have increasing difficulty in staying on your program. You may insist that your cessation plan is sheer torture, and eventually you might just come to the conclusion it's just too darn difficult to quit. It isn't worth the trouble, and why not just chuck the whole idea. In essence, you are back to square one.

Now put yourself in the suicidal person's moccasins. His or her problems make our hypothetical 20-cigarette-a-day habit look like a Sunday picnic. Can you fantasize the incredible hurdles such individuals may have to vault over after they conquer the initial difficulties? And, needless to say, a return to their own private square one is a lot worse than a measly case of tobacco dependence—it's living hell. I believe those of you who have been truly suicidal know exactly to what I am referring.

One question with which I am forever confronted when I talk with concerned citizens is whether depression is physical or purely psychological. Is this state of exaggerated sadness caused by chemicals, or is it all in your mind?

Strange as the answer may seem, it can realistically be fostered by both. Studies in laboratories the world over have demonstrated that the physical and chemical state of the body has an effect on the mind and in turn the mind can alter the chemical balance of the body. The first part of this statement seems easy enough to accept. Who among us has not been in a rotten mood due to an annoying earache, toothache, or sore throat? The second part of the statement, however, implies that the mind can influence the body. Many people with whom I speak find this very difficult to believe.

Truthfully, despite the fact that I was trained in the social sciences and was supposed to believe in mind over body control, I must forthrightly admit I too always had a small degree of skepticism until the mid-1970s when I began working with biofeedback. Biofeedback is a procedure in which extremely sensitive electronic equipment is used in order to reveal very minute changes in the body. A client, for example, who is constantly plagued by cold hands (such as in Raynaud's disease) is hooked to an ultra-sophisticated thermometer which indicates what thoughts, feelings, and ideas can raise or lower the temperature of the hands. After several sessions of monitoring his/her own hand temperature the individual can actually influence his/her body by raising the hand temperature by will! Muscle tension, blood pressure, heart rate, and even brain waves can be brought under conscious control by this process. So yes, your mind definitely can help make you sad, and it can make you sick. The antithesis is also true, however. If you believe in psychosomatic illness (i.e., your mind can make you sick), then you also should believe in psychosomatic health (i.e., your mind can make you better). This is something I will expand upon in future chapters.

So many theories exist regarding depression that a truckload of books would be needed to even scratch the surface of what could actually cause this dreadful malady. I have found, nevertheless, that one theory in particular sometimes known as "learned helplessness" seems to fit the bill quite nicely when examining the suicidal personality.

The concept of learned helplessness grew out of the laboratory observations of experimenter Martin E. P. Seligman and his colleagues Bruce Overmier and Steve Maier. Dogs were strapped into an apparatus called a Pavlovian harness which kept them from moving when they received a traumatic, but not physically damaging, electric shock. Then the dogs were taken out of the harness and placed in a two-compartmental box where they were ideally learning to escape electric shocks by jumping over a barrier into a safe or non-electrified section of the box. The researchers found, much to their surprise, that harnessed dogs (which had no control over the situation, inasmuch as their initial escape attempts proved futile) howled, ran around, whined, and then sat down and simply gave up! They never even tried to jump over the barrier.

Another set of dogs was placed in the experimental box but they were not restrained via harnesses. These dogs learned fairly rapidly to jump to safety when zapped with electric current. In fact, dogs that were not held down actually learned to escape the shock altogether when a light which preceded the shock was dimmed just before the shock to warn them of the painful situation.

In essence, the dogs in the harnesses learned that nothing they did made a difference. Now let me relate the experimental observations to a 17-year-old teenager with whom I am acquainted and who attempted suicide but now knows better and is out lecturing to people on the topic of suicide prevention.

Now I wish you could see the look on the members of the audience's faces when this young woman marches in to give on of her presentations. She is just the sweetest, most wholesome looking teen you've ever laid eyes on. Then the whispering among the participants begins. "Not that girl. She's too attractive, too sweet; that's not the suicide attempter. It can't be her." But, of course, it really is. I urge you not to judge other people's insides by your perception of their outsides.

This youngster explains that for as long as she can remember she craved praise from her father, though sadly enough, it just never seemed to be forthcoming. No matter what she accomplished, it simply wasn't good enough to be rewarded with a good old fashioned "nice going, honey" and a heartwarming pat on the back.

For years, this young lady sat around burning the midnight oil in an attempt to somehow come up with a scheme to impress dear old dad. Then one day it hit her. What a brilliant insight, she thought. Her father loved football. You could almost say it was his favorite thing in life. Why not become a football player—a powder puff player on a woman's team, that is. So it was off to the gridiron for practice, practice, and then a little more practice. Finally, it was the day of the big game, though her father was nowhere to be seen in the stands. Still determined, she played her little heart out that day, setting a number of school records in the process. She was terrific.

Ecstatic, she rushed home to give dad the exciting news. She just knew he would be pleased. She pushed open the front door, ran over to dad, and recounted her success on the field. Dad listened intently but void of emotion for several minutes until his daughter, who was brimming with joy, finished speaking. He then shrugged his shoulders and said, "Big deal, your mom and I are going to San Francisco for a vacation this weekend."

Now imagine the impact this statement had on this youngster who was just looking for a kind word. It's rather analogous to holding out your hand in anticipation of a handshake and the other person begins jumping up and down. It was just too much for this teenager. It didn't seem to matter what she did, she was out of control, nothing she did seemed to have an impact on her environment. When a person feels that nothing can be done to change things, he/she often becomes very hopeless which translates to suicidal in everyday language.

This is the teenage equivalent of a wet baby who cries but no parent response to change the diaper. Eventually our infant gives up and suffers in silence. But our teen had more options than our infant and decided to put an end to her anguish by ingesting 120 plus pills from the family medicine cabinet. Thank God she was saved.

What transpires eventually is that the dog part of the human personality encounters the final shock it needs to decide it cannot escape. Of all the signs of depression, "what difference does it make what I do," hopelessness which seems to be the most deadly. And yet, in reality hope is present: as eight steps to eliminate suicide pave the road to rescue. Light is at the end of the tunnel. You will see it by reading the next page.

6

THE ROAD TO RESCUE:
Eight Steps To
Eliminate Suicide

Dim lights, soft music, elaborate decor, and a mouth-watering medium well done strip steak set the stage for what could have been a beautiful evening. There I was, dining out at one of the plushest restaurants in the midwest with a small group of friends and acquaintances.

As I patted the bottom of the steak sauce bottle I cringed as I heard the lady sitting across from me joking about committing suicide again. This was the fourth time she had brought the topic up. I winced and glanced up from my plate.

"Hey, the only way to do it is with a gun, you know. You get the job done the first time." Everyone at the table with the exception of myself chuckled nervously. The situation would have been much less complicated had the woman responsible for the suicidal jesting not been an administrator of a suicide prevention center in another state! I mean I could confront my clients and those phoning the crisis intervention center for help where I work, but this lady knew more about suicide than practically anybody I know. I couldn't ask her—or could I?

My conscience began working a mile a minute as I reminisced how I had lectured to literally thousands upon thousands of people regarding the first cardinal rule of suicide prevention: Take all suicidal remarks seriously and always ask the individual if he or she is suicidal. Here I was, however, a mental hypocrite debating whether or not I could pose the question to my dinner companion. I could ask anybody else, I rationalized to myself, but not this woman. She knew so much about suicide that in her case she was just truly joking. Wasn't she?

Eventually, the evening drew to a close and everybody prepared to go their separate ways. I waited until everybody else left and then decided I would walk the woman in question to her car. As she reached for the door handle of her automobile I mustered up the courage to ask her.

"Look," I said, "you know as well as I do that those who talk about suicide are often seriously considering it themselves. Are you thinking about suicide?" For several moments, complete silence. The woman then began shedding tears as she ever so carefully opened the door, reached inside the vehicle, and handed me a loaded 22-caliber pistol.

"I've been thinking about doing it for months now," she confided. Everything seems so bleak, I've been so depressed lately, and a person in my position isn't supposed to get depressed."

In retrospect, I think you will agree that asking the woman whether or not she was suicidal was the right thing to do. In fact, the moral of the story is to always ask the question in a forthright, direct manner. Don't beat around the bush. If you know someone who is displaying the smoke signals of suicide. **Step One of suicide prevention, ask them if they are suicidal.** You don't need to pull any punches either. Simply ask the question. Here are some ways to go about it:

"Are you thinking about committing suicide?"

"Would you try to kill yourself?"

"Have you been thinking about hurting or harming your-self lately?"

"Do you see suicide as the only way out of your situation?"

"It sounds like you want to end it all."

"Would you consider taking your own life?"

The most common objection I have heard in regard to asking the question is that it could put the idea into the person's head. Actually, nothing could be further from the truth. Suicidal ideation begins when stress becomes overpowering, the suggestion is not put into somebody's head simply by asking the question. I have been doing clinical hypnosis for almost ten years now and can assure you that to suggest something to somebody even under optimal conditions is extremely difficult.

Returning to my potentially disastrous dinner companion, I tactfully explained to this woman that her position as a suicide prevention center director did not automatically grant her nervous system immunity to stress, and I recommended she seek professional guidance, which she did. Today—over a year later—she is doing fine and considers her decision to live the finest choice she ever made.

Another principle in reference to this story is what I like to call the "Kojak Complex," not to be confused with the "Quincy Complex" discussed earlier in this book. Almost everyone has seen rough, tough episodes of cops and robbers shows like Kojak, Magnum P.I., or Miami Vice. A typical scenario you might view on one of these television crime-buster series is a guy with a gun to his head threatening to take his own life. Next, Kojak, or whoever the hero is, utters a few tough words, hits the guy with a surprise Chuck Norris karate kick, and everyone lives happily ever after.

The Kojak Complex asserts that life is decidedly more cruel than the Hollywood tinsel town version. In 4 out of 100 cases, suicide occurs along with homicide, meaning that the person takes somebody with him/her. In most cases the suicidal person kills someone he/she knows personally, generally another family member. I thus state flatly that you should not physically try to overpower a suicidal individual with a weapon unless you are suicidal yourself! Try to talk the person into surrendering the firearm. If the person hands you the weapon, such as in the aforementioned situation with the suicide prevention center director, then by all means take it, but using physical violence to disarm the person is generally out of the question.

A truly wonderful organization known as the American Association of Suicidology acts as an umbrella group for professionals and volunteers interested in suicide prevention practices and research. If you wish to join or merely want to share their informational resources, you will find their address and phone number in the Helpful Havens chapter in the back of this book. One of the things the association does is to provide recommended standards for the certification of crisis intervention and suicide prevention centers. The association seems to feel strongly that anyone who calls a hotline should be given a suicide assessment which begins by asking the caller whether he or she has considered suicide as an option. I personally want to ease your mind by mentioning that I have never seen negative repercussions which resulted from asking the question.

Step Two of suicide prevention is to inquire about the person's suicide plan. Don't moralize, don't criticize, and for God's sake don't say something like, "Why would a nice lady like you with a handsome husband, two beautiful children, and a plush condo want to commit suicide?" Such verbalization invariably makes the person feel worse. Once again I urge you to be direct.

"What method do you plan to use to end it all?"

"How would you commit suicide?"

"What is your plan to take your own life?"

This is extremely important for a number of reasons. First, it will let you know how serious the person is about his/her decision. Generally, an individual who is not very serious about the act will not have a plan. A person who is truly intent on doing it, nevertheless, usually has a mental outline of how he/she can get the job done. The risk increases markedly as (1) the details of the plan become more specific and (2) the individual has the means to implement the strategy.

When you hear a plan such as "I'm going to do it with a gun," you should respond with a question which will yield additional information. You could inquire, "Do you own a gun?" If the individual answers, "No, but I'm going to register to vote at the beginning of next month, then I'll apply for a gun permit. After that I'll be traveling to Marksmanville where they have a number of stores which sell firearms...." in most instances an answer such as this indicates a degree of low risk since the person is not in immediate danger. If, on the other hand, the person responds with, "Do I own a gun! Heck, I've got a nickel plated 44 Magnum with a pearl handle, and it's sitting in the glove box of my Olds 98 which is parked in the driveway. I'm marching out of this sweat shop at lunch, and I'm gonna put another hole in my head," this, indeed, is high risk. Action to save this person needs to be taken, and I mean fast! This is high risk par excellence.

On the next page you'll find a **Lethality Assessment Scale** which is a simplified version of what crisis intervention centers use to help determine the seriousness of a suicidal person's intentions. Please keep in mind that the scale depicts Mr. and Mrs. Joe Average and does not apply 100% to the person with whom you are dealing. I thus insist that to over-react a bit is far better than to take the situation too lightly. When I consult with individuals who are worried about a significant other I invariably find myself clarmoring that I'd rather have the person angry and alive than dead.

In the case of the aforementioned person with the flamboyant 44 Magnum waiting to be fired at high noon, I would take the situation seriously even if he/she managed to plug into a number of low risk categories on the lethality scale.

Research regarding suicidal notes—despite the previously mentioned fact that they do not paint a complete picture of the distressed individual—do in fact indicate that persons who are hell bent on ending it all often fixate on a method of self-destruction. Bluntly stated, suicidals believe the only solution to their diffi-culties is suicide and only one method is available to accomplish that goal. Suicidal people are adamant and inflexible. They shy away from changing their self-destructive strategies, and this in turn helps us save their lives. If you can throw a monkey wrench into the plan, then an attempt can be circumvented. If, for example, your daughter says she will kill herself this Friday while baby-sitting for the Smiths, then the most effective initial measure to combat the suicide attempt is not to allow her to babysit for the Smiths.

LETHALITY ASSESSMENT SCALE

FACTORS	LOW RISK	HIGH RISK
Demographics		
* Age	less than 44 years	45 years or older
* Sex	female	male
* Race	black	white
* Marital Status	single or married	separated or divorced
* Sexual Orientation	heterosexual	homosexual
Suicide Indices		
* Plan	none or vague plan	detailed plan
* Method	pills or wrist-cutting	highly lethal, e.g., guns, poison, gas, hanging
* Availability	have yet to obtain	in hand or already used
* Time	in the future	immediate or specific date and time
* Prior Attempts	none or of low lethality	one or more of high lethality
* Family History	no history of suicide	suicide in family history
* Tunnelvision	none; wants to escape a painful situation	marked; desire to die very strong
Social Factors		
* Living Arrangement	lives with others	lives alone
* Significant Others	has several who are available	none or has only one
* Isolation	none or vague feelings	withdrawn
* Loss of Loved One (real or imagined)	none or some time ago	very recently
* Other Loss	none or some time ago	very recently
* Vocational	employed	retired, unemployed, recent loss of job
* Financial	financially secure	little or no money
Medical History		
* Physical Health	good	poor; recent treatment or recent treatment failure
* Psychiatric History	none	extensive; negative view of past treatment
* Depression	mild	severe; may appear calm or happy once decision to suicide has been made
* Substance Abuse	none	high level of abuse

In accordance with this principle, then I routinely advise parents, spouses, and friends to dispose of pills, weapons, and dangerous objects (including the family car keys if carbon monoxide is mentioned in the plan) in order to rid the person's environment of lethal objects revolving around his or her plan. *Step Three of suicide prevention is to eliminate the means to carry out the plan whenever possible.*

Cases involving prescription drugs or medicine cabinet remedies must be handled with a special degree of common sense since the person in question may genuinely need the medicine for his/her physical or mental well-being. A noteworth point to remember is that one of the leading methods of attempting suicide in the U.S. currently is overdosing on Tylenol which, as you well know, can be purchased in nearly every drug or food store in the country. Tylenol attempts often leave the person with tremendous physical pain and liver damage. Aspirin tablets, which also are available nearly to everyone, also rank fairly high on the list. Thus, in cases where medicines or drugs are involved, the best procedure is to merely leave the person with a daily supply of pills inasmuch as extra pills might be ingested for the wrong reason.

When I'm out lecturing on this principle of eliminating the means necessary to carry out the plan, I am often asked by parents, teachers, administrators, school counselors, social workers, and even teenagers whether to break confidentiality in cases where a life is at stake is ethical. If Johnny, for example, tells his fourth hour high school history instructor in confidence that he is going to kill himself with his dad's old army rifle, should the teacher then sever the confidential bond by phoning mom and dad? The answer is an unequivocal yes. The same is true in a situation involving an adult. If Mr. Johnson tells us at a discussion that he is definitely going to do himself in at 6 p.m. by overdosing on his back pain medication, the ethical thing to do would be to pick up the phone and call his wife. After all, we are trying to save a life here.

Interestingly enough, professionals may actually be a bit more uptight about breaking the silence than lay people, with all the suits now pending against practitioners these days. In nearly every case I have seen related to suicide, however, the legal battle ensued because the professional did too little rather than too much. Again (and I probably can't say this too many times) to over-react is better than to do too little or to do nothing at all. Professional organizations for counselors, psychiatrists, psychologists, and related mental health professionals generally stipulate in their code of ethics that members will breach confidentiality in and only in those cases where a client displays life-threatening behavior toward self or someone else.

Along these same lines prevention programs in the schools springing up throughout the nation are teaching kids never to keep a secret about suicide comments. If a friend or classmate threatens suicide, the child is instructed to take the communication seriously and tell an adult.

Step Four of suicide prevention is critical: give the person the telephone number of suicide prevention center or crisis hotline. Such centers are generally staffed by crisis workers who have received intense training in suicidology and crisis intervention. The bottom line is that these centers are good at helping people on the brink of self-destruction. Many centers run 24 hours a day 365 days a year, which means that there will be someone there to share your difficulties with, even when they pop up unexpectedly at 3:30 on a Sunday morning.

How about the troubled individual who tells you flat out that in no way is he/she going to spill his/her guts to some dumb telephone counselor or some stupid lifeline shrink? Isn't it a waste of time to give that individual the telephone number of the local suicide-crisis intervention center?

Actually, an incredibly high number of individuals who claim they would never take advantage of the service do so without informing the person who was thoughtful enough to volunteer the information. I've seen it happen many times and in a variety of situations. Mrs. Jones phones the hotline for a consultation as her brother who is a stockbroker on Wall Street says he is going to jump out of the fourteenth floor window if Widgets fall even one more point. Last night he gave away his treasured coin collection, and now he is threatening self-destruction. Mrs. Jones showed him the suicide prevention number in the phone book, but he merely laughed nervously as he ripped the phone book page into tiny pieces.

"What the hell could they do?" he snapped at her, "nobody can help me now."

Just minutes after terminating the call from Mrs. Jones the center receives a call from an anonymous male stock broker whose whole life has been shattered by falling Widgets. His suicide plan is well thought out, and he just parted with his coin collection the night before. He is now fixating on a jump from the fourteenth floor of a Wall Street office building.

Now you are ready to implement **Step Five which is the formation of a verbal agreement or written contract.** Ask the person to promise you that he/she sill not try to harm himself or herself without calling and talking to someone first. Here, again, you can see the reasons that giving the number of the nearest suicide hotline is preferable to giving your own number. Oh sure, you know the person's situation better than the fellow or gal manning the lines, but what happens when your friend becomes suicidal and you are out cruising up and down the interstate? Even assuming you carry a beeper at all times, you could easily be 40 miles from the nearest phone and when you reach it could discover it's electronically dead as a door nail. In addition, helpline crisis workers generally have a wealth of experience working with self-destructive individuals which could definitely make the difference in a life or death situation.

Though a verbal agreement is better than no agreement at all, *a signed contract is the treatment of choice.* Written contracts hold more weight in our society since legal documents are always put in writing. And when you draw up the contract, please don't forget to give the suicidal person a copy of it. If you have never been suicidal yourself, then what I'm about to say might come as a bit of a surprise or sound unrealistic. The mere act of carrying a contract symbolizes to the self-destructive individual that somebody cares. The distressed person can glance down at any time day or night and literally see the caring. And believe me, when you are at the end of your rope and the mental torture seems unbearable, that paper and pencil affirmation of compassion may actually be the one thing keeping you alive. A good contract might read:

> I, Hank Sampson, promise not to harm myself or attempt
> suicide. If I feel like hurting myself I will call the Pleasant-
> ville hotline (Tel. 284-1234) and speak with a crisis worker.
>
> Signed   <u>Hank Sampson</u>
>
>   <u>John Doe</u>

Please notice that John Doe, who drew up the contract, also puts his John Hancock on the document as a written expression of his concern for Hank's well-being. You should remember to do likewise. The phrase ". . .and speak with a crisis worker" is also intentional. An incredible number of people in our society take everything they hear literally.

I'll tell you a humorous story. Some years ago my brother owned a car which rode extremely rough. In order to abate the undesirable condition he left the car at the local service station and instructed the mechanic to "check out the shock absorbers." The next day my brother picked up the car and was merely told that "the shocks were okay." The car, nevertheless, still rode like the inner workings of an old washing machine. My brother thus immediately took the car to another mechanic for a second opinion. The second mechanic momentarily glanced underneath the carriage of the vehicle and said, "No big deal, sir, you've simply got a rear shock absorber unhooked."

After the repair was completed, my brother returned to the original mechanic in order to give him a piece of his mind. When my brother finished voicing his dissatisfaction the fellow replied, "Listen, mister, you asked me to check out the shocks. I did, and I told you they were fine. You never asked if they were hooked up."

When a suicidal person behaves in a similar manner, however, the results are less than humorous and on occasion, deadly.

A colleague of mine recently worked with a young woman who was threatening to slash her wrists after a break-up with her boyfriend. A contract was drafted and signed by both parties. When the woman ended up in the hospital for, as she put, "carving on myself," my colleague was extremely disappointed and reminded her of the contract. "Oh," remarked the your woman, "I telephoned and got a busy signal. You told me to call but you didn't say I had to talk with anybody."

When a person is at the end of his rope he will virtually hand on to every word for dear life. Be certain you give him the words worth hanging onto.

Now step number six, though desirable, is much to our dismay not always possible. ***Step Six of suicidal prevention is to remove the stressor which is causing the person to feel suicidal.***

In reality, never is just one incident the cause of suicide inasmuch as suicide is the result of numerous situations which pile up and instill a sense of hopelessness. Nevertheless, despite the true theoretical picture, the person who is about to do away with himself will *often blame his/her feelings on a given situation.*

A suicidal teen may blame the unhappy state of mind on the fact that he/she is getting beat up on the school bus. An adult might believe his/her mental sadness resulted from the husband's/wife's vow never to speak with the person again. As a concerned helper you always should try to change or eliminate *this straw that seemingly broke the camel's back.* For instance, you may suggest to the person getting beat up on the bus that he/she try walking to school or driving by starting a car pool with other kids in the neighborhood. You might offer to have a talk with the school bus driver or the bully's parents.

As for the depressed person whose spouse refuses to speak with him/her you might offer to speak to the spouse to explain how upset the other spouse is and to help open the line of communication between the two of them.

I once attended a lecture by a world famous suicidologist who told an incredible tale. Once when he was working as a college advisor one of his advisees came to the office in a suicidal panic because he was going to receive a B in an economics class. This B would serve to kill his straight A perfect grade point average for the past four years.

The suicidologist tried every trick in the book to talk him out of it, to no avail. He thus picked up the phone, called the economics instructor, and argued with him to give the young man an A. All of this, mind you, in front of the suicidal student! At that point in the lecture I raised my hand and asked, "But did the student deserve an A?" The expert replied, "You just missed the whole point of the story."

I'm certain I'll never forget it again, however. Always try to abate the primary stressor and let the person know you are doing it. In other words, when you're in a state of suicidal duress it helps to know somebody is on your side. Don't be a silent hero or heroine; let the person know you are helping. The security of knowing you are not going at it alone helps to abate the helpless, hopeless thoughts and feelings. Furthermore, even in those cases where you genuinely can't eliminate or lessen the dreaded stressor, you are modeling for the individual that the situation can be approached in a calm, collected manner.

When dealing with suicidal children and teens I forever find myself saying: "Look, you need someone on your side, someone to go to bat for you. Parents don't always listen to kids, but they'll listen to me. I'm an adult and maybe someone needs to tell your parents to quit demanding so much from you; it's just not fair."

Whether the parents really are being fair or the student deserves a B are irrelevant issues at that point in time. Your job is to let the suicidal person know he or she has an ally—and since it is not a silent ally, you'll need to make a production of it.

Step Seven is crucial because all your and the suicidal person's work will be completely undone if this step is not carried out. **Step Seven in suicidal prevention requires that you or someone else stay with the suicidal person.** You cannot leave the person all alone even if the person seems to be okay or at least doing better. This is so because the suicidal person's emotional state is fragile and unstable, therefore making it easy for the person to slip back into a suicidal state. Also, the duration of most suicidal states is about 24 hours. So if you can get the person through this period, or at least through the night, then you're fairly safe. For some very determined people they can fake an improved mood in order to be left alone so the plan can be carried out. Moreover, most people who commit suicide do so when they are alone, and leaving such a person could be fatal.

Suppose you are speaking with a suicidal person over the phone. After calming the person down, you need to remember that you must find someone to stay with the person for a significant amount of time. Tell him/her you are going to call someone to come to where the person is and get the telephone number of a friend or relative who can stay with him/her as long as need be. This will secure the person's safety through the crucial period and until professional help can be sought.

Thus, the last step, **Step Eight in suicidal prevention is to encourage the person to get professional help.** Getting professional help is not a weakness, as most people wrongly hypothesize, but rather a strength. In school we teach reading, writing, art appreciation, geometry, political science, and, on occasion, volleyball. Nobody in his/her right mind would seriously suggest that your lack of knowledge which caused you to sign up for eighth grade geometry made you a weak or genetically inferior individual. Along these same lines, nobody should seriously consider himself or herself a second class citizen for wanting or needing emotional education or what we have traditionally labeled psychological treatment.

Emotional education (like learning geometry) is a strength as it provides knowledge to better master your environment. If you (or somebody you know) are ready for a coach to help you pump some psychic iron to gain some emotional muscle, then read on.

7

SMART SHOPPING FOR A SUITABLE SHRINK

The time is two o'clock in the morning and a severely depressed woman finds life so utterly distasteful that she ponders the termination of her own existence. Plagued with intolerable emotional anguish, she reaches for the phone and calls her rabbi as a last resort. The rabbi, who knows the family quite well, is a bit taken aback since her husband is a well-known psychiatrist.

Realizing that the simplest solution is often the most elegant, the rabbi advises the distressed woman to wake her husband for counsel.

"Wake my husband at two in the morning," snaps the lady, "you've got to be kidding, he'd kill me."

Though I've told the story and heard it told with a minister, principal, boss, or police sergeant in place of a rabbi, it never fails to produce at least a chuckle from the audience while accurately driving home the point that many suicidal individuals have a tendency to shy away from talking about their own problems. The truth is, in fact, that very frequently after a suicide the family and friends of the deceased will comment that the individual listened to everybody else's difficulties while never mentioning his or her own.

How in an enlightened high-tech age can a person too distraught to go on living actually fear professional intervention? Inquisitive researchers have asked the same question and have often come to the conclusion that persons who harbor serious suicidal fantasies often fear they are going crazy. This, combined with the sense of extreme hopelessness of which I wrote earlier, results in a state of mind in which individuals feel that they are not only losing their grip but also that nothing can be done by them about it. This, in essence, would be the suicidal person's worst nightmare: He or she goes to a mental health professional who affirms that he or she is truly crazy and cannot be cured. You know the old joke. A guy visits a psychiatrist and says, "Listen, Doc, I'm here because I feel I'm suffering from an inferiority complex." The psychiatrist listens closely to the patient without uttering a word. At the end of the session the patient asks, "Well, Doc, what do you think? The psychiatrist responds, "You're not suffering from an inferiority complex, you really are inferior, mister."

For those readers who are at the moment anxious, depressed, extremely unhappy, or just plain suicidal, I want to emphasize that by virtue of reading this very passage you've just demonstrated that you're not a complete crazy, a weirdo, an individual operating with a screw loose, the victim of lost marbles, a gal whose elevator doesn't go all the way up, or any of those other derogatory terms society has cast upon the unfulfilled. Instead, you are simply an individual who can benefit from professional psychological intervention or per- haps what might be better described as one-on-one emotional education.

Again, I repeat, get professional help. It's decidedly a strength, not a weakness. Treatment will not only help you eliminate your seemingly intolerable state of mind but will provide you with a psychological road map so you won't sink back into a suicidal state when confronted with similar circumstances in the future.

Now that I've hopefully convinced you to acquire the services of a professional, I must warn you that the task of choosing a helper can be overwhelming. Purchasing a helper can be tougher than picking out a new car, a microwave, or even a toaster. Many models of therapists and therapies are available from which to pick and relatively few consumer guides to help us make the selection.

I'm afraid that the shelves of our psychotherapeutic super-markets are overstocked with psychological canned goods. Let's see, now, we have the Freudians, the Jungians, the Adlerians, the Rogerians, the cognitive therapists, the gestaltists, the reality therapists, the behaviorists, the logotherapists, the Chicago School, the Minnesota viewpoint, systems therapists, attack therapists, Orgone box therapists, RET, RBT, TA, AT, and the alphabet soup therapists, sex therapists, psychodrama therapists (to name a few!), and God knows what gems of wisdom our "therapy of the month" columns will cast at us next.

Now to make matters more complex, we have almost as many kinds of individuals performing the aforementioned helping strategies as we have helping strategies themselves. Though nearly every individual who receives psychological help claims that he or she sees a psychiatrist, or psychoanalyst, the fact is that very few see either.

In this chapter I hope to clear up the confusion and help you make a decision about who might be best for your particular needs. If this is all new to you, don't be surprised. While teaching college I routinely come in contact with social science majors in psychology, sociology, and social work who cannot discern these distinctions.

Let's begin by discussing psychoanalysts first, since nearly every time we see a psychological thriller at the movies the helper is an analyst. Psychoanalysis is both a theory of personality and a helping strategy (i.e., a form of psychotherapy) pioneered by the legendary Sigmund Freud. True to the silver screen, the patient lies on a couch and babbles whatever comes to his or her mind. The analyst sits with back turned amassing information from the patient's three to five 50-minute sessions weekly for about three years or more. The patient goes into great detail about early childhood and the analyst generally says little or nothing.

Though psychoanalysts are primarily medical doctors, other professionals may become so-called lay psychoanalysts by attending a psychoanalytic institute, foundation, or school. The analytic training takes approximately five years to complete, and the analyst receiving the training must successfully undergo and complete an analysis himself/herself supposedly to enhance his or her own mental health.

If you are reading this page and feeling genuinely suicidal at this very moment, let me assure you that a full-blown psychoanalysis is not the treatment of choice for your malady. I am not saying this with any bias toward psychoanalysis, and I am certain that any psychoanalyst reading this chapter would concur. Psychoanalysis (Freudian, Jungian, Adlerian, or otherwise) is a lengthy process and is not intended for the person in crisis. Furthermore, most psychoanalytic practitioners require a screening process prior to psychoanalysis which can often take six to eight weeks. Individuals contemplating self-destruction often won't be able to hang on for that period of time.

If, nonetheless, delving into your past, your dreams, and your childhood fantasies appeals to you, you may opt for psychoanalytic treatment, with the hope of total personality reorganization, at a later date. This would, of course, occur after you've visited a mental health professional for another type of treatment and your suicidal feelings have subsided. If you find yourself attracted to psychoanalysis but short on time, you might wish to pursue a brand of therapy known as psychodynamic which is similar to psychoanalysis except that the patient is face to face with the therapist and the treatment is of slightly shorter overall duration. Moreover, sessions are one to two times weekly and the therapist says a bit more.

Next, let's talk about psychiatrists. All psychiatrists are medical doctors with additional psychiatric training and thus sport an M.D. or D.O. after their names. One advantage of going to a psychiatrist is that they can give prescription medicines and may admit patients to hospitals. If you have reason to believe that a medical or organic condition has led to your suicidal feelings, then by all means don't hesitate to see a psychiatrist. I want to caution you, however, that the popular phrase "talking to my psychiatrist" is by and large a misconception. The talking cure, also known as counseling or psychotherapy, is often not practiced by many psychiatrists due to time or training limitations, or both.

Since I personally believe that all suicidal individuals should be receiving psychotherapy even if they are taking psychiatric medicines, I can't urge you enough to ask your psychiatrist if he or she does psychotherapy. I would recommend a bare minimum of one hour a week if you are feeling depressed or suicidal.

Many individuals in this day and age still falsely believe that if they can secure counseling or therapy from a psychiatrist it is somehow better, deeper, or more intense that if it is administered by a non-medical practitioner. In reality some psychiatrists actually hire or recommend non-medical psychologists or social workers when psychotherapy is indicated, as their own expertise may lie in other areas. I might add that if you feel suicidal and are seeing a psychiatrist who is utilizing only chemotherapy (i.e., psychiatric medicinals) you should add psychotherapy to your treatment regimen as quickly as possible.

Psychologists provide another viable choice for talk therapy. Psychologists come to the therapy room armed with a four-year college degree plus two years' graduate training if they possess a master's degree (M.A., M.S.) or approximately five years if they hold a doctorate (Ph.D., Ed.D., Psy.D.). If psychologists have one over-whelming strong point, it seems to be their vast knowledge of psychological and educational testing. This could indeed be of benefit if the suicidal stressors are seemingly the result of educa-tional difficulties such as learning disability or an inability to grasp subject matter. Inasmuch as 1 in 10 teens who attempt suicide have problems in school, a practitioner trained in testing (also known as a psychometrician) could constitute a wise choice in terms of a mental health provider.

Now when utilizing a psychiatrist I mentioned that you should always insist on psychotherapy in conjunction with chemo-therapy. Likewise, never allow a psychologist, or any other mental health provider for that matter, to perform a battery of psycho-logical tests without providing concurrent psychotherapy. (I hope by now you're getting the message that talking to a mental health professional regardless of background ranks number one in my book—no pun intended.)

Another key point is that the individual giving the tests should always give the suicidal client a rationale for taking them.

I'll tell you a short story which illustrates the necessity of giving the client a reasonable explanation as to why a given psychological or educational instrument has been chosen.

A lady I know was legitimately worried as her 16-year-old daughter had mentioned suicidal impulses. She thus sought the help of a clinical psychologist who gave the child a Minnesota Multiphasic Personality Inventory or MMPI for short. For those readers who have never taken the MMPI let me assure you that the test is quite long (over 500 questions!) and because of scales to assess personality traits as well as to eliminate cheating, lying, or faking the client is asked a number of strange questions repeatedly. A question similar to "I believe people from outer space are controlling my mind" would be an example.

After taking the test the young lady's anxiety escalated into a complete state of panic which intensified her self-destructive tendencies. As her mother drove her home from the test site the poor girl said, "Mom, they kept asking me the same silly questions over and over and over again; they're trying to prove I'm crazy and put me away in a mental ward. Then I'll never get out."

This rather typical fear of going crazy which is precisely what prohibits the suicidal from seeking help in the first place was unfortunately inadvertently increased in this situation by the therapeutic testing. Mom, who didn't know an MMPI from apple butter, was thus as perplexed as her teenage daughter and called the psychologist, who offered to talk with the girl immediately. Matters were made even worse, however, when the psychologist refused to give meaningful information. Instead, he responded to the distressed teen with lines like, "You seem to have a fear of hospitals," or "It sounds like you are worried about going crazy." I guess I don't have to tell you that the secrecy on the part of the tester served as the crowing blow to what little self-esteem this young lady still possessed.

The next day during her home economics class the child became frightfully suicidal. She informed her teacher, who took her to the principal's office. The principal was a warm and caring individual who listened to the youngster's tale of woe. When the girl concluded the principal perked up and said, "You and I are going over to the psychologist's office this minute and he's going to explain to both of us why that test asked so many stupid questions."

The psychologist reluctantly acquiesced, and both women left the office in markedly better spirits!

Again the issue here is not to blast psychologists or any other mental health professionals but to convince you that emotional first aid for suicidal impulses begins with mouth to ear resuscitation.

One last tip regarding the use of psychologists: don't refer high-risk suicide clients to university psychology clinics without the express permission of the clinic director.

On a number of occasions throughout the nation, suicide prevention hotlines have been told by university clinics to hold up on the suicide referrals. The reason for this is twofold. The first is that often these clinics are staffed with graduate students who at this stage of the game may not possess the knowledge or experience to tackle life and death situations. The second is that some clinics like for every client to complete a battery of tests "before" the counseling or treatment begins so the students can acquire much-needed testing experience. As we have already seen, suicidal individuals are in no position to wade through a battery of tests while waiting for therapy to begin.

Social workers also are often well equipped to provide competent treatment. You can spot them by the M.S.W., M.A.S.W., A.C.S.W., or L.C.S.W. after their names. Social workers hold a four-year degree and a master of social work which takes one to two years to complete depending on their undergraduate social work background. Though a doctorate is not necessary for therapeutic practice, some spend a few extra years and add a Ph.D. or D.S.W. after their name. In many doctoral social work programs the emphasis is on research or administration, hence most social work helpers hold master's level credentials.

Social workers are more likely to do networking and make home visits than other types of mental health workers. By networking, I mean that they will often hook you up with agencies which deal with a specialized need you are having. If, for example, the stressors relating to your suicidal feelings revolve around being a shut-in, suffering from a handicap, a medical disability, transportation needs, food, clothing, public assistance, or shelter, then as a start you should consider a therapist with social work letters after his or her name. Simply put, schools of social work generally emphasize these areas more than schools and training institutes cranking out helpers from other disciplines. They are a bit more holistic if you will and tend to be concerned about all your needs, not merely those which reside from earlobe to earlobe.

After working with and supervising social workers for a number of years now, I am convinced that although most social workers may know a tad less about in-depth therapy and psycho-pathology than psychologists and psychiatrists, they are more apt to refer you to another mental health professional without feeling guilty or inept if that is not their area of expertise. Again, I would speculate that this comes from their training which emphasizes referrals to the hilt.

Social workers, as a general rule, are schooled in short-term therapies which focus mainly on the here and now rather than splitting hairs over traumatic incidents which occurred when you were a toddler. They also tend to favor family therapy which, as the name implies, brings everyone in the household and sometimes relatives and friends outside of the home into the therapeutic arena.

If and when a therapist prescribes family therapy, insist that the suicidal individual be seen for at least the first session, if not longer, alone. This applies to all age categories, but I am convinced that this is absolutely imperative in the case of teens and younger children. Suicidal individuals often feel weak, ashamed, or guilty about discussing self-destructive thoughts and therefore clam up during a family session. Somehow once the feelings or thoughts are out in the open with the therapist in private he or she can gently help explain this to family members in a group setting.

I am adamant about the fact that the initial session should be a private one. If your therapist refuses to see things my way, I'd suggest bringing in a copy of this book and shoving these paragraphs under his or her nose or doing some additional shrink shopping.

Quite frankly, I came across this all-important principle after violating it myself. The suicidal family member would verbalize the rationale for his or her feelings, and other members of the household would laugh, minimize, criticize, or just plain discount the individual's innermost concerns.

Before moving on to another breed of therapeutic animal, let me stress that social workers, for the most part, are not trained to administer or interpret psychological or educational tests.

The last basic type of therapist I want to mention is the professional counselor. Mental health workers of this persuasion are able to snare a four-year degree and then go on to secure a master's (M.Ed., M.A.Ed., M.A., M.S.) or a doctorate (Ph.D., Ed.D.). Interestingly enough, although counselors spend more time learning to do counseling than other mental health professionals, their status has not always been commensurate with their superior knowledge.

An acquaintance of mine who is a therapist told me that when he was ready to graduate his advisor told him that a hierarchy existed in the social sciences. Psychiatry, he explained, was top dog followed by clinical psychology, social work, and counseling holding steady as the low person on the totem pole. During my colleague's vast educational career he was enrolled in departments of psychiatry, clinical psychology, social work, and counseling. The irony, he claimed, was that he felt he learned the least about helping people from psychiatry which focused primarily on biochemical issues and psychiatric diagnosis. Psychology had an edge over psychiatry, he felt, but was overly concerned with psychological testing and research design, which really didn't directly deal with human unhappiness. Social work was still one step further in the right direction yet was too preoccupied with the family system and material or physical needs to adequately investigate the client's emotional discontent. Only counseling, he insisted, hit the nail directly on the head and delineated exactly what to do when you found yourself face to face in a therapy room with a client.

Professional counselors often view themselves as emotional educators and with good reason, I might add. Counseling programs are often taught under the auspices of departments of education, and hence graduates see themselves as teachers. Human unhappiness occurs because the client has learned to feel, think, and behave in an unproductive manner. He or she can, nevertheless, be taught the skills to lead a more fulfilling life.

Counselors, in addition to their straightforward stance, generally have at least a smattering of knowledge about occupational tests and educational measurement. Their knowledge of individual personality testing, nevertheless, is usually not as vast as the clinical psychologist's.

So now you have it, a cook's tour of the therapeutic players colloquially referred to by the populace as "shrinks." Before moving on, however, I must tell you that the aforementioned descriptions are at best intended to serve as rough guidelines or stereotypes. Some, psychiatrists, for example, shy away from doling out medications and only believe in psychotherapy. On the flip side of the coin, I've worked with social workers who practice classical Freudian psychoanalysis and whose expertise lies in personality testing. And some clinical psychologists and professional counselors despise testing but spend a majority of their time networking and doing clinical casework. Let me conclude this disclaimer by insisting that you should always feel free to interrogate your would-be therapist about his or her training and experience. If a therapist balks at the questions, especially in regard to training and experience in suicidology, I'd shop elsewhere.

If you want a religious or pastoral counselor you should still ask about graduate training relevant to psychotherapeutic intervention. Each year I lecture to literally thousands of volunteers and lay pastoral counselors in regard to suicide prevention. Now although I feel comfortable about their performing the eight crisis intervention steps in the last chapter, I am still squeamish about letting them continue seeing the client for long-term counseling or in-depth psychotherapy. Fortunately, nearly everyone in these audiences realizes that this, indeed, can be a life or death task and they have no qualms whatsoever about turning the case over to someone who has acquired the necessary sheepskins.

If you don't know where to begin shopping for a shrink, you should contact your nearest suicide prevention center or hotline, your family doctor, or your local mental health association. I've also given you some institutes, centers, and national organizations in the "Helpful Havens" chapter which can point you in the right direction. Remember that professional organizations, hotlines, crisis intervention centers, and mental health associations screen those professionals included in their referral lists. This is extremely important since they can often tell you which mental health professionals have acquired specialized training in suicidology and have experience working with suicidal individuals.

The rationale for my giving you guidelines about therapists' biases is so you can pick a helper in whom you will have faith and with whom you will feel comfortable working. If you can't talk with a man, then for Pete sakes insist on a woman, or vice versa if you're uptight about spilling your guts to a female. Those parents reading this chapter may find be interested in knowing that teenagers and children may do better with a young therapist—or at least a therapist who looks young—than an older one if the child verbalizes this preference.

In addition to types of therapists I shall now give you a thumbnail sketch of the schools (or types) of therapy. Even if you have supreme faith in your therapist, doing so is of no value if you don't believe in his or her technique. Those with a penchant for who-done-it mysteries may choose psychoanalytic or psycho-dynamic therapies mentioned earlier. Here are the other major helping strategies.

Client-Centered Counseling. Also known as non-directive therapy, person-centered, or the Rogerian School (after the late great psychologist Carl Ransom Rogers), this point of view sees man as basically rational, forward-moving, and realistic. Helpers who favor this treatment modality do not give advice nor do they try to interpret behavior. Instead, they believe that the individual has the capacity to guide, regulate, and control self if certain conditions exist which can be set up in the therapeutic relationship. Counselors of this persuasion don't push their clients to change, feeling that they will, in fact, improve when they feel accepted and prized by the therapist. Rogerians are nice guys who are very warm and shun criticism like the plague.

If you are tired of being told what to do, despise others analyzing your behavior, and like the idea of moving at your own place, then client-centered counseling could be your meal ticket to happiness. If, nevertheless, you find yourself using the therapy as an escape from reality and as an excuse not to change, then be honest with yourself and switch to a therapy which will give you a gentle push in the proper direction. P.S. Never stick with a non-directive therapist yourself (or let someone else you know and care for) if the therapist remains non-directive when the client is seriously contemplating suicide. In such a situation, even the most non-directive or analytic therapist should throw the um-hm school of therapy act out the window and do something! That something entails the first seven steps in the last chapter.

Behavior Therapy. This brand of therapy and its second cousin, behavior modification, have excellent track records with concrete problems in which the client knows why he or she is unhappy. Clients who verbalize that they have no idea why they feel the way they do might have a better shot with a Rogerian or an analytic therapist. On the other hand, clients who say they are unfulfilled because they are overweight, nonassertive in social situations, or scared to ride the elevator in the office building would probably be an excellent candidate for a behavior therapist or a behaviorist as they are often called. Behavior therapists want to know exactly what actions and reaction patterns you want to change.

One of their techniques, for example, called systematic desensitization, which calls on the client's powers of imagination and ability to learn to relax, has been extremely successful for persons suffering from fears or phobic reactions.

If you know what specific stressors are contributing to your suicidal feelings and would like a therapist who doesn't believe you are the way you are because of early toilet training difficulties, then a behaviorist would serve your needs well.

A word to the wise, however. If you're looking for a warm shoulder to cry on so you can repeatedly verbalize your discontent for an endless number of sessions, forget it. Buy Rogerian or go analytic because behavior therapists don't believe you need to know the underlying causes of your difficulties, nor do they feel an intense, meaningful relationship with the counselor is necessary in order for change to occur. This means the therapist will be giving you homework assignments and will be expecting rapid progress. In essence, behavior therapy, perhaps because it has its roots in animal research, is short, sweet, and geared toward changing specific behaviors.

Rational-Emotive Therapy. This system of therapeutic intervention is the brain child of New York clinical psychologist Albert Ellis, a prolific writer who now has published over 45 books and more than 500 articles. Rational Emotive Therapy, or RET for short, insists that people are disturbed not by things but rather by their view or perception of them, a position taken by the Greek stoic philosopher Epictetus who lived in the first century A.D.

Therapy in this mode is an educational or so-called didactic process in which the therapist acts as a teacher giving homework assignments and outlining strategies for straight thinking. The counselor who utilizes this technique literally hammers away at the client's irrational beliefs which are seen as the core of the unhappy individual's disturbance.

Unlike some behavior therapists who insist that man is simply an animal, the practitioner or RET concludes that humans, unlike the lower species (e.g., rats or birds used in many of the behaviorist experiments to derive therapy principles) are self-defeating, self-evaluating beings which get into trouble when they falsely see simple preferences as dire needs.

If you want a therapist who will tell you what to do, how to think, and may talk as much if not more than you do during the sessions, then RET is for you.

Overall, RET moves at a fast pace and is in my opinion a superb therapy for those experiencing a suicidal crisis. It focuses on the exact thoughts responsible for one's self-destructive state of mind.

A hybrid of Ellis' RET formulation is Dr. Maxie, Maultsby's Rational Behavior Therapy or RBT which is structured similar to RET except that RBT includes a written self-analysis by the client.

Offsprings of RET and RBT including cognitive therapy, cognitive-behavioral modification, or active-directive therapy also have the goal of assisting clients in recognizing and discarding self-defeating cognitions. Smart shoppers of therapy should be aware that RET and the cognitive therapies are considered by many professionals as excellent treatment for clinical depression and by now you are more than acquainted with the relationship of clinical depression and suicide.

Reality Therapy. This method of helping insists that individuals are responsible for their own behavior. Psychiatrist William Glasser, who pioneered the approach, suggests eight steps necessary for efficacious Reality Therapy:

1. The helper must develop a good therapeutic relationship with the client.

2. Focus on the current behavior of the client.

3. Ask the client to evaluate the current behavior.

4. Develop plans for change.

5. Get a commitment from the client regarding changes which need to be made.

6. The therapist will not accept excuses.

7. Punishment is never utilized (unlike RET and behavior therapy).

8. Never give up on the client.

Because reality therapists utilize contracts, it could be a logical treatment to follow the crisis intervention steps listed in the last chapter. The client, already introduced to the idea of contracting, may be receptive to the paradigm.

If you want to talk about your unconscious, early childhood traumatic experiences, or your dreams, then reality therapy is not for you. Reality therapy, though very effective with some individuals in a very brief period of time, has been criticized on the grounds that it may tend to oversimplify some complex issues.

Gestalt Therapy. The basic goal of Gestalt therapy (incidentally, the German word gestalt means form, figure, or configuration) is awareness rather than analysis. Fritz Perls the originator of Gestalt therapy, emphasized the here and now and the process of reowning parts of oneself that have been disowned. If you find your non-verbal behavior interesting, your past unimportant, and your dreams relevant, then this school of therapy could well appeal to you.

Unlike RET and the cognitive therapies, Gestalt deemphasizes and discourages the act of thinking about one's difficulties and has been criticized for doing so.

That rare breed of therapist who integrates Gestalt work with cognitive strategies could, indeed, help a wider range of distressed individuals.

Group Counseling. Although any of the previously mentioned therapies can and have been used in a group setting, the type of support group most focused toward the suicidal individual is the *attempters group*. As the name implies, everyone in a suicide attempters group has attempted suicide and thus members can often learn from each others' coping strategies. The common feeling—to take one's own life—is often missing from typical counseling, therapy, or support groups, and hence suicidal members feel misunderstood.

One word of caution regarding group psychotherapy. If you are currently experiencing suicidal ideation and attending a group, you should always be receiving individual therapy concurrently— yes, even if the group you are attending happens to be an attempters group. The suicidal client needs the personalized attention afforded by individual intervention. In fact, many attempters groups have a rule which stipulates that only persons who are engaged in individual counseling may attend the group. A note from the psychotherapist performing the individual therapy is often a prerequisite for admission.

In summary, get professional help. Pick a therapist and therapy combination with which you feel comfortable and in which have faith. If you are short on money and don't have insurance to cover the services, then look for a therapist who sports a "sliding fee scale" in which the amount you pay per session is based on your ability to afford it. And if you are seeing a therapist and it's not working, always discuss it with him or her before you pack up your emotional bags and leave. You might just be on the verge of dealing with a sensitive issue and this could be abetting your resistance. Nevertheless, if you feel you are becoming more suicidal by the session, then change therapist, therapies, or hospital programs.

Although many therapists and counselors are available to assist individuals, many people wrongly assume that nobody wants to help them.

Much of my lecturing on suicide is done in St. Louis, Missouri. Nearly every time I speak someone raises a hand and voices the opinion that, "There's no one around to help". I therefore interject a little levity by mentioning a certain part of town which literally houses hundreds of mental health professionals and comment that I'll give anybody in the audience a five dollar bill if he or she can walk through the streets of the vicinity without bumping into a therapist!

Now let's look at what you can do to help yourself.

8

GIVE ME ONE GOOD REASON TO LIVE

I can still remember an incident as if it happened yesterday. My fifth grade teacher handed me a rather large manila envelope with the words "Confidential. Do not open." stamped boldly across both covers.

"Howard," she said sternly, "I want you to take this envelope to the principal's office, and whatever you do, don't open it."

After my typical "Yes, ma'am" I found myself halfway down the stairs which led to the principal's office, envelope in hand, and a burning desire to open that envelope and peruse the very document which held the key to my future.

You see, I knew that there was but one thing which was confidential, just one fact so top secret the student was never allowed to see it, and that was his or her IQ score.

The way it was explained to me during my elementary school years was that your mind was like a funnel. If you had a high IQ your mind was analogous to a very large funnel which could hold an incredible amount of information. This was the guy or gal with the right stuff who could really go places in life—a real somebody, if you will.

On the other hand, a low IQ was the kiss of death. It symbolized a pint-sized funnel incapable of storing much knowledge. The owner of the little pip-squeak was doomed to a life of mediocrity. As a matter of fact, a score below 135 supposedly ruled out a college education while a figure of 120 or under meant saying adios to high school prior to graduation because you just didn't have enough upstairs to cut the mustard.

Now imagine my initial moment of sheer terror after I looked up and down the hallway to make certain the coast was clear and then came face to face with a piddly, almost insulting, slap in the face score of 118. Oh, sure, I scanned the rest of the class roster and found some even more debilitating figures, yet I also came across a few lucky souls boasting funnels in the 140 plus range.

From the fifth grade on, the stage was set for my intense, exaggerated fear. The dread that sometime, someplace, when I would least expect it, some overzealous teacher, guidance counselor, or peeping-tom administrator would purposely or accidentally discover my pygmy-like figure of 118 and pull the plug on my educational career. ("Why waste your time trying to teach him," I'd fantasize them saying, "his funnel just isn't big enough, he can't possibly graduate. Stop squandering the teachers' time and the school's money.")

In fact, it wasn't until I began giving IQ tests myself that I discovered how little they actually meant and came across the fact that Nobel Prize winners possess statistically average IQ's (i.e., about 100—God only knows where my mentors came up with 135 for college, 120 for high school guidelines. And furthermore, why a funnel? Why not a water glass, a pot, or a jar—funnels have openings at the bottom and could leak valuable IQ points.).

Anyway, after I snared up four college degrees which included a full-fledged doctorate, I made up my mind I was going back and let my fifth grade teacher know the anxiety and paranoia I felt after eye-balling my IQ score. I wanted her to know the feeling—like something in my personality was broken, yet I couldn't fix it.

As I began to tell my story my teacher began to snicker, chuckle, and ultimately she broke into an uncontrollable fit of laughter to the point where she was almost falling off the chair. "How can you laugh?" I protested. "I've been upset about this for over twenty years."

"You fool," she told me, "we weren't allowed to see the IQ scores either. You saw a chart of the class weights."

"You mean I've been depressed for over 20 years because I tipped the scales at 118 in the fifth grade?"

"It's not really so funny," she added, "kids in the 80's are killing themselves for a lot less."

As a suicidologist, I could have interjected that she was correct to the tune of 125 teens a week in this country with approximately one thousand others who will try and fail. Amazingly enough, both teens and adults often kill themselves due to misinformation which leads to misperceptions and/or a low opinion of the self.

Recently, somebody told me about a situation in which an elderly gentleman was informed he was the victim of a horrendous incurable disease. The man killed himself and left notes to three relatives stating he just couldn't tolerate the pain he heard was associated with this malady. The day after the suicide doctors discovered that the man had received the wrong medical report. His actual examination revealed he was not only in good health but on par with men nearly one-half his age! This brings me to the *First Good Reason to Live:* **You may have acquired incorrect information about your situation or yourself which you will later discover is inaccurate.**

In the case of my IQ score, this took approximately twenty years, so don't be too impatient. You'll want to be around to reap the benefits or have a good knee-slapping laugh as I did. People who see themselves as frogs often end up being princes. When suicide prevention and crisis intervention centers train interventionists they generally teach them that you can't give a suicidal client on the line a good reason to live since he or she will merely say "yes, but" and provide a rationale why they cannot go on. Truly, trying to save a life on the line by giving one good reason to live is often futile. A person at that point in time is not willing to listen to such reasoning.

In the case of those reading this book, however, you are currently calm enough to digest this vital information. Thus, the reasons to live set forth in this chapter could very well have a tremendous impact and serve to ward off future unwanted suicidal thoughts, feelings, and ideas.

The *Second Good Reason to Live* states that **PEOPLE CHANGE.**

Not long ago a rather handsome 21-year-old man sat across from me in a therapy session. The discussion—so illustrative of the second reason to live—went something like this:

"Overall it sounds like everything in your life is starting to fall into place."

"Aw yeh, I'm doing fine, my job, my social life, you know, I'm feeling super."

"And Dawn?"

"Dawn?"

"Yes, Dawn, of course."

"Dawn who? I mean it doesn't ring a bell or anything."

"Oh come on now, you can't be serious; level with me, how do you feel about Dawn?"

"Dawn, let's see, um . . . gosh, I'm drawing a blank. . ."

"Dawn, for land sakes, the girl you slashed your wrists over two years ago when you were 19."

"Oh, right, um, Dawn, I remember now."

"Do you still have any emotions or feelings related to Dawn?"

"Well, no, man, not really . . . like I say, I um, couldn't hardly remember who she was."

"But I don't understand. Two years ago you were butchering yourself because she left you."

"Aw yeh, well I was just a 19-year-old kid. Like now I wouldn't walk across the street to talk with her. I've changed my ideas a lot since then. Besides, I only date college chicks now."

To say "People change" doesn't sound all that profound and certainly doesn't seem like a life or death earth-shattering matter. But as we have seen from the previous example, it can be just that.

I also want to mention that in my clinical practice I have seen this phenomenon time and time again. Matters which appear worth taking one's life for on one day can seem trivial or non-existent at some point in the future.

Often individuals change physically. One day a social worker and I were having lunch together at a cafeteria. Since my social worker friend is about six feet five inches tall, he doesn't generally run into a lot of people taller than himself. That particular day, however, he tapped me on the shoulder as we were standing in line and said, "My gosh, would you take a look at that guy up there, he makes me look like a midget, he must be at least seven feet."

As we walked over to sit down my friend recognized the fellow we were looking up to. He had been an ex-client of his years ago and ran up to see him.

"Roy, Roy, is that really you?"

"Yep, all seven feet of me. Good thing that suicide attempt didn't succeed in the eighth grade. I'd never have gotten to play college basketball."

My social work friend later explained that Roy tried to take his own life in junior high because he was the shortest guy in the class and always felt funny standing next to his classmates. Now, needless to say, he towers over all of them and just about everybody else! According to Roy it was all mother nature, too, no hormone injections or dangerous steroids.

Now certainly nobody should ever attempt suicide over their height, but imagine if you did when you were destined to be a late bloomer who would ultimately hover around the seven foot mark!

Along these same lines, I know a therapist who has a picture of a very ordinary, if not downright plain looking, teen-age girl sitting on her desk. Though the girl in the picture is not ugly, she certainly isn't the type you'd take a second look at walking down the street.

Since the picture sits in a very conspicuous place, most of her clients ask who it is. The picture, she explains, is movie star and bathing suit poster girl Farrah Fawcett when she was about fifteen. She utilizes the photograph to convince clients that you never know how things are going to turn out. "Slow starters often finish first," she reminds them. "You know," she told me once, "Every picture tells a story, but that one has saved a few teens' lives."

People change in terms of their beliefs and their preferences. Even societal customs can have a profound influence in this respect, which brings me to the *Third Good Reason to Live:* **CUSTOMS CHANGE.** If you don't understand what I'm getting at here, try pulling out one of your old photograph albums. There you'll find yourself psychologically strolling down memory lane. Perhaps you'll spy yourself sporting that hair style you just had to have at the time—the Sal Mineo Wave, the Jack Kennedy Bush, the Beatles Mop, the Bee Hive look, or even a bouffant. Let's face it, I'd have to pay you handsomely now to get you to even step foot out of your house looking like that! But back then, it was important; again you just had to have it. It was a necessity.

While you're thumbing through the album, catch a glimpse of your clothes. There you were in your leisure suit, white plastic belt and shoes, and a tie so wide that quite truthfully it could have doubled as a Cadillac hood ornament! If you're a woman, perhaps you will find yourself balancing on your platform shoes, hat in your hand, and wearing a mini-skirt so tiny it would probably turn men's heads in a strip joint. This is one picture you may decide never to show your grandkids.

Not long ago I was lecturing to a youth group. After the lecture a young woman came up to me in tears and discussed her plan to commit suicide. The problem, she informed me, was that her parents weren't rich and couldn't afford to buy her a new wardrobe each month. She then went into great detail about which alligator was "in" this month and which polo player the next. Designer labels had literally become the measure of her happiness.

I tried to convince her that basing one's happiness on social customs or trends is ludicrous since today's most sought-after designer labels will eventually go the way of the leisure suit. A course of therapy has begun to reduce her self-defeating tendency.

Even more amazing is that social customs and trends can even dictate the way one is supposed to look. Today thousands of individuals are indirectly committing suicide (or just plain ruining their health) with a knife and fork—or perhaps I should say a lack of them. Here, of course, I am referring to the dreadful problem of eating disorders such as anorexia and bulimia. Would you believe that when I first began seeing clients in the early 1970s my colleagues and I had never seen a "real" anorectic or bulimic? These were at the time, obscure terms housed in the pages of our psychiatric dictionaries. Today nearly any classroom teacher has a number of students with eating disorders in his or her class.

In a sense, society has fostered this widespread condition by insisting that modern men and women be extremely slender. In an attempt to reach this ideal (which was decidedly not an ideal just a few years ago when we referred to the condition in a derogatory fashion as being skinny) people have taken to literally starving themselves.

If you still don't think this is a bit bizarre, then try this on for size. One day I was talking with a gentleman who owns a chain of gyms and has been making a small fortune off society's new desire to look, as he put it, "like Twiggy only smaller." When I asked him what he thought of the trend both from a health as well as a physical culture standpoint he said, "Look, if this afternoon Marilyn Monroe walked into our gym for a membership one of my instructors would assess her as a fat overweight slob who needed to drop twenty pounds immediately. Now I'd say that's insanity! But if what people want is a body that resembles a telephone pole, then we'll certainly teach 'em how to slave for it while taking their hard earned money. I can't honestly say it's that healthy for you, though."

The gym owner failed to mention that we have good reason to believe Marilyn Monroe may have taken her own life, which suggests that even if you do somehow match up to society's current standard of perfection it does not assure contentment or happiness.

If, nonetheless, you insist upon trying to match society's sometimes counterproductive customs, you may become a skinny Minnie just about the time some new-fangled stockier look comes into style.

In essence, if you want to be happy, stop trying to please society and start trying to please yourself! Remember that what seems important to you now may appear trivial or meaningless at some point in the future.

Now I shall explain how to get tough with your suicidal personality and take it down by the knees! Not just for today or tomorrow, but forever.

9

HOW TO BRING YOUR SUICIDAL FEELINGS TO A SCREECHING HALT

I'll never forget my enthusiasm the first time I went to hear a behavioral scientist speak on the topic of suicide prevention. My pen was moving a mile a minute jotting down information from the lecturer's numerous overhead projector charts which dealt with every possible statistic I could ever imagine related to self-destructive behavior. By the end of the lecture my note pad was brimming with facts, figures, line graphs, dotted-line graphs, bar graphs, multi-color graphs, and a few graphs so complex I was unable to even give them a label.

Finally, the moment for which I was waiting came. "Any questions?" asked the expert.

"Yes, sir." (I couldn't believe how lucky I was, a huge audience and I had the good fortune of landing the first question. This was the kind of day I should have purchased a lottery ticket, visited a horse race track, or something!)

"Yes, doctor, um, I was just wondering what causes suicide?"

The expert's face rapidly contorted into a rather unfriendly grimace. For a moment complete silence was present in the audience and the speaker. I leaned forward to make absolutely certain I could hang onto every word and tightened the grip on my overworked pen.

"I'm sorry, sir, we don't know what causes suicide."

That was it, his complete answer in its entirety. No tag lines, no "let me qualify that," just a simple "We don't know what causes suicide." Boy, was I ever disappointed.

Now unfortunately, in the literal sense the expert was essentially correct in saying that we don't know what causes suicide. Doctors, biologists, and physiologists cannot let you see the culprit under a microscope. Psychologists have not as yet invented an instrument capable of always pinpointing the exact individuals who will suicide. And lastly, despite athropologists and sociologists' vast knowledge of cultural and social patterns, they have been unable to target specific societal situations which always lead to the final act.

Shall we then just throw up our hands and calmly accept suicide as an inevitable act? I think not, and I shall not disappoint you as the aforementioned expert did me. My work with self-destructive individuals has led me to propose a number of personality traits (i.e., ways of thinking, perceiving, and behaving) which I have seen time and time again. And I am optimistic. Optimistic, because I firmly believe that if you can sit down and take a cold hard look at yourself you can (1) put your finger on your own specific troublesome behaviors and (2) take the bull by the horns by eliminating these self-defeating tendencies.

Some of you will find yourself fitting into one category, others more than one; and still others will see a part of yourself in all of them.

Let me say right off the bat that if you are suicidal you should never use this chapter as an excuse not to go to therapy, nor should it ever take the place of competent medical, psychological, or psychiatric care.

Having said that as emphatically as I know how, I am still convinced that despite my numerous directives to secure professional help many of you reading these words simply will not do so.

Some of you won't go out of fear, while others out of inconvenience or inaccessibility. The nearest mental health provider, for example, could be 75 miles away and you are lacking a viable source of transportation.

Other readers will deny themselves a visit to a professional because of a negative past experience which left them with bad tastes in their mouths regarding mental health practitioners.

The saddest scenario, nonetheless, is the reader who has, in fact, visited therapist after therapist, participated in an endless string of inpatient and outpatient programs, and still feels hopelessly suicidal. This chapter was written for all of you who feel that way.

In addition those of you who are receiving counseling services will want to use this chapter as an adjunct to your treatment program. It will be ideal for those eager beavers who say, "What can I do to help speed up the therapy process or make it work a little better?" So if your therapist gave you this book as a bibliotherapeutic (i.e., using selected readings as an adjunct to the counseling process) homework assignment, now you can see why!

In this chapter I have pulled out all the stops and provided you with the best possible information to annihilate your unwanted suicidal thoughts and feelings. Not everybody who has these personality traits will be genuinely suicidal and hence I have not discovered the "true causes" of suicide. I will, nevertheless, forthrightly contend that even if you are not suicidal but fall into the troublesome areas I have outlined, you could still feel happier by following my advice.

As stated earlier in this book, a major part of feeling suicidal is harboring a sense of hopelessness, a distinct feeling that you are out of control and are powerless to change your situation. The guidance provided in this chapter will help you regain a feeling of power and control, thereby gnawing away at those nagging, no-good feelings of hopelessness.

One question you should ask yourself when you read any self-help literature or embark on a self-improvement program is whether or not the techniques set forth have, in fact, ever really worked for anybody. In the case of strategies provided herein I can assure you that they have. Persons for all walks of life and nearly every age bracket have derived benefit from the advice contained in this very chapter.

Now let us take a cold hard look at those personality traits which could very well be responsible for those nagging self-destructive feelings and use some common sense and sheer brute psychological force to take them down at the knees.

The Suicidal Individual Is a Perfectionist

At the core of every suicidal individual's personality is a demanding perfectionistic streak consumed with criticizing, cutting down, nit-picking, and downright tyrannizing every major, minor, and even minuscule behavior.

The perfectionist is appalled by mediocrity and insists upon keeping a mental score card at all times of the day and night. (Yes, unfortunately, even when the perfectionist sleeps he or she often dreams in the form of a rating!) Every act becomes a performance and an object of ridicule. Simple activities are no longer a source of enjoyment but rather factors which need to be scrutinized and evaluated. Life in general is an assessment process, and the perfectionist leaves no stone unturned in order to yield an unfavorable report card of one's self.

Stop right this very minute and ask yourself whether you are a perfectionist. The tell-tale signs will be evident by your statements and thought patterns. Here are a few typical give-aways that you could be suffering from the curse of perfectionism.

"I demand an A in every course I take."

"If I don't make $100,000 this year I'll consider myself a failure."

"I'll kill myself if I don't make the varsity football squad."

"If I can't be the best I won't even bother attending."

"I couldn't stand it if he told me she was prettier."

"I must get accepted to Harvard . . . that's all there is to it."

"I ought to have twice as many friends as I do now."

"I must master the job or they'll see how stupid I really am."

"I know it's not important to anybody else, but I must accomplish it; and if I don't, it will be the end of the world as far as I'm concerned."

"Oh, sure, I'm very hard on myself at all times."

"What an idiot, I did it again."

"How stupid of me."

"I can't say anything good about myself."

"Everybody thinks I'm a success but deep down I know I'm really a failure."

"Nobody gives a damn what happens to me."

"Yeh, I should be able to, but I can't."

"Don't worry, I'll blow it and choke up, I always do."

Now from time to time all of us have said similar things. Nevertheless, when the tendency becomes very commonplace or when we begin to obsess about our faults, then we are literally programming ourselves for extreme unhappiness, depression, and possibly even self-destruction.

The very first thing you can do to turn the situation around is to be aware of every time you cut yourself down.

I nearly always recommend that suicidal clients *keep a record* of every instance in which they are displaying self-critical behavior.

At first, you needn't try to change your behavior since you've been doing it so long that this would probably result in failure—just another thing to beat yourself over. Instead, merely keep a record or a chart of each time you engage in any self-critical action. Unbeknownst to most individuals, the mere act of charting the behavior is aversive, or at least somewhat undesirable, and hence can actually lessen the frequency with which it occurs. So begin keeping a sheet of paper in your pocket, purse, lunchbox, or on your desk top so you can begin your tally. The paper and pencil record also will allow you to chart your progress.

Another neat little trick is what is known as *"thought stopping"* and is easily accomplished by mentally shouting "STOP" to yourself every time you engage in your typical put-down behavior. It takes a little practice and imagination, but in a very short period of time you will be capable of silently shouting "STOP" so loudly in your mind that you wouldn't dare clobber yourself over the head with your mental baseball bat when you get a less-than-perfect mark on the scoreboard in your mind. Implementing this methodology along with tallying makes the process even more effective.

When looking for perfectionistic thought patterns be aware of those statements or declarations which contain the words "should," "ought," "must," "always," and "never." Such words can indicate that you are getting ready to nag yourself.

Again, suicidal individuals are often their own worst critics, and the idea of these psychological exercises is to teach you to *be a little kinder to yourself.*

Another viable strategy is to literally *reward yourself* for not engaging in any self-critical behavior. Simply pick a length of time—and at first I'd keep it short so you can be successful—and give yourself a reward for not castigating yourself. (M & M's, chocolate chip cookies, and French vanilla ice cream, though traditional favorites, may contain a bit too much sugar, which can actually depress some people, thus inadvertently making them feel worse. Therefore, you may wish to find sugarless rewards or go easy on the desserts!) As you become more proficient you will want to stretch out the time before you reward yourself.

I'm very fond of this strategy, since I'm convinced every suicidal individual needs to be nicer to himself or herself and the idea of giving oneself a reward is unequivocally a step in the right direction. Life is tough enough, so try going a little easier on yourself.

In order to further combat your pernicious self-critical attitude I'd advise you to *draw up a list of positive attributes about yourself.* This will no doubt be a very difficult task inasmuch as suicidal individuals generally expend so much energy giving themselves a pain in the duff that they rarely find time to pat themselves on the back.

When I recently gave this assignment to an eighth grade youngster who was contemplating suicide, the first sentence on her list read: I'm really smart when it comes to math but check my spelling and you will see how dumb I really am.

When it comes to doing this exercise you simply want to generate positives. Write: I'm really smart when it comes to math, period! No additional tag lines which suggest you need to improve your spelling, typing, or gardening.

As I said, this will be a tough assignment since you may be unaccustomed to treating yourself with respect. Once you have a list of ten or twelve positives I want you to force yourself to *think about your desirable qualities* as often as you can, again setting up a system of rewards to reinforce this therapeutic activity. You may, for example, allow yourself the luxury of a new leather handbag or that quartz wristwatch you've always drooled over after you compliment yourself say 50 or so times.

Here is a letter one of my clients sent me after we discussed the concept of perfectionism in regard to suicidal feelings. I've chosen to include it because it is illustrative of the mixed feelings you may experience when embarking on your self-improvement program.

Dear Dr. Rosenthal,

As you may have guessed by now, I won't make it home in time for my weekly therapy session. I'm keeping the slip of paper you gave me with the local crisis center's number on it just in case I start feeling really down again.

Being in a strange town reminds me how lonely I am and how poor I am at meeting new people. Darn it—you were right—there I did it again; put myself down as usual. Bet you've never had a client as quick to criticize himself as I am.

Hold on, I have to mark my chart. (Well, that's 32 critical thoughts so far today dummy and it's only 2:00 o'clock in the afternoon.) Whoops! Make that 33 times.

Actually, I am doing a bit better though. The day after I left your office I racked up 113 and came to the conclusion I'd better cut it out or I'd be spending my whole day updating my chart.

My current goal is to lower my self-critical thoughts to just 25 per day. No, it won't mean I'm cured, but it sure as heck will indicate some significant progress. When I reach 25 my reward will be the expensive light blue silk tie I told you about. Normally, I'd never shower myself with a gift like that but I'm convinced that eliminating my put-down behaviors is truly something worth celebrating.

Now making the list of positives has been a much more difficult task. Every time I try to think of a positive a negative pops into my mind. Nevertheless, perhaps we can work on this in my next therapy session. It's really tough to think about your positive attributes when you've been focusing on the negative for over 30 years.

Anyway, despite the fact that I still have an occasional suicidal impulse I still feel better knowing that I'm doing something to fight it in the opposite direction.

See you soon.

Respectfully,
Dennis

Give these exercises a try and you will find yourself gaining control over self-destructive behavior.

Suicidal People Have Distinct Difficulties Expressing Anger

The existential philosopher Albert Camus once asserted that suicide was the only question worthy of philosophical inquiry. For the majority of cases, nevertheless, Camus was wrong. Suicide is not a question of philosophy but rather one of mental health and more specifically an inability to effectively express pent-up feelings of extreme anger.

As stated earlier, this anger may manifest itself in the 4 out of 100 cases in which suicide is accompanied by an act of homicide. A not uncommon act is for the suicidal individual to pack an extra bullet in his or her weapon.

The Freudian notion that the self-destructive individual really wants to kill somebody else seems to ring true in many instances.

The suicidal person saves up angry feelings in the same manner that other individuals collect trading stamps. Because they never fight with others (or at least wait until the last few days before the attempt), they generally end up fighting themselves.

When you do counseling with survivors of suicide you are immediately struck with the seemingly ironic fact that a goodly number of individuals who took their own lives never seemed to express anger or disagreement with anybody for any reason.

I have actually come across cases in which the suicide note provided family and friends with the first clue that the person was seeing things with intense anger and hatred.

Inasmuch as suicide and homicide are acts of anger, I often think of them as second cousins. Several years ago when I was supervising social service caseworkers I would routinely assign them readings related to the mass-murderer personality (e.g., Charles Manson). They were shocked to find that in many, if not most cases, the personalities of these individuals have been described in positive terms by those who knew them personally. More amazing was that many of them were referred to as "quiet," "polite," or simply a "nice guy." Phrases like "all-American boy," "a very peaceful man," "extremely well-mannered," "terribly sensi- tive," and "a polite person" also accompanied some of these descriptions.

In many instances, the friends and acquaintances of these nice-killers were initially convinced that the "police got the wrong man" or that "the person was not himself at the time." I have routinely heard survivors say similar things about the victim who took his or her own life.

Could anger turned inward serve to abet depression in these gentle, yet rigidly controlled individuals? Might the suppression of aggressive feelings lead to an eruption of violence toward the self, others, or in some cases both?

Let me reiterate that all types of people from every walk of life commit suicide—tall, short, black, white, underweight, overweight, bankers, doctors, teachers, and, yes, even candlestick makers. Nonetheless, in my work I have observed two groups which seem to have more than their expected share of difficulties: on one hand is the individual who never shows a trace of anger, and on the other is the belligerent hot-head who comes across in a severely aggressive manner. Not surprisingly, neither one of these extreme personality types is able to achieve satisfactory personal fulfillment. The first is so namby-pamby he never gets his or her way, while the latter comes across so forceful others often don't respond as expected out of fear, protest, or an attempt to show the person he or she cannot push others around.

One evening I received a call from a gentleman who was highly suicidal after breaking up with his girlfriend. He was so inflamed he was shaking, throwing objects around his apartment, and had literally put his fist through two rather thick panes of glass.

Had he told his girlfriend he was mad? "Not really," he explained, "I graciously agreed that if she wanted to break up I'd be willing to go along with the plan."(!)

So instead of fighting with the object of affection, he ended up doing battle with himself.

Assertiveness training is a psychological paradigm which is geared toward helping clients express their own rights without violating the rights of others. Assertiveness trainers often classify behavioral responses as non-assertive, assertive, and aggressive. The aforementioned client was undoubtedly displaying a non-assertive posture.

Individuals are said to be non-assertive when they don't verbalize their wants or needs and end up letting everybody walk on them. In essence, they become human doormats. The aggressive individual does the direct antithesis of the non-assertive person.

He or she steps on everybody's toes without concern, which can often lead to guilt despite the fact that the aggression usually doesn't yield the desired results.

I'll never forget the only time I almost lost my cool in front of a large audience. I was summoned to a rather small town after a popular teen took her own life. After I finished some basic bereavement work with the group, I offered to take questions regarding suicide prevention in general.

A lady stood up in the back of the room, placed one hand on her hip while the other was pointing at me in a punitive fashion. She leaned forward and began yelling: "Hey, listen to me, mister. I knew that child and it's her own fault she killed herself. I scolded her many times and tried to correct her stupid behavior. But no, all my fussing didn't help a bit. What in the hell good did all my yelling and screaming do? So tell me, Mr. hot-shot expert, what the heck do I say when a kid feels like killing herself? Hum? When I demand things from kids they don't respond. Are they deaf or what?"

"Look," I told her, "you can begin by lowering your voice and eliminating your threatening body posture. I wouldn't respond to you either!"

The auditorium became very quiet as everybody stared at her. She blushed and ever so slowly lowered her finger which was still pointed at me in a accusatory fashion and sat down in her seat.

Though this woman didn't know it, she was displaying textbook aggressive behavior. The sad fact is that I believe her when she says that "when I demand things from kids they don't respond."

If you are feeling suicidal I would wholeheartedly suggest you seek out an assertiveness training group. If you don't know of any, you can call your local mental health association, crisis center, hospital stress unit, or college psychology department for a referral.

You also can help yourself by becoming *acutely aware of your own behavioral responses* or what assertiveness trainers refer to as "discrimination exercises." In a discrimination exercise you examine actual, everyday situations in your own life in order to ascertain whether you are coming across in an assertive, non-assertive, or aggressive manner. You then make a concerted effort to change those situations in which you are falling into the non-assertive or aggressive categories.

You may choose to write down assertive responses and then practice verbalizing them when you are alone, or better still, role-play the scenario with a trusted friend who has been made aware that you are working on such issues.

Let's take a look at a typical example so you understand precisely what I mean by a discrimination exercise:

> **Sample Situation:** A door-to-door encyclopedia salesman calls on you during final exam week.

> **Non-Assertive:** Although your budget would never allow you the luxury of purchasing a set of encyclopedias at this time, you invite the gentleman in and listen to his lengthy sales pitch. You also have access to the school library which is just one block from your apartment and, of course, houses a number of different encyclopedias. Nevertheless, the salesman seems like a swell guy and has spent almost an hour of his valuable time discoursing on the merits of these beautifully bound tomes.

> "What the heck," you say, "you've convinced me; what is life without knowledge? I'll take a set."

> Later that night you will toss and turn unable to sleep. You'll replay the scenario over and over in your mind while you castigate yourself for being sold a bill of goods you obviously didn't need. In addition, anxiety and severe panic set in since you have absolutely no idea where you will be able to summon up the money to pay the bill.

> And last but not least, you will lie awake fuming over the fact that the guy took away a valuable period of study time which could very well lead to a lower final exam grade. Before falling asleep you will administer the crowning blow to your ego by saying to yourself, "nice going, twerp, you wimped out again. You just dug yourself a little deeper hole to climb out of. You ought to just blow your brains out."

Aggressive: You cut the man off immediately and begin yelling, "Listen, bimbo, you're the third damn door-to-door salesman I've seen this week. Now get the hell out of here before I take one of those crummy-looking books and shove it where the sun doesn't shine. You've got your nerve, pal, even showing your face during final week." You then slam the door so hard the glass cracks.

Like the non-assertive person, you too will have ill feelings about the situation, not to mention a costly front door repair. You will feel a touch of paranoia wondering whether the neighbors over heard the exchange and may thus ostracize you from future activities in the apartment complex. You also will wonder if the guy selling the encyclopedias wasn't also a student at the university who could further turn fellow students against you. "What a mess," you tell yourself, "I should just get the gun and mow down that jerk and then put myself out of commission. Face it, I'm useless."

Assertive: You respond in a conversational, firm voice: "No thanks, I have access to numerous encyclopedias through the college library and so I'm just not interested in purchasing a set. Thanks for stopping by. Good night." You can continue your studies without looking back at this situation as unfinished business. Mission accomplished, and without obsessing about any bad feelings either!

As you come across situations which caused you distress due to an aggressive or non-assertive response, sit down and calmly imagine how you could behave in a more assertive manner in the future. Even if you can't role play the situation with a friend you can always role play it in your mind! Instead of falling into the suicidal trap of giving yourself a mental lashing for your inept behavior, you can spend those precious moments planning for a happier future.

Now perhaps I need to state with a high degree of authority that not being an assertive individual does not automatically mean you are suicidal. What I am saying, however, is that if you are currently suffering from suicidal impulses, then increasing your assertiveness will help ameliorate one of the major contributing factors to your unwanted state of mind.

Here is a final grain of advice for those of you who are too shy to honestly express your feelings. Since mental health starts with the minutiae (i.e., the small things in life) and then generalizes, you can begin your self-assertiveness campaign by asserting yourself in trivial, non-threatening situations. Here are a few examples:

> Go into a service station and ask if you can borrow a tire pressure gauge to check the air in your car tires. Better yet, ask the attendant to do it for you.

> Ask for a glass of water in a restaurant or extra salad dressing (catsup, mustard, napkins, etc., etc.).

> Start a conversation with somebody you really don't know.

> Ask a friend for a favor which you normally wouldn't have the guts to request.

> Return an item to the store which is marginal and with which you are not really satisfied but would traditionally have been too meek to complain about.

> If you are a student, raise your hand and answer a question or volunteer information you wouldn't normally share.

> Ask your boss for the rationale behind a policy you find distasteful. (Some of my non-assertive clients have tried this and their bosses couldn't come up with valid reasons and actually changed the policy!)

And when you perform these exercises, or simply converse with others in daily situations, *try using the word "I," especially in conjunction with feelings, likes, and dislikes.* This practice will help make you feel comfortable as you express yourself and lets everyone know you are taking responsibility for your own feelings.

Since we are talking about counterproductive habits of communication which afflict the self-destructive personality, I cannot forego mention of a pattern known as the "hidden bargain." Now in the "hidden bargain," an individual performs a number of tasks with the hope that someone else will notice and respond in a desired manner. The exchange is known as a "hidden bargain" because the person who wants the other person to notice the tasks never lays his or her cards on the table and explains why he or she is behaving in a special manner.

Here are some examples of "hidden bargains" my clients have shared with me in therapy sessions:

> "For six months I always cooked my husband's favorite dish twice a week. I kept thinking that if I did this he wouldn't divorce me. I never said anything, I just kept cooking those meals ... treating him like a king. Two weeks ago he served me with divorce papers. That's when I decided I couldn't go on and took an overdose of pills."

> "I tried so hard in school. And I thought, gee if I get all A's maybe Dad will stop drinking, but it didn't happen. It just never happened, and I started thinking about suicide. I didn't ever tell Dad how much I hated his drinking. I thought he'd become angry."

> "I was at that damn office until nearly midnight on some occasions. I mean I was a slave to that job. I would work until my tongue was hanging out but I'll tell you what, I could taste that promotion at the end of the rainbow. Hell, that promotion meant everything to me. It was like my whole life was riding on it., and then Harry gave the position to his brother who never spent one day of his life in the restaurant business. I said the heck with this. All the other problems in my life and now this ... Forget it. Life just isn't worth it. I fired up that classic Corvette race car I told you about and took her out on highway 32 to see how fast I could fly off that second hairpin turn. The doctors said I was lucky I didn't lose both legs."

If you have a "hidden bargain" in your life I urge you to come out of the closet with your wants and needs right now. The more time, money, and emotional investment you put into your "hidden bargain" the harder the consequences will hit you. Tell the person (or persons) what you want, and if it doesn't happen don't catastrophize. Don't sit around mumbling how terrible it is, how life can't go on, and how this meant everything to you. Such thinking will indeed do nothing more than intensify your state of unhappiness.

Teenagers and adults can sometimes rid themselves of the pernicious effects of the "hidden bargain" by understanding that the roots of this self-defeating behavior stem from your childhood. Generally, what has transpired is that you were placed in a situation or situations in which you were genuinely unable to change. You may have verbally or physically tried to remedy this situation to no avail. At the time you didn't just feel helpless—you really were helpless. Your only recourse was your childhood notion that good things happen to good kids. It may have even occurred to you that bad things happened only to bad kids and therefore you were bad and had to become good.

Maybe dad was sexually abusing you and you begun thinking, "If I become the perfect little girl this will stop."

Perhaps mom was bruising you severely with those belt thrashings and you came to the conclusion that, "If I can keep my room extra clean the punishment will cease."

Or maybe your parents were talking about separating and you convinced yourself that if you got a night job selling papers your folks would stay together. And why not, they nearly always argued over financial matters?

Now despite your tendency to become a more perfect child, the sexual encounters with dad, the sting of the leather belt, and mom and dad's separation all continued to transpire. And at that point in time, it might have even crossed your mind that you were good, but not good enough. In the future you made a mental vow to yourself to try even harder, and this eventually evolved into your current adulthood pattern of the "hidden bargain."

Another possibility is that the sexual abuse, the beatings, and the separation ceased to occur and you thus wrongly came to the conclusion that your propensity toward perfection warded off the threatening situation. I say wrongly because as a child you were unaware that other factors were responsible for the alleviation of the unwanted traumatic predicaments. (For example, dad began molesting your younger sister, mom was reported to the child abuse hotline, and your parents no longer found it necessary to date someone outside of the marriage.)

An important procedure is for the suicidal individual to begin expressing his or her feelings in a direct and socially acceptable manner, lest those feelings will return to haunt the person. You can begin by reviewing your past in order to uncover experiences which may have caused you to become non-assertive, aggressive, or the perpetrator of hidden bargains. The mere act of discovering the roots of your behavior will often provide a degree of understanding and insight which can facilitate change.

Once again—and I shouldn't have to reiterate this statement, but it is so critical I will—when *you start behaving in a way that is desirable, reward yourself for doing so.* You deserve it and you know it.

Suicide Can Result from an Unrealistic Fantasy Self

At the expense of sounding a bit pejorative, every person who has killer instincts against self has a wish to become Superman (or in the case of a woman, Superwoman). The exaggerated sense of perfectionism at the core of nearly every suicidal person's personality leads to the psychic creation of a fantasy or ideal self which can only be described as unrealistic.

To be sure, each of us can and should have an ideal self-image. An image which will cause us to be goal directed and allow us to improve the quality of our own lives as well as the quality of others'.

The problem is that the suicidal often set extremely high standards for themselves which are at best unattainable. The suicidal individual's fantasy self is omnipotent and immortal. The poor owner of this fantasy does not see his or her conceptualization as impractical nor impossible. Though most of us will view our ideal self as something worth working toward, the suicidal mentally turn the situation around and view the inability to reach this goal as another example of their gross incompetence. This leads to a state of continual unfulfillment and extreme unhappiness. Worse yet, when a crisis occurs (e.g., losing a job, a break-up of a relationship, a death in the family, or an inability to pass a college course), the suicidal person not only comes to the conclusion that he or she is powerless to change the situation, but adds insult to injury by being hit with the realization that he or she will never reach this fantasy self. Instead of discovering at that point in time that this fantasy self is not even a positive state worth striving for, the suicidal ask self why go on living when the person he or she truly wants to be is unattainable.

I'll never forget a shy, retiring young lady I was seeing for therapy who had a dream of being a beautiful, outgoing, highly-paid fashion model who was out on the town with a different male movie star every night. In reality, she was lonely, never dated, and worked in an office secretarial pool. Not long after beginning therapy she was transferred to another state and thus had to terminate therapy.

She did, nevertheless, continue to keep me informed via a series of letters and postcards which seemed a bit far-fetched. Her correspondence implied that she was no longer a homely secretary in search of a date but rather the girl of her dreams—a much sought after covergirl who drove a Ferrari, wore mink whenever it was appropriate, and had her pick of New York's best-looking male models.

Somehow I just didn't buy it and called long distance to make certain she wasn't becoming acutely suicidal. The day I called, the young lady wasn't at home and her landlady answered the phone. When I told her to leave a message that Dr. Rosenthal called the landlady said, "Oh, doctor, I'm so glad you called today; this poor girl really needs help. She goes to work, comes home, and never goes out of the house. Maybe if she had even a friend or two she would care a little more about her appearance and the shabby way she dresses. I'm sorry, doctor, I know it's none of my business; it's just that she looks so sad and depressed, it makes me want to break into tears. She's awfully nice and actually quite attractive. Can't you do something to help?"

Fortunately, I was able to contact a relative who, in turn, was capable of convincing her to continue her therapy. In this parti-cular instance, the need to become the idea or fantasy self generated an overpowering desire to prove to a significant other (in this case, me) that she had, in fact, become the person of her fantasies.

If you are suicidal, then you need to evaluate your ideal self with a fine tooth comb to see if it is (1) realistic, (2) really a meal ticket to happiness, and (3) primarily created to please others rather than yourself.

I once counseled a rather successful 30-year-old gentleman named Al who was suicidal for a number of reasons. One of the factors, which manifested itself during a counseling session, was that in his mind he felt a burning desire to be big and burly or, as he put it, "built like a football player." he was naturally tall, lanky, and literally hundreds of malted milks and protein drinks had failed to put on even a pound.

Now the interesting thing to note is why he wanted to look like this.

"Well," he told me, "women go ape over guys like that; they just love that big-as-a-house look. It's macho. If I looked like that, Cindy would be falling all over me."

"But doesn't she love you now?" I asked.

"Aw, yeh, sure she loves me, but it would really turn her on if I looked like a fullback."

During the next session I brought in some pictures of football players and asked him to pick three or four who looked similar to his fantasy self. He had no trouble in choosing several. I then invited his companion Cindy in and said, "Cindy, how would you feel if Al looked like these guys?"

"These guys? . . . How disgusting," she remarked. "They look like overgrown pigs." She then glanced over at Al and added, "That's the way a fellow ought to look."

Al looked downright confused. "Wait a minute. What's wrong with those guys? I thought you'd find them attractive."

"Why in the world would you think that?"

As you may have guessed, a rather interesting discussion ensued. The moral is that before you create a fantasy self you think others find desirable, at least have the decency to ask them!

Now realistically, I said this partially in jest since I sincerely believe that suicidal persons should immediately (if not sooner!) give up their tendency of trying to please others. First of all, because you cannot do it. Even if Cindy loves big burly football hunks, Sarah, Mary Beth, Terri, and your mother may find them a total turnoff. And second, because if you base your self-worth on the opinion of others, you have sold out your own value system and are making the opinions of others more important than your own. From that point on in time, others—not you—will be in charge of your mental health and relative level of happiness.

Here are some concrete strategies to rid yourself once and for all of that unrealistic fantasy self:

1. Imagine this very moment what would happen if you became your fantasy self. Would it, in fact, be correct to say that all of your problems would be solved? If you did look like a gridiron star, what would happen if you met the love of your life and she detests athletes? Or if you achieve covergirl status and your next heartthrob is crazy about the shy, homely type?

2. Some suicidal people come extremely close to actually reaching their fantasy self and still aren't happy. (In one case, I heard about a young woman who lusted after a young man for three years. He was the most popular fellow on campus and nearly every girl wanted to date him. Finally, when she succeeded in catching him she committed suicide. In her note she said she was disappointed and still very unhappy.) So ask yourself: If tomorrow morning I could become my ideal self, is it possible I would still be disappointed? Would I use that as an excuse to make a suicide attempt?

3. Try to determine what difficulties are bothering you that would not be solved by your fantasy self. For example, once you look like a famous covergirl, a well-known quarterback, or date Mr. Wonderful, how will it affect your phobia of elevators, your ongoing feud with your Aunt Peggy, or your lack of communication with your children?

4. What statements in your childhood led to the formation of your ideal self? Did your father tell you that real men always serve in the armed forces? Did your mother insist that smart girls never

argue with men? Perhaps your father wanted nothing more than an athletic son and because you never got along with him you chose an ideal self which was the direct antithesis? Could your ideal self serve as a protest against messages you heard and found less than palatable in your childhood, or is it a way of unconsciously pleasing significant others out of your past?

5. Ask a professional counselor or your trusted friends what they think of your fantasy self image. Even if some of them feel it is realistic and desirable, do all of them?

6. Come up with an alternative fantasy self. This will help to convince you that perhaps there are other—even totally opposite—paths to happiness. There truly is more than one way to skin a cat!

7. Use thought stopping (remember your mental bullhornlike technique of yelling STOP) every time you catch yourself worrying more about what others think than what you think about yourself.

8. Reward yourself when you do any of the aforementioned seven steps.

The Suicidal Person
Wants to Punish Self

Suicidal persons go beyond the mere act of criticizing themselves—they literally want to hurt themselves. Often one is accurate to say that they are masters of self-harm and live in self-induced psychic prisons.

In essence, they are serving emotional sentences for their self-proclaimed evil streak every day of the year.

The truth is that if we look at ourselves in an honest manner, each and every one of us has done a number of things of which we were not proud, incidents which caused us to experience guilt and shame. In a relatively short period of time, nevertheless, most of us admitted we were fallible human beings who made a mistake, and from that day on we forgot about our shortcomings and went on with the business of living our lives. The self-destructive personality will hold the incident captive and use it to haunt himself or herself throughout eternity.

Those individuals are easy to spot because they are intent on badgering themselves. Their verbalizations indicate that they will persistently hold on to the notion that because of their own wicked act or acts they must be sentenced to death. Here are some statements demonstrative of this pattern:

"I had an abortion. I killed . . . I actually killed . . . now I must be killed too . . . even if I have to do it myself."

"Jeff was in the car when I ran off the road and he ended up dead. Now I'm going to end up dead and I'm going to do it on the anniversary of his death."

"Sure, I'm a terrible person. I've done all kinds of bad things. But in the end I'm going to get mine. I'm going to make myself suffer; I promise you that."

As children, many individuals who fit this pattern only received attention when they did something wrong (e.g., hitting another family member or stealing something). That, of course, led the person to often engage in guilt-producing behavior in order to secure attention. The person craved the attention but hated self for the way he or she went about it.

If you are condemning yourself to the point where you are feeling suicidal, you need to be aware of something: punishing yourself will not rectify your heinous deed. Instead, why not consider ways you can personally improve similar situations in the future? If your best friend died as a result of your driving while intoxicated, you could volunteer several hours a week at a local hospital unit which specializes in substance abuse treatment.

Now if you truly want to feel better about your life, you must vigorously apply the strategies herein and adamantly refuse to punish yourself for your past behavior. Rewarding yourself when you don't punish yourself sounds contradictory, but it helps to ameliorate the difficulty.

And just in case these techniques in this chapter don't stomp out all your feelings of self-destruction, fear not, my next chapter will allow you to make even greater strides toward personal fulfillment and happiness.

10

ROCK MUSIC, IMITATION, SUICIDE, AND YOUR PERSONAL HAPPINESS

The tiny island of Oshima is just 59 miles from Tokyo and covers only 36 square miles of the vast surface of the planet earth In fact, prior to 1933 it attracted only a few tourists who went to see the massive sulfur clouds which boiled from the crater of its mighty volcano, Mount Mihara. Three times weekly, a small steamer, the Kiku Maru, would leave Tokyo to visit the small body of land.

Now before the year 1933, behavioral science historians would have been hard pressed to give you statistics on the number of people who committed suicide by jumping into a volcano, because for all practical purposes, it just didn't happen. On January 7 of that very year, however, a 24-year-old student named Mieko Ueki from the exclusive Jissen Higher School in Tokyo would change all that. In fact, Mieko's behavior would literally initiate an astonishing chain reaction which would not only incite hundreds upon hundreds of suicides but would ultimately render Mount Mihara the number one spot on the face of the earth where people killed themselves!

On January 7, 1933, Mieko confided in her 21-year-old classmate and friend Masako Tomita that she wanted to jump into the Mount Mihara crater. Though she knew the act would surely result in her death, she had visited the volcano a year ago and was convinced the fiery pit would cremate her and the smoke would transport her to heaven. In Mieko's mind, this was a beautiful, poetic form of death. Interestingly enough, she did jump to her death on that date with her last request being that Masako keep her death a secret for five years.

Masako kept her promise for all of two weeks and then spilled the beans to a 21-year-old schoolmate, Kiyoko Matsumoto. Though it may sound difficult to believe if you are not suicidal yourself, Kiyoko expressed an urgent desire to follow Mieko to paradise. On February 12, Kiyoko leaped to her own death in Masako's presence.

Another companion noticed Kiyoko's strange disappearance, the police were contacted, and in no time newspapers were plastering the gory details on page after page and in article after article.

An endless string of reporters hounded Masako, and in April she became ill (no doubt stress was a significant factor) and died. Now magazines jumped on the bandwagon and overnight Oshima became a national attraction.

The Kiku Maru could no longer carry the numerous passengers and a larger boat was constructed. During the first Sunday in April six persons took the plunge to end it all while 25 others were prevented by using physical force.

In almost no time crowds were coming to see the suicides rather than the volcano! Record has it that on one occasion a man dared someone from the crowd of tourists to jump and somebody did! Oshima began to resemble Niagara Falls or Atlantic City as 14 hotels and 20 restaurants sprang up. A post office was even constructed at the crater's edge.

By the end of 1933 Mihara claimed the lives of 143 individuals.

By 1934 police noted that they had forcibly prevented 1,200 such deaths. An anti-suicide league was formed, yet 619 persons still jumped to their own deaths in 1936.

Eventually, guards and a high barbed wire fence helped to put the lid on this morbid reign of self-destruction.

Suicide, seemingly, is contagious. If you have one suicide in a school, business, prison, or even a volcano, the odds increase that you will have others. When a person who is unhappy sees another flee the pain of everyday life via suicide, the person seems now to have permission to do so himself or herself. And though the second, third, or hundredth person to take his or her own life does not always know the other persons who killed themselves, he or she knows of them.

This phenomenon has been known as the contagion, ripple, or copycat effect, and it happens in places other than Japan.

To be sure, Japan's hari-kari tradition, and the 5,000 World War II kamikaze pilots, would cause one to wrongly assume that this unfortunate dynamic belongs only to the Japanese. Nothing could be further from the truth. And although adults are susceptible to contagion, our teens seem to be the ones at the greatest risk.

In Plano, Texas, once thought of as a "perfect city," a rash of 8 youths suicides occurred in a little over a year and a ninth on the third anniversary of the teenager who was the first to take his own life. The town literally lived in the fear of a suicide epidemic which spanned from February 1983 until February 1986.

The wealthy vicinity of Westchester County, New York, also has been a site for a cluster of suicides, some of them linked to an ABC-TV movie *Surviving* and the box office smash hit *An Officer and a Gentleman.*

The most recent chain of incidents took place in Omaha, Nebraska, during a brief five-day period when three students from Bryan High School killed themselves in February 1986. An even greater number of teen attempts was made in the month surrounding the days in question.

To the aforementioned incidents, we could add 12 teens who suicided in an 18-month period in Larimer County, Colorado; a domino reaction of suicides which at first glance appeared to be accidents in Leominster, Massachusetts; and the horror of the

1980-81 school year, in which 20 teens took their own lives in Fairfax County, Virginia, to cite a few major teen clusters.

Suicide is a form of communication, and whether we are ready to admit it or not, we all seem to live in monkey-see, monkey-do societies. We like to think that we are captains of our own ship, but are we really? When another individual does something against his or her own best interests, does that in turn give us a blank check to follow in the same footsteps?

I remember one day I was sitting around chewing the fat with some other therapists between workshops at a mental health conference. One of them commented, "You know, I bet you at least 25% of my clients who attempted suicide saw a family member do the same thing." At that point a psychiatric nurse who worked in a hospital ward said, "Of the patients I've seen, I'll bet the figure is well over 50%."

I began making mental notes from the survivors with whom I had worked and I came to the conclusion that about one-half of the individuals who suicided saw (or were aware that) another family member make an attempt. Always keep in mind that most forms of emotional education originate in the home, especially during the early or so-called formative years.

Ask yourself these questions: If right now you discovered that another individual you knew committed suicide, would you be more prone to attempt? Would a series of news stories depicting the self-intended deaths of others cause you to think more about suicide as an option? Would you compare your own situation to the predicaments of those individuals talked about in the media tales?

If your answer to any of the previous questions was "yes," you could very easily be a potential victim of the copycat syndrome. The possibility increases by leaps and bounds if one of your family members suicided or attempted suicide.

One of the finest ways I know to fight the tendency is to first be aware that you were taught that suicide was a viable option for solving your problems. Realize honestly that you were the recipient of a less-than-desirable emotional road map since in many, if not most, families children are taught other coping skills. Suicide, if you will, is not discussed as an option, nor is it acted out when the going gets tough in the healthy family.

In addition to family patterns and media tales, the self-destructive personality is susceptible to things he or she reads in books. The scientific terminology suicidologists utilize to describe the imitation factor is "the Werther effect." In 1774 Johann Wolfgang von Goethe wrote a romantic novel, *The Sorrows of Young Werther*, which caused a wave of suicides. In the story, Werther takes his own life using a gun which belonged to a rival who won the girl of his affections.

Within a brief period of time copies of the book were discovered next to people who had suicided, and a wave of so-called "Wertheritis" swept across Europe. The book was banned in several countries, and when an Italian edition appeared in Milan the Catholic clergy stopped the dissemination of the work by purchasing every available copy.

In 1974, a sociologist working out of the University of California, David Phillips, noted a significant increase in self-destruction after front-page suicide articles, a phenomenon he called "the Werther effect." Needless to say, the description was right on target, and other professionals began using it in regard to copycat or ripple effect deaths.

Phillips also discovered that well-publicized suicides of famous people also can give the suicide rate a boost in the arm. When Marilyn Monroe committed suicide, almost 200 people more than would normally have killed themselves took their own lives in the month after the star's death.

Again, we can turn to Japan for the most blatant example of how a famous person's suicide can provide the impetus for others to do the same.

On April 8, 1986, Yukiko Okada, an 18-year-old rock star, jumped from the top of a seven-story recording studio building. The report was that Yukiko was extremely upset over the fact that her love affair with an actor who was many years her senior wasn't working out to her satisfaction.

A number of media releases billed Ms. Okada as Japan's top rock star, and rightly so, inasmuch as in the year prior to her suicide she received an award as Japan's top new singer.

The cluster phenomenon took off just two days after Okada's suicide when two sisters, one 18, the other the tender age of 12, jumped to their deaths. The snowball effect was not in full force, and in just seventeen days after her death 33 other teens decided to terminate their own lives. Approximately one week later the tab increased to 34 when a 21-year-old male jumped from precisely the same roof as Okada. The link between the suicides became even stronger when pictures of Okada were found in the victim's pocket. What might be the most striking statistic, however, was that 22 of the 34 suicides resulted from jumping off buildings—Okada's method of choice.

Not only does one suicide increase the chances that another will occur, but it ups the ante that subsequent acts of self-destruction will be enacted in exactly the same fashion as the initial incident.

Perhaps nothing reflects the magnitude of the suicide problem in our country more than the fact that approximately one out of every ten new movies currently features a suicide or a suicide attempt carefully woven into the plot. Suicide scenes have now infiltrated their way into mystery, action, drama, sports-related, and even comical movies. In the humorous film *Dr. Strangelove* actor Slim Pickens seemingly performs the ultimate act of suicide-homicide when he rides the atomic bomb to earth, cowboy hat in hand, as if it's a horse. Portrayal of suicide in the movies seems endless. Just as examples, I can personally attest to the fact that the last two box office flicks I've seen were replete with some mention of the issue. In Stallone's video arm-bender *Over the Top,* the viewer gets into the first few moments of the movie and only as far as the right mud flap of Sly's tractor-trailer truck before the word suicide appears, in this instance inscribed on its surface. In the other movie I viewed, *Lethal Weapon,* the message is even stronger—star Mel Gibson plays a somewhat psychopathic suicidal maniac who is working as an undercover cop. Throughout the movie he gives repeated consideration to taking his own life.

Several movies, most notably the ABC-TV broadcast of the television film *Surviving,* have been implicated in a number of real-life suicides. In the movie, the act of suicide is seemingly romanticized as stars Zach Galligan and teen idol Molly Ringwald die in each other's arms from carbon monoxide poisoning. Two days after it aired, one father blamed his son's death on the movie. The 17-year-old youngster told friends he felt the drama "was really good" and then died in his car of carbon monoxide poisoning.

Data from various cities throughout the U.S. indicated a greater proportion of suicides resulting from carbon monoxide after the movie. Distressed teens who saw the story may have consciously or unconsciously identified with and imitated the behavior portrayed by Galligan and Ringwald in the movie.

If, however, concerned citizens and suicidologists have repeatedly pointed the finger at any movie as provoking out-and-out acts of self-destruction, it would be *The Deer Hunter.* As part of the plot actor Christopher Walken and others are forced by Vietnamese Communists to play Russian roulette. Later, Walken, reflecting on his war days, decides to play Russian roulette again and ends up shooting himself.

At this point in time, approximately 40 suicides and a number of attempts have revolved around this movie. In many cases, I might add, Russian roulette was the method of choice.

But movies, newspaper stories, books, and the suicides of others, including the rich and famous, are not the only culprits. The connection between rock music lyrics and teen suicide is now well documented and has already been the subject of an occasional legal battle.

Take the original version of *Suicide Solution* by Black Sabbath and Ozzy Osbourne which contains a number of suggestions to take one's own life. In the fifth stanza the listener is exposed to the message that "Where to hide, Suicide is the only way out." Then, in the final stanza, recorded at 1½ times the normal recording speed are the words which communicate why try therefore get the gun and shoot.

Since the portion of the song is recorded at 1½ times the normal rate of speech it may not, in fact, be intelligible to the average listener—at least not consciously. I have clarified this by saying "at least not consciously" because some research into a phenomenon known as subliminal perception suggests that messages we can't hear consciously can actually have a much greater impact on our thoughts, feelings, and behaviors than those we can. In all fairness to Osbourne's original version from the *Blizzard of Oz* album, at this time a raging debate is ongoing as to whether or not subliminal suggestion works.

Tom Anderson is a California lawyer who represented a father whose 19-year-old son shot himself in the head in October 1984 after he listened to Ozzy Osbourne albums for five hours. Anderson claims to have received at least twenty calls from parents who said their teens committed suicide and were avid listeners of Ozzy Osbourne.

Interestingly enough, Osbourne mentioned in an interview for KABC-TV in Los Angeles that the song was actually "anti-suicide."

In a revised version by Osbourne and Randy Roads, the final stanza is tamed down a bit, though the line about suicide being the only way out since there is no place to hide remains intact.

Not long after the Osbourne lawsuit was dismissed on constitutional grounds, a so-called heavy metal British rock group, Judas Priest, was hauled into court over a youth suicide pact. The suit claimed the band's message was to commit suicide as the ultimate act of societal rejection.

Another heavy metal group, Metallica, has been taken to task for their song *Fade to Black,* which advises: that yesterday was undesirable and death now would be better, therefore goodbye. In one situation when a 17- and a 19-year-old woman took their own lives a suicide note was discovered on the windshield of the vehicle containing lyrics from the rock band Metallica.

Perhaps even more remarkable is the fact that teens also will mimic the fictional acts of rock stars which coincide with the music even when they lead to death. In October of 1984 a youngster hanged himself after he saw super rock star Alice Cooper complete a mock hanging as part of a musical act!

In an analogous fashion a 17-year-old took his own life after dressing up like rock star Prince as he appeared in the hit movie *Purple Rain*. In the film Prince, who plays "The Kid," fantasizes about killing himself. Though no formal suicide note was found, the names of the child's mother, brother, sister, girlfriend, and Prince (!) were scrawled in purple crayon on the walls of buildings very near the location where the body was found.

With all the overwhelming evidence, the reader is now probably convinced beyond a shadow of a doubt that newspaper articles, books, movies, television shows, rock music, and suicides themselves cause suicide. I will say this forcefully:

I Do Not Believe That TV Shows, Radio Programs, Movies, Books, Rock Music, Newspaper Stories, Or The Suicides Of Other Cause Us To Attempt Or Successfully Complete Suicide.

I sometimes humorously tell the audiences to whom I lecture that Billie Joel doesn't cure suicide and Ozzy Osbourne doesn't cause it; though they both work in opposing directions (Note: Billie Joel's *Second Wind, You're Only Human* is an example of a rock tune and complementary video which speak out against suicide.) To find a Bible next to the person who suicided is very common, though to be sure, the Bible was generally not the cause of the tragedy.

Things like rock music, newspaper articles, and the suicides of others are merely triggers, permission slips of sorts, for the distressed individual to follow in the footsteps of others who experienced similar hurt and anguish.

Whether you are suicidal or not, you no doubt have a number of triggers in your life which cause emotional or behavioral reactions.

For some of us, getting in our car, drinking a gin and tonic, or completing a business task may well be a trigger to smoke a cigarette. A mid-term in physics, a blind date, or a business presentation may become triggers which cause us to bite our nails. Fortunately, such behaviors don't have consequences as serious as suicide. Remember that we often perform such acts without conscious awareness. In essence, they occur automatically.

Now if you read the previous paragraph, it may have dawned on you that if you don't bite your nails and are not a smoker, the triggers I mentioned would not affect your behavior.

The truth is that the same could be said of suicide related triggers. Literally millions of people have listened to Ozzy Osbourne records, read *The Sorrows of Young Werther,* or seen *The Deer Hunter* without taking their own lives. An individual who is healthy and happy does not go out and blow his or her brains out after hearing that a movie star did so. In fact, in some suicidal individuals these factors actually cause persons to seek help for their difficulties. Calls to hotline centers often go up after suicide shows air. However, researchers can more easily tabulate those who turned up maimed or, worse yet, dead than those who sought help for their disturbances.

If you are suicidal, the first important thing you need to do is to *take the zap out of these triggers* by making them *conscious.* Ideally, you should sit down and discuss such matters with a trained therapist; nevertheless, some self-analysis also can be a life-saving measure.

Think back to the times when you were highly suicidal—the times when you came frighteningly close to making an attempt or literally followed through on one. Was something in the environment baiting you? Did you see a television news story about an individual in a predicament similar to yours who took his or her life? Did you sit down and listen to some musical lyrics that seemed to make sense because you sought freedom from intolerable mental pain? If so, keeping a list of these things can help fight their debilitating effects. Smokers and nail biters who are acutely aware of the precise situations which trigger the behavior find that they are less likely to engage in the acts.

Also an absolute imperative is for you to realize that if members of your family made attempts when they were depressed, you will be much more likely to do likewise when the going gets tough. If they did, probably you will accept much easier the suggestions of movies, news stories, or music.

In order to fight this horrendous tendency you will need to do exactly what I advise my clients. *Begin by making a comprehensive list of options other than suicide.* Often when clients perform this exercise as part of the therapeutic process they discover that even when they include the option to kill themselves, it does not appear at the top of the list. And so, my stock comment goes something like, "Why do it now? What's the hurry, you've got a lot of other things you need to try first."

Let's examine a common situation. Let's say your girlfriend of three years left you and claims she is never coming back. You are devastated and initially decide life isn't worth living since you convince yourself you will never find another girlfriend. After all, who would go out with a guy like you? You really look like such a nerd.

This time, however, instead of reaching for the pill bottle you compose the following list and make a vow to try each and every alternative before harming yourself in any fashion.

1. Go to the malt shop and try to meet some other eligible women.

2. Read a book which deals with the art of meeting women.

3. Take an ad in the personal column of the county journal, "Dumped Capricorn seeks a new shining star. . ."

4. Visit the video dating service which just opened up.

5. Give my girlfriend three weeks before I do anything—last time she broke up with me she came running back on the 21st day.

6. Give my girlfriend four weeks. She seemed madder than last time.

7. Talk with my best friend, my favorite professor, a peer counselor, or someone in the university counseling center.

8. Call the suicide prevention hotline.

9. See an image consultant so maybe I won't be such a nerd.

10. Ask my sister to fix me up with somebody.

You could also make a list of things which have kept you alive so far. Try to put your finger on the source or sources of your motivation. After all, the break-up took place three days ago; why haven't you committed suicide yet? A hypothetical motivational list might read:

1. My studies mean far too much to me. I've lusted after my art degree for almost four years now, and I'm not going to throw it all away over the break-up of a relationship.

2. I secretly always wondered whether I could do a little better than Sylvia. Although I was head over heels in love with her, she always was very self centered.

3. My brother and I have a vacation set for July and I want to be around at least long enough to enjoy it.

4. I've got an art contest I want to compete in next month and despite the fact I have been devastated these last three days I've been making a lot of progress on this project.

Even if your reasons seem like contradictions or rationalizations, write them down, because they are the very things that are in some way, shape, or remote fashion keeping you alive. Having read this far you now know that life-threatening self-destructive feelings generally subside in a relatively brief duration of time. If you can just keep your motivation alive for another day or so, possibly your feelings of doom will pass.

**Prepare Yourself for Troubled
Times by Desensitizing your
Self-Destructive Feelings**

I am now going to reveal to you an excellent strategy for warding off feelings of self-depreciation in advance. The technique, known as *desensitization,* can literally cut suicidal feelings off at the pass before they even begin to show their ugly little faces.

The reason that desensitization paradigms are so extremely effective is that feeling anxiety and relaxation at the same time is nearly impossible. They seem to be mutually exclusive entities—two different animals, if you will.

When you are relaxed, to feel a sense of extreme panic is mighty difficult. Very often when individuals call suicide prevention centers they are in a panic and can't think straight. A situation has caught them off guard and hence they are totally unprepared to deal with it. Amazingly enough, many of these distressed individuals could easily handle the difficulty without the threat of suicide if they were responding to the situation in a calm, relaxed, confident state of mind.

The idea of desensitization is (1) to teach you how to achieve a desirable relaxed, logical sense of inner stability; (2) to prepare you for potentially dangerous situations; and (3) to instruct you on how to return to the desirable state of mind during the midst of a crisis.

The first step is to *master the art of deep relaxation.* Although, per usual, the most elegant solution is to practice the technique under the watchful eye of a trained therapist, you can learn to do it yourself if you are really willing to throw your heart and soul into the process. And when you consider that the strategy could save your life, you darn well better!

Several very effective methods of relaxation exist and can be described thusly:

1. First you get into a comfortable position, either sitting or lying down, in a room which is preferably dark, quiet, and free of distractions. You may even wish to take your phone off the hook or turn on your answering machine if you own one. I would recommend that you follow the aforementioned guidelines regardless of which mode of relaxation training you choose. The only exception might be those people who intuitively know that they are most at ease in the warm sunlight or perhaps under a cool shade tree. These individuals can merely apply the instructions in a peaceful outdoor setting.

    Initially, close your eyes and try to relax as much as you possibly can. Now what you will do is to consciously tighten and relax every major muscle group throughout your entire body. The best procedure is to begin at the top of your head and work downward until you reach the tips of your toes.

Though different experts recommend different time spans for the tensing and relaxation cycles, my advice would be to use your own judgment and discover what works best for you. About five or six seconds of tensing and about ten seconds of sheer relaxation before going on to the next group of muscles is what most of my clients utilize, but once again, you are the one we are concerned about here, therefore use what feels most comfortable to you.

As you perform the exercise you can mentally give yourself the following instructions, changing the wording here and there to adapt the instructions to the way you normally think.

Here is basically what you will say to yourself: OK, you're beginning to really relax now. First you'll* furrow your brow ... come on, really tense it good, very good ... now just let go. All right, now contort your face, harder, harder, harder ... now relax again. Your entire face is completely relaxed. Time to release the tension from the neck. Start making it tight, even tighter, keep tightening ... more ... stop . . . just relax and feel the wonderful peaceful sensations. Now let's take care of the shoulders. Push them up, higher, toward the ceiling . . .and . . . stop. Mmmm, relaxation feels so good, so comfortable, so pleasant.

The back is next. Pull the shoulders backward and tighten your back ... come on ... really tighten it ... a little more ... OK ... let go. Good, very good. Since the relaxation needs to spread, tense your stomach and chest muscles ... see them ripple like a washboard ... suck your gut in, more, more ... let go, let go and breathe deeply and slowly. Your entire upper body is extremely relaxed and it feels good. Now let's rid the rest of your body of any remaining anxiety. Straighten your legs and tighten them all over . . . your upper leg ... lower leg ... even the calf, ankles, and toes, just a little more . . . more . . . now relax. Your entire body is completely relaxed, calm, and very peaceful.

---

*These instructions are written in the second person(i.e., you will do this or that). Some clients find that it makes more sense to use suggestions given in the first person since you are talking to yourself (i.e., I will do this or that).

Once you have released the tension from your entire body, then visualize yourself in a very relaxed setting. Perhaps you will see yourself lying in the green grass on a warm sunny day, lounging in your favorite easy chair, sleeping on the beach, or floating down a calm quiet river in a small boat.

The most important thing is to make your mental picture of the scene as vivid and realistic as possible. Try to create the details in your mind. See the color of the trees, feel the texture of the sand, and hear the small waves which protrude from the body of water.

2. In this method the individual only gives suggestions related to relaxation and a peaceful scene. Some clients find this strategy more effective inasmuch as the tension exercise reminds them of instances when they have been stressed and this prevents them from relaxing totally.

    The person may even become rather forceful and command the various muscle groups to relax.

    A person going about it this way might silently say to himself:

    My entire body is going to relax totally. My face, neck, and shoulders are completely relaxed, totally void of tension as I float down the river on this beautiful warm sunny day. The relaxation feels so good that I'm going to command my chest muscles to rid themselves of every last bit of anxiety ... so relaxed ... it feels so good ... and the gentle waves push the boat ever so slightly rocking me into a tired pleasant state. (Pause) I haven't felt this good in a long time. Now I'll move on to my abdomen, etc., etc.

    If you are prone to muscle cramps, then this method should be used over the first choice.

3. The third strategy is to utilize either of the two previous methods except you will talk aloud as you give suggestions the first time you perform the exercise so they may be tape recorded. Once you have them on tape you can merely play

them back and you won't even have to think about what you need to say to yourself next. Moreover, many people truly respond best when they literally hear the suggestions. If none of the aforementioned suggestions seem to work for you, you may consider purchasing a commercial relaxation or hypnotic relaxation tape through one of the bookstores.

4. Purchase a portable biofeedback relaxation device through a biofeedback supplier or distributor of scientific equipment. If you have always been fascinated with gadgets, this might be the best route for you.

Regardless of which method you choose I want you to do one other thing. Once you reach a totally calm, peaceful, and general overall state of relaxation I want you to tightly clench the fist of your dominant hand several times. I will come back to the rationale for this in a few moments, but suffice to say here that this will work for you like post-hypnotic suggestion.

Now forget about relaxation for a moment because I want you to construct a list of situations that have made you suicidal in the past or situations which you foresee as possible evoking suicidal feelings in the future. (I bet you never knew suicide prevention consisted of making so many lists!)

Here is a list an 18-year-old client named Dan composed:

1. Giving my required mid-term history presentation to 80 students in my class.

2. Being grounded by my parents for a month again.

3. Asking a girl for a date and getting turned down in front of my older brother who is a "real ladies' man."

4. Receiving a rejection note from the state college.

Your next step is to pick the situation on the list which you personally feel will be the easiest to overcome. If they all seem like insurmountable barriers, then pick one at random. In this particular case my client chose the first one on the list—presenting his mid-term to 80 classmates.

At several points during therapy sessions he said, "I'd rather die than get up in front of 80 people, I really mean it."

The next order of business, then is to create a series of similar situations which moves from the ones which are least threatening to those that are the most anxiety provoking, including the actual monster on the list (in this case giving a presentation in front of 80 people). When I say a "similar situation" here I am referring to any set of circumstances which resembles the problem area but evokes slightly less anxiety. Although initially this might sound technical it really isn't. The situations may be ones you have really experienced or they may be totally fictitious.

Here are the situations my client came up with in regard to his phobia of public speaking.

1. Giving his lecture to the guys on the basketball team. In his opinion, this would be very easy to do and would only incite a very low level of fear or anxiety. If he makes a mistake, so what, these guys are his friends.

2. Presenting to the girls' basketball team! This, of course, was a hypothetical situation. He claimed he would be just a bit more nervous since he was always afraid of making a mistake and looking foolish in front of girls his own age.

3. Delivering a speech in his woodworking class. The class has 29 members, some girls, and would be presented in front of his teacher. Dan gets extremely uptight in front of adults. He does, however, feel less threatened by his shop teacher than his history instructor.

4. Moving right along to the high anxiety steps, Dan decided that the fourth level would be: mentally rehearsing the material on the night before the speech. According to Dan, that one would really scare the pants off him. The only situation more scary would be . . .

5. Giving the actual lecture. As I said before, the final situation is always the one you dread the most and comes from your original list of situations which could leave you contemplating the act of suicide.

Now, here is precisely how you can begin to desensitize yourself so you will no longer experience fear and panic. Begin by relaxing totally utilizing one of the techniques set forth earlier in this chapter. Just relax and remember the relaxing scene. Now switch your thoughts from the relaxing scene to the first one on your list, the one which incites the least anxiety. Imagine it as vividly as you can and keep imagining it until you experience any degree of anxiety, tension, stress, or uneasiness of any sort.

If you don't feel any fear, then it's wonderful—you may actually be in control of the situation. If you do, however, you must immediately return to the safe, relaxed place in your mind. Try clenching your dominant fist which has now been programmed to muster up the relaxing state again. If that fails to do the trick, return again, go rapidly through your relaxation steps again until you feel calm and secure again.

If you are unable to imagine the first scene without exper-iencing anxiety then you can bank on the fact that it's just too difficult for you at this time. When this occurs the only sensible thing to do is to create a less threatening scene.

Take Dan's list as an example. Let's say that he relaxes completely and then becomes panicky as soon as he imagines giving a lecture to the guys on his basketball team. He could then begin an easier one such as giving his speech to his 12-year-old brother.

Often the difficulty does not manifest itself on the first step but rather while imagining later stepping stones. This implies that the jumps between situations on the list are too big. The solution is merely to add an intermediate step wherever the jump is too large in order to close the gap.

To return to Don's original situation, let's assume for the sake of discussion that he was able to complete step one but the jump from one to two seemed insurmountable. That is to say, he could imagine lecturing to the men's basketball team without tension yet became stress-ridden and began shaking when the thought of giving a presentation to the girls team was introduced. To remove this stumbling block Dan would need to come up with a set of circumstances which are ever so slightly more anxiety provoking than lecturing to the men's squad but less scary than speaking to the gals' team. He could imagine speaking to just three members of the girls on the team and would do so until the fear, anxiety, or tension related to this step have disappeared.

If you need to add steps to your hierarchy but repeatedly keep coming up empty-handed, you may construct another step in which you merely visualize yourself thinking about the step you cannot master.

If Dan was readily able to imagine lecturing to the girls' basketball team but became anxious while visualizing a delivery to his woodworking class, he could create a step in which he imagines that it is the day prior to the woodworking lecture and he is thinking about it at the dinner table. The idea of the strategy is merely that it is less frightening to imagine that you are thinking about a difficult situation than to think about actually performing it.

Another valuable self-improvement maneuver is to literally attempt the actual activity after you are able to successfully imagine it without fear or panic.

I can only point out that desensitization paradigms are very effective and can do wonders in terms of bolstering your confidence and allowing you to like yourself better. Like a fire drill, they prepare you in advance for the worst possible scenario so that when the situation really hits it is anticlimatic. You have virtually taken away all the huff and puff which once left you in a state of emotional shock. A state which in the past might have been enough to make you go get the gun, the pills, or the rope now will only have enough impetus to strike you with the force of a deflated beachball.

Even more important perhaps is that utilizing the strategy now gives you control over the environment and puts you in charge of the way you think, feel, and ultimately behave.

So how about it, huh? Make me a promise, and make one to yourself, that you will give the method presented a try. Set up a stepladder hierarchy around every set of circumstances on your list which could potentially generate self-destructive behavior.

I know you can do it—for many suicidal people total emotional fitness requires just 30 minutes of desensitization exercise per week!

Now get going; I'll be rooting for you every day.

11

HOW TO COPE WITH THE SUICIDE OF A FRIEND OR LOVED ONE

Wendy, a survivor of suicide I know, was shopping at a local grocery store when she spied an acquaintance she hadn't seen in over two years. "My gosh," she thought to herself, "Carole doesn't even know my son Robert committed suicide seven months ago. Can she handle it?"

Wendy and Carole did cross paths in the frozen food aisle and talked about everything from knitting to microwave oven delicacies. Wendy could feel it coming on, however, the moment she dreaded.

"Say, Wendy, how's Rob getting along these days?"

After an extended pause, Wendy hesitatingly responded, "Robert killed himself just seven months ago."

"Well...well hey, things have been just as bad in our family—the steel market dropped markedly last month."(!)

I guess I don't have to tell you that the moral of the story is that people are scared to death—well, almost—when it comes to talking about suicide; hence, the plight of the unfortunate survivor. The best medicine for a person who has experienced the loss of a significant other resulting from suicide is to talk about the incident again and again until the individual no longer feels a need to do so. The problem is to whom do you talk?

Or as another survivor said: "When I entered the lunchroom at work, the place cleared out like there was going to be a bomb search. When I hit the copy machine, the fellow in front of me would always scurry away like a scared rabbit. People in the halls suddenly came down with temporary laryngitis, and I never again want to hear anybody say 'if I just wasn't so darn busy I'd like to sit down and talk.'"

In the United States each year we have approximately 250,000 new survivors of suicide.

For the person experiencing horrendous difficulties, suicide represents an end to the pain. For family and friends, however, the tragedy itself is merely the beginning. The death of a loved one, regardless of the circumstances, is a traumatizing event indeed. The grief resulting from a death via suicide, nevertheless, is characterized by a number of unique features.

When suicide has taken place, the survivor cannot possible blame a virus, an earthquake, a cancer, or an intoxicated driver. Instead, the survivor must come to grips with the fact that the person made his or her own decision. And while the causes of most deaths are eventually forgotten, the survivor is still targeted as "the person whose son shot himself."

When a family loses a member through an accident or ill health, others often show sympathy, caring, and warmth. In the case of suicide, the family may be viewed as outcasts.

Now let me say something very important about the grief related to suicide: **There Are No Timetables Or Schedules Of Bereavement Related To This Tragedy. Nobody Can Tell You Exactly What You Will Feel Or When You Will Feel It.**

This is one area in which a great deal of popular psychological pap has actually caused more anguish than it ever cured. Now mark my word, if you are survivor of suicide, sooner or later you will come across a book, a newspaper article, or an expert on television who will tell you precisely how you "should" feel. The "should" always gets people in trouble.

The expert will throw something at you like: "... approximately ten months after the suicide you will go from the anger phase into the guilt stage."

The difficulty is that you may look critically at your own situation and decide that your grief reaction is abnormal or pathological. You will then, most likely, intensify the hurt by questioning your own response to the tragedy. "It's ten months," you will say to yourself, "and I haven't even felt the anger yet. What in the heck is wrong with me?"

The fact that one expert tells us that a given stage terminates at ten months, while another stipulates that it occurs after only six months, should warn us that such schedules are at best hypothetical tools which can be useless, if not harmful, when viewed in a literal fashion. Most bereaved individuals, however, are too preoccupied to scrutinize the work of several experts and thus latch onto the first timetable with which they come in contact, and rightfully so, inasmuch as they are seeking anything which can help treat their emotional wounds.

Lay persons are also guilty of making the grief process even more painful. Not unlike the experts who delineate times, dates, phases, or order of stages, the average person in society often stifles the grief process by minimizing the hurt associated with being a survivor.

A survivor I know was told by his best friend, "Come on, Ed, forget about your daughter's suicide and get on with your own life. It has been about six weeks now." (Little did Ed's friend realize that I have seen survivors seek counseling for suicides which took place over 20 years ago and here he is demanding Ed work through all his grief in under six weeks. What a tall order!)

Teachers and school administrators also need to take note of this undesirable practice. One of the worst things school personnel can do in the aftermath of a suicide is to act like everything is still business as usual, something I have seen happen more than I care to remember.

Policy statements like "I'm sorry Pete killed himself yesterday and I'm sure we all feel terrible, but you still need to take the math exam. You may not use this incident as an excuse to weasel out of it" cause additional problems.

Sometimes just a faction of the faculty will take this position. I remember one instance after a suicide took place when I was asked out to the school to help with bereavement counseling. After the sessions, several teary-eyed girls approached me on the parking lot and told me they really wanted to attend but the gymnastics coach laid down the law and said that if anybody missed practice for the suicide counseling they would be cut from the gymnastics squad! Needless to say, the principal received a call from me the very next morning and provisions were made for the girls to be seen.

Any attempt to minimize the significance of a grief reaction will hinder the healing process and may actually increase the suicide risk in the survivor.

If my work with survivors has taught me one thing, it is that survivors often ponder suicide themselves. Survivors are more likely than non-survivors to commit suicide. Unlike the population at large, survivors think somewhat seriously about committing suicide themselves. This does not mean, however, that we should take the matter less seriously. All the suicide precautions mentioned previously should be carried out with suicidal survivors.

The wish for the survivor's own death is manifested in statements such as:

"Without my husband I don't want to live."

"I want to kill myself so I can be with Grandpa again."

"Tom wouldn't want me to go on living without him."

"We had a suicide pact, you know; I should be dead too."

"There was another bullet in that gun and it was meant for me. Maybe I'll get to use it."

Here are some rules of thumb which will help you or your friends in the wake of suicide.

1. Find an outlet so you can talk about the incident again and again. Contrary to popular belief, reliving the tragedy can be therapeutic.

2. Realize that there are absolutely no bereavement time-tables or precise stages of grief. Everybody improves at his or her own pace.

3. Although it does get better (the most frequently asked question is "Does it ever get any better?"), in the process often a series of ups and downs occur. Just when you think that the most horrendous feelings are behind you, you will probably experience another setback or setbacks. These may last for just a few brief moments or can span a week or more.

4. If you have physical problems, see a physician. The grief process can, in fact, cause your body to become sick. Don't assume it's all in your mind—get it checked out immediately! Actually, as a matter of course, survivors of suicide would do well to secure a medical examination.

5. Familiarize yourself with the thoughts, feelings, and reactions survivors typically experience. By acquiring a knowledge of these responses you will be less likely to castigate yourself when they manifest themselves in your particular situation.

In order for you to follow directive #5 I will share with you some universal or common reactions to suicide. Remember, nevertheless, that you may experience one of them, some of them, or all of them. Experiencing one is no better or no worse than experiencing all of them. Moreover, they may occur in the order listed and they may not. You could experience these reactions over a period of years, and on the other hand they might transpire in a matter of minutes. As a survivor you need to go easy on yourself, and that means forgetting about the concepts of bereavement timetables, schedules of grief, or the order of your emotional reactions.

One common reaction is shock and denial. Much like the medical phenomenon of phantom limb (in which the individual feels sensations from a lost limb), the survivor may believe he sees or hears the person who committed suicide. A survivor once told me she followed a gentleman on the freeway for nearly twenty minutes because she was nearly certain it was her husband who supposedly suicided. Similar stories are quite common.

The survivor who experiences denial will go to great lengths to "prove" that suicide was not the cause of death. Statements like, "We haven't ruled out homicide," or "It was strange she didn't leave a note" are sometimes indicative of this tendency. As I pointed out earlier, from a purely statistical standpoint, most persons do not leave a note.

I recall counseling a couple who was convinced that their son's suicide was really a homicide. Since the tragedy occurred in another state the couple had literally spent a small fortune with a private detective agency trying to validate this hypothesis. Finally, during one of our sessions the man said, "For land sakes, Martha, give it up. The boy committed suicide, but that doesn't mean we were bad parents. There were other things in his life too, you know."

Another common reaction, and a perfectly normal one I might add, is anger. "How could this person do this to me?" is a phrase survivors use to verbalize the ostracism and ultimate rejection they feel. Often the anger increases as one ponders the fact that the individual gave him no chance to intervene. Throwing things, tearing them, and even yelling and screaming loudly are typical.

One survivor I knew expressed it best after his girlfriend suicided by saying: "I don't want her to go to hell, but I sure hope God paddles her fanny but good!"

The anger also may be directed toward another individual such as a teacher, employer, friend, or relative who was intimately involved in a crisis situation which took place in close proximity to the suicide. In such cases the anger shows its teeth in the form of blame. Mental health providers involved with the person in question also may be the recipients of this unleashed rage.

One woman told me that she honestly felt no anger for the first eight months after her husband's suicide. Then one day she was under the sink trying to fix the plumbing and came to the realization that she wouldn't be wrestling with the job if her husband was still alive. At that point she commenced banging the water pipes so loudly with a pipe wrench that her neighbors came over to see what was causing the ruckus.

Guilt is another emotion which is usually present. Phrases like "What did I do wrong?" or "Was it my fault?" typify this self-reproach.

The National Institute for Mental Health estimates on the average five survivors are intimately affected by each suicide. A somewhat typical occurrence is for the survivor to think that he or she should have been the one to have prevented the tragedy. Often when I have worked with schools or business settings after a suicide, I have met literally hundreds of people who feel guilty because each one felt he or she was the one who could have prevented it.

The guilt is often inseparable from the anger.

On one occasion when I was doing clinical supervision for the local suicide hotline a man came to see me who was irate, belligerent, and downright nasty because he felt one of our helpline volunteers killed his wife. Though true his wife did call for assistance and then went on to kill herself, and also true she told him she would attempt suicide that very night. Moreover, he was sleeping in the same room with her when the incident took place. He had promised to check on her every hour on the hour but had dozed off.

After listened intently to his saga for a little over an hour, the man began sobbing and pleaded, "Please, please tell me I didn't kill her. She said if I didn't get an extra part-time job she'd kill herself ... and I fell asleep and she did."

By now, of course, the reader knows that the break-up of a relationship, grounding your son or daughter, or not securing a part-time job does not cause suicide—though admittedly each situation may somehow be related to the final incident before the ultimate act of self-destruction.

Though nearly every survivor experiences guilt for at least a brief period of time, remembering that you didn't literally cause the suicide (since suicide is always precipitated by a multiplicity of factors and people) will help to keep this undesirable emotion in check.

Underlying all of the previous feelings is generally an intense sense of loss which results in extreme sadness and depression. You feel so incredibly lousy, your only wish is that the situation would disappear so you could stop thinking about it.

Here is how an individual might experience numbness, sadness, denial, anger, shock, and guilt all in a period of a few brief moments. You could be riding down the highway and hear the person's favorite song on the radio. You begin to feel elated. All the good times you shared together come back to you. Then it hits you that the person is gone—gone forever—and the sense of loss causes a wave of sadness to come over you. The sadness and depression, nevertheless, are rapidly replaced by guilt, guilt generated by the fact that on two separate occasions you told your friend you were too busy to talk. Could those two phone calls, if handled differently, have saved his life?

Within seconds, the guilt turns to anger as you recall that you were supposed to be on vacation with him in London this week. Didn't he care about your feelings?

Again you consciously hear that tune on the radio and start feeling elated. But wait; how can you feel elated when your best friend has killed himself? Guilt returns as you assure yourself that you should not be enjoying yourself, even for a brief moment, at a time like this.

Lastly, you will wonder if your friend is really even dead; after all, you never actually saw his body at the funeral and he had everything going for him. Denial will dictate that you check into other realistic possibilities.

Survivors often have to contend with scary dreams. Sometimes even adult survivors can be comforted by having a night light in their sleeping room. Persons who live alone may feel more secure if another individual moves in for a few weeks after the suicide.

Providing adult or teen survivors with a wealth of information about the topic of suicide is also desirable. The factual information somehow seems to ease the pain and incidentally reduces the risk of suicide for the survivor.

In this society, suicide is a verboten topic. This makes the bereavement process incredibly difficult, inasmuch as nobody wants to talk about it.

The most therapeutic activity for survivors seems to be talking about the suicide again and again. Because of this very need, survivors of suicide support groups are beginning to mushroom throughout the nation. Because survivors have a unique common bond, they trust one another and learn from their mutual experiences. Believe me, when one woman who lost a son via suicide six years ago tells a group member who lost hers only six weeks ago that it gets better, it can mean a lot to her.

When the average person on the street says, "Yeh, Joe, that's just terrible that your wife committed suicide, I know just how you feel," Joe will accurately assume that a person who is not a survivor himself will not know how he feels.

Although a survivors group is not a replacement for individual therapy, I would advise all survivors who are undergoing therapy to *consider attending a survivors of suicide support group* as a supportive adjunct to the treatment process.

Since this book does not fully address the problems of being a survivor I have provided you with some excellent resources in the Helpful Havens chapter. There, too, you will find a list of survivors support groups. I would highly recommend you join a group, and moreover, suggest you exchange phone numbers with willing members so you will have someone who will listen when the hurt seems unbearable. Survivors also should feel free to utilize suicide prevention and crisis hotlines when they need to talk with somebody.

One activity which seems to help survivors is to literally sit down and *write a letter to the person* who has suicided in which you express your innermost thoughts, feelings, and fears. Another helpful technique is to *engage yourself in activities which seem to help others.* Survivors I know have felt a sense of accomplishment, for example, by creating suicide prevention brochures, posters, helping with fund raising and planning mental health seminars, or assisting with survivors groups. As one mother told me, "I want to know that at least one other individual was helped by my son's suicide. I want his death to count for something."

No, after a suicide your life will never be the same, but fortunately you can still be happy.

12

A NO HOLDS BARRED QUESTION AND ANSWER SESSION

A fellow who is up for an extremely high paying executive position is given a very in-depth personality test to take home with him after the initial job interview. He is told that the job is far too important to leave the decision up to a mere interview.

Since the guy really has his heart set on the position—not to mention the big bucks that go along with it—he contacts his neighbor who teaches psychology at a local university. For the next three or four nights these two gentlemen stay up late burning the midnight oil to answer the test questions in precisely the right way so that the test reveals an almost perfect personality profile.

Sure enough, the guy gets the position. Some six months down the road, however, guilt sets in and he goes to see the president of the firm to tell him the truth though he expects to be terminated immediately. When the poor man finishes his task of trying to absolve his guilt, the president speaks up and says, "Oh calm down and shut up. We knew you faked the blasted test the day we received it; nobody has a perfect personality."

The embarrassed executive, hanging his head by now, sheepishly asks, "Then why did you hire me?"

"Why," barked the president, "why do you think? The time, the effort, the creativity, and the sheer persistence it must have taken to do that . . . that's the kind of man we want around here . . . one who's willing to try to answer all the questions no matter how difficult the task becomes."

After lecturing to approximately 35,000 individuals on the subject of suicide prevention I can promise you one thing—certain questions invariably crop up after a lecture. No matter to whom I lecture, regardless of the location, I find myself confronted with a number of recurrent issues surrounding the topic of suicide. This means that despite the fact that we may not be able to meet face to face I can still answer most of your questions, and you won't even have to raise your hand or wait to be called upon!

Question: *I know that most people are surprised when they discover the high rate of suicide in the U.S. Yet earlier you hinted at the fact that suicide attempts are running rampant. It sounds like attempts constitute an even bigger problem. Any statistics on this topic?*

Answer: The statistics are mind-blowing. Five million living Americans have tried to take their own lives. Estimates run as high as 600,000 annual attempts in the U.S. For every completed suicide in the U.S. we have approximately 14 attempts. In the teenage years we have about 200 attempts for every youngster who succeeds, while in the elderly the ratio is 4 attempts for every senior citizen who completes the act. Out task is to stop self-destructive behavior at all levels and in every possible age bracket.

Question: *As a Black female I can honestly say that I've never heard of another Black female who ended her own life. Is my experience typical?*

Answer: Out of 29,286 U.S. suicides in 1984, whites accounted for 27,002 while 1,760 were Blacks. Simply put, Blacks don't commit suicide as often as whites—at least that we know about. The Black female rate is a mere 2 per 100,000 which is extremely low. I would say your experience is typical.

Question: *Does the U.S. have the highest suicide rate in the world?*

Answer: No. In reality, the problem in America is considered moderate in nature when compared to Hungary (which generally has the highest rate on the globe), Austria, Switzerland, Denmark, and Japan.

Question: *Which state has the highest suicide rate?*

Answer: I'm afraid Nevada, year in and year out, has everybody else backed off the boards with a rate which repeatedly hovers in the 20 per 100,000 rate. Incidentally, loneliness and sparsely populated areas probably do more to jack up the rate than misfortune at the blackjack tables! The other so-called mountain states, including Wyoming, New Mexico, Arizona, Colorado, Montana, Idaho, and to a lesser extent Utah, all have well above average suicide rates despite their lack of slot machines.

Question: *Every time I see a television special on suicide prevention, alcoholism and drug abuse are implicated as prime culprits. Are these problems really widespread or is this merely a lot of hoopla about nothing?*

Answer: We are talking about more than just hoopla here. Approximately 25 million Americans (i.e., roughly one in ten) have tried cocaine. Drunk drivers currently account for 60% of accidents on our roads and highways. Alcohol is involved in one out of every ten deaths in this country. Cannabis sativa, or marijuana, is a $10 billion industry in our country, and anywhere from 35 to 60 million Americans have tried pot. And heroin—often considered the most addictive of all drugs—has become an addiction for approximately 550,000 citizens. I could go on and quote statistics for methadone, LSD, mescaline, STP, Valium, and a whole new breed of designer drugs, but I think you get the message that these figures spell big trouble not only in terms of our suicide dilemma but also contribute to a host of other societal problems.

(Note to the reader: I know that if you are a high school, college, or graduate student you're pleased as punch that I've thrown all these wonderful statistics at you so you can complete your thesis or class presentation. Students always call me to ask for "suicide numbers" in order to complete a paper or project. If you're not a student, nevertheless, you may be beginning to yawn and well, quite frankly so am I. Therefore, I promise no more data will be cast at you from here on in so feel free to ask questions!)

Question: *I heard you say that suicide cuts across all ethnic, age, race, and economic classes. If this is true, then why is it that persons who have really accomplished a lot in out society never seem to commit suicide? Let's face it, suicide merely afflicts the crazies and the losers!*

Answer: Where in the world did you get your information, mister? Would you refer to Arthur Chevrolet, one of the designers of the Chevrolet automobile, as a crazy or a loser? After all, he committed suicide. Or how about George Eastman, who founded Eastman Kodak of camera fame? He too took his own life. And while we are on the subject, let's mention Dr. Wallace H. Carothers, inventor of nylon and co-inventor of synthetic rubber; Edwin H. Armstrong, who created the electronic circuit which took radio beyond the crystal set design; novelist Virginia Woolf; French painter Vincent Van Gogh; Dr. Benjamin F. Sieve, who developed birth control pills; and Melvin Purvis, the FBI agent who became a hero by capturing John Dillinger; all succumbed to death via their own volition.

In more recent times we could add Marilyn Monroe, Freddie Prince, and John Belushi. Bright, creative, artistic, and humanitarian individuals can and do take their own lives on occasion. I strongly suggest you seek a new source of information!

Question: *Do vitamin and mineral deficiencies cause suicide?*

Answer: I'm not going to say that nutritional difficulties per se cause suicide. They may, however, be a contributing factor as is a divorce, a break-up of a relationship, a loss of a job, or a nagging mother-in-law.

An entire branch of treatment known as Orthomolecular Psychiatry now exists which hypothesizes that everyone has a particular biochemical makeup and hence possesses individualized vitamin and mineral requirements.

In researching the problem of schizophrenia, for example, orthomolecular psychiatrists discovered what they referred to as

10- or 50-gram-a-day schizophrenics. In other words, a schizophrenic who needs 50 grams a day of a certain vitamin to function normally may lose touch with reality if he is given 49 grams. Likewise, an intake of 9 grams produces this reaction in a 10-gram-a-day patient, despite the fact that these amounts may be 10,000 to 50,000 times what Mr. & Mrs. Joe Average may require.

Cases have, indeed, been cited in the professional literature which indicate that vitamin and mineral deficiencies can aggravate a depressed state of mind. If you are currently suicidal, a wise procedure would be to make certain that you are receiving an adequate amount of vital nutrients.

I often have to chuckle when I meet clients who don't believe in this theory. "My psychiatrist prescribes medicines like lithium," they will say, "who needs vitamins and minerals?" Lithium—though available only by prescription—is in fact a mineral.

Let me warn you, however, that dietary rehabilitation is more than making a mad dash to the nearest health food store and then purchasing and popping every capsule, pill, or tablet in sight. Certain supplements may contain excess copper, yeast, or unwanted binders which can actually inhibit or negate the desired effect.

Because the average run-of-the-mill physician may know less about nutritional science than you do (especially if you have been on a diet) I suggest you consult the referral list of active members of the Academy of Orthomolecular Psychiatry or the Linus Pauling Institute listed in the Helpful Havens section of this book. Trying to play orthomolecular-shrink with yourself could be dangerous!

Question: *Can exercise really cure the depression which leads to suicide?*

Answer: Though a healthy mind and body no doubt contribute to a state of general well-being and happiness, these factors may be the equivalent of trying to stop an elephant with a pea shooter when it comes to overpowering a bout of suicidal feelings.

Some studies have indicated that exercise can relieve depression while others say no. Still others indicate that excessive exercise can virtually incite a depressed state of mind.

The discrepancy in these findings reinforces what common sense has told us all along: What works for one person may not work for another and can even be dangerously detrimental to a third individual.

Since this is the case, you might want to keep a diary of your feelings if you embark on an exercise program in an attempt to ascertain whether or not it really works for you. You must keep in mind other variables such as how much exercise, what type, how often you are performing it, and even more importantly, what else is going on in your life.

The current popular theory which suggests that exercise causes the body to produce endorphins, a natural antidepressant, is meaningless in your personal case if exercise doesn't work for you. I've seen athletic guys with arms like Swarzenegger's and gals sporting curves on a par with Jane Fonda's successfully terminate their own existence, indicating that 50 push-ups is not always the answer.

When all is said and done, however, I must admit that if I were suicidal I would try getting a little more exercise and make certain my nutritional intake was up to snuff.

Question: *I work as a middle-school counselor and have helped a lot of suicidal students. Recently, however, I came across an unusual situation in which I contacted a suicidal teen's parents and they flat out told me they were refusing to get help for the poor child. What in the world do I do now?*

Answer: Your situation, surprisingly enough, is not that unusual. A lecture rarely goes by in which I am not asked this very question.

Get on the phone and call your state child welfare division or the abuse and neglect hotline. In many places this department is known (or listed in the telephone book) as "protective services for children." If the number is long distance it is generally toll free.

Be aware that not seeking psychological help for a youngster who is suicidal is often classified as a form of child neglect.

Now since child protection workers usually come out to the home or contract with other mental health workers to do so, mom and dad's protests that they simply don't have the time or the money to take little Johnny to see a therapist are no longer issues.

In those rare instances in which mom and pop refuse to see the child protection worker, the worker has the duty to refer the family to the juvenile court and the child can, and often will, be removed from the home if cooperation is not forthcoming.

Question: *I'm glad to know teachers have some recourse if they see a dangerous set of circumstances, but what does a housewife such as myself do when I encounter a similar situation? I'm not a teacher, a counselor, or a mental health professional; I can't call the child abuse hotline, can I?*

Answer: You can and you should! Child abuse and neglect laws usually stipulate two types of reporters: mandated and permissive. A mandated reporter is usually defined as a mental health, medical, education, or social service professional who could actually be legally liable if he or she doesn't make a report when made aware of an incident involving abuse or neglect. Other citizens, though they are not legally mandated reporters, can and do save lives by bringing such incidents to the attention of the authorities. So go ahead and call the hotline; in most instances if you are not a mandated reporter, you can remain anonymous and won't even have to reveal your own name. As a permissive reporter you should pick up the phone and be a good Samaritan!

Question: *What do I do when my 57-year-old husband becomes hysterical and threatens suicide? He's no longer a little kid. I can't throw him in the car and cart him off to some psychiatrist's office.*

Answer: No, but you can call the police if he is actively threatening self-destructive behavior.

You also could contact the nearest state mental health facility and request that a "mental health coordinator" be dispatched to your household. Many are available on a 24-hour basis. If your husband is endangering his own life, he may be admitted to a psychiatric center whether he wants to go or not.

Question: *Can you recapitulate one more time the best methods one can utilize to convince a spouse, friend, or child to willingly seek professional help?*

Answer: First have someone who the person really trusts explain that treatment is a strength and not a weakness. Try to pick an individual with whom the suicidal person trusts and seems to agree on other topics. ("Tom and I see eye to eye on literally everything" is the type of statement which may have been made before the person became actively suicidal, and this clues us in that Tom is the man for the job in this instance. Try to enlist his cooperation.)

Next, have somebody, preferable the trusted person (e.g., Tom), offer to take the suicidal individual to and from the treatment setting. Just knowing that a friend is sitting in the waiting room tends to lessen anxiety and provides moral support.

Question: *My cousin admits to being suicidal but she stubbornly refuses to sign a written contract stating she will call me if she feels like hurting herself again. Help!*

Answer: Her will to live is obviously waning. If somebody won't sign a contract, I'd seriously consider hospitalization.

Question: *Would you ever recommend challenging the individual? You know, "You want a gun, here's a gun" or "Hey, if you want to jump I'll open the window, fellow," that type of thing?*

Answer: No, I would never advocate such directives.

Question: *As a teacher I'm wondering whether any programs exits to teach suicide prevention in the classroom.*

Answer: Yes, simply contact the American Association of Suicidology listed in the Helpful Havens section of this book.

Question: *Isn't there a form of suicide related to sexual practices?*

Answer: Yes, the act known as auto-erotic asphyxia is what you are referring to here. The individual—in nearly every instance a male—places a rope or a towel around his neck while masturbating, often while viewing sexually explicit or erotic materials. The rumor going around is that when the towel or rope tightens, the air supply lessens and the person experiences a heightened sense of sexual awareness and ultimately an orgasm which is more powerful that that achieved through normal sexual activity.

What can happen, nevertheless, is that when the individual tugs on the rope or towel the blood supply to the brain is lowered, which produces a mental state similar to a drug-induced high, impairing the person's judgment and deadening sensations related to pain. The result is that the person often tugs too hard and literally hangs himself.

Even if we choose not to call it suicide, we must acknowledge the fact that the individual was in essence so unfulfilled he was willing to flirt with death.

The warning signs related to this behavior parallel those pertaining to suicide except that we could add a fascination with knots, bruises or excessive red marks around the neck, and bloodshot eyes.

So forget about those rumors floating around—sex is best when you are alive and can enjoy it!

Question: *I've heard everyone thinks about suicide at some time during their life. Well, surprisingly enough, I never have. Perhaps I'm just blessed with better mental health than most people? Truthfully, the word suicide has never crossed my mind.*

Answer: Baloney! The word suicide did cross your mind or you couldn't have utilized it in your question. Yes, everybody who is familiar with the word suicide and its meaning has thought about the act. Thinking about the word or the act in passing certainly doesn't mean you have a problem.

Most people have thought about what it would be like to fly unassisted by mechanical devices, but few of us have ever tried it. Suicide is the same way. You can and probably have had the thought flit through your mind. If, however, you begin to repeatedly think about suicide and realistically consider the act as an option to your present situation, then seek help at once.

Question: *When I was 16 years of age I attempted suicide twice in one year. I'm currently 41 years of age and don't feel suicidal at all. I've heard that once an individual is suicidal, he or she will always be that way. Is there any truth to this statement?*

Answer: No. People change and thus the statement "once suicidal, always suicidal" is definitely not true in many cases.

Question: *Can a loss of interest in sex be a sign of depression?*

Answer: Yes.

Question: *My aunt killed herself nine years ago. What test can I have performed to see if I inherited her suicide gene.*

Answer: As far as we know, suicide is not genetic and ergo no such test exists.

Question: *I've heard that ions or bad electrical charges in the atmosphere can cause depressed or suicidal feelings. Is there any truth to this, and if so, what can an individual do to protect herself?*

Answer: Some evidence does exist which indicates that humans (and, for that matter, even plant life) thrive best on a negative ion balance in the air. An abundance of positive ions in the air has been implicated in a less than desirable fashion in matters pertaining to physical and mental health.

Throughout the world, stories run rampant that so-called "Witch Winds" are responsible for increased traffic accidents, health problems, plane crashes, murders, fights at home, unsuccessful medical operations, and even suicide.

The Witch Winds include the Santa Ana in California; the Chinook in Canada; the Sharav (or Hamsin) of the middle east and primarily Israel; and most notable, the Foehn in Switzerland, southern Germany, and Austria. All carry with them air laden with a heavy concentration of positive ions.

Scientists have discovered that artificial environments such as the airtight cockpit of a jet, the interior of your automobile, a centrally heated and air conditioned building, or wearing synthetic clothing can all generate positive ions.

One method of protection seems to be the ion generator which, as its name implies, produces a desirable supply of negative ions in your car, home, or office. Generators can be purchased by contacting a supplier of scientific equipment in your area.

Again, if you are suicidal, seek competent medical, psychiatric, and psychological help. But if you have done that and still feel distressed, research has shown no contraindications or negative side effects from the use of ion generators.

Question: *Have biorhythm charts been useful in terms of predicting suicide?*

Answer: No.

Question: *I've heard that suicide occurs because of a chemical imbalance. What substances exactly are responsible for suicidal tendencies? And by the way, if suicide is the result of this certain chemical, how can the psychological strategies in this book be of any value? Shouldn't we be treating the biological basis of suicide?*

Answer: Some researchers have felt that low levels of serotonin or 5-hydroxyindoleacetic (5-HIAA, for short) in the brain might help to spawn self-destructive tendencies. The studies, however, have been inconsistent even when performed by the same investigator. Studies which demonstrated that low levels of 5-HIAA, or an imbalance of other chemicals, caused suicide have not been replicable in many cases. Even if and when we capture the chemical culprit remember that your psychological state can affect the physiological state of the body.

Question: *Do working Women have a higher rate of suicide?*

Answer: To the best our our knowledge, they do not.

Question: *Do teenagers who are survivors of suicide take longer to work through their grief than adults?*

Answer: In general, I would say that teens bounce back to normal a little quicker than their adult counterparts.

Question: *My husband took his own life several weeks ago. I told my boys, who are 11 and 12 years old, he died of cancer. Am I doing the right thing, or can my sons handle the truth?*

Answer: I would advise you to level with them and I'll explain why. In nearly every case I have seen in which a family suicide is kept a secret, the truth somehow eventually leaks out. At that point the enlightened individual is mad, and I mean extremely mad, that he or she was lied to. In this case the anger would be directed at you. The added anger makes the grief process that much more difficult to work through.

Question: *Yesterday we had a suicide at our high school. Is it all right to give the students factual information about suicide, such as the information in this book, or will this simply make the situation worse? As a school principal I'm worried about this event and want to do everything possible to help those students.*

Answer: First, remember that once you have a suicide in your school the chances go up that you will have another student make an attempt in precisely the same manner. So first, try to eliminate the means. If a student jumps out of certain window or hangs himself from a ceiling beam, then the administrators should do their best to make the area off limits to students for a brief period of time.

Next, make certain that the school has counseling resources. Disseminate the appropriate hotline numbers and don't be afraid to give them factual information. In fact, dispelling the myths can actually help deter future attempts. Feel free to let students read this book. It will help to convince them that they have alternatives to suicide.

Question: *I'm a youth leader for a teen group which meets at our church. I know teens love movies and I had considered renting a suicide prevention film. After reading your chapter on imitation and suicide, nevertheless, I am wondering whether this might be a dangerous practice.*

Answer: I have shown films to literally thousands of teenagers without any adverse effects. The interpretation you provide as their group leader, however, is absolutely critical to the outcome of the session.

If the thrust of your explanation is that suicidal behavior will make one the center of attention, or that suicide is a dramatic or a romantic act, then your teens could be in for trouble. If, on the other hand, you focus on facts, warning signs, utilizing adults as helpers, and the fact that self-destructive behavior is not the answer, then you shouldn't have any difficulties. Just in case a group member reveals a personal problem, you should have a list of qualified mental health providers available for the youngsters' parents or caretakers.

And just to be certain you make a wise choice in terms of audio-visual aids, I have included a brief explanation of the materials I have found most valuable in my own work in the Helpful Havens chapter of this text.

Question: *In this book you mention that there is always a better answer than suicide and go on to state that suicide is generally a question of mental health rather than philosophy. How about situations involving elderly persons who are suffering intolerable physical pain which cannot be alleviated?*

Answer: You will note that I say "in the majority of cases" suicide is a mental health related issue. You are correct in asserting that in instances of unrelenting physical pain, which torture a dying person, we are looking at an extremely complex medical, ethical, and philosophical problem and certainly one which is beyond the scope of this text.

The idea of this book is to stomp out suicide in cases where emotional difficulties have made life unbearable.

Question: *Throughout the text you have given us the impression via the case histories that one's feelings about his or her looks can have a profound influence on their decision whether to live.*

Answer: Yes, this is very common. A poor self-image may not be the sole cause of suicide but it sure doesn't help any.

13

IT'S A WONDERFUL LIFE

Years ago I worked at a state office building in which the front door was manned at all times by a very imposing security guard. He always stood straight up, shoulders back, with his chin high in the air as he checked each and every person who walked through the doors.

Every day when I would approach the entrance to the building I would be confronted by the guard whose stoic, unemotional voice would boom out, "Good morning, sir. How are you?"

My stock answer—which seemed to be the answer of everybody in the building, was "Just fine, how are you?" to which the guard would respond, "Thank you, sir, I'm fine too."

Since his answer always seemed a bit automatic and not very genuine I decided to try a little experiment.

The next day when he greeted me with his usual, "Good morning, sir, how are you?" I came back with, "Absolutely terrible, I had a dreadful night."

He replied, "Thank you, sir, I'm fine too."(!) At that point I realized that I was truly conversing with a human robot.

Just for the fun of it, I tried something else. Instead of flashing my official state identification card in his face, I would pull out my driver's license, credit card, or plastic bank machine plate. And every time, like clockwork, the guard gave me the okay sign and thus I entered the building. In almost no time, other employees caught on and were presenting everything from hospital insurance cards to laminated social security cards.

Since the guard's desk and the front door were adjacent to the waiting room, invariably clients were roaming around the area. One day after I said I felt dreadful, flashed a Sears credit card, and the guard responded with his usual "Thank you, Sir, I am fine, too" remark, a young girl of perhaps six or seven years of age witnessed the travesty and followed me to the elevator. As the elevator door opened, I looked down and saw the youngster tugging on my pant leg. Her huge blue eyes looked up at me in an inquisitive fashion as she tilted her head slightly and played with her long blonde hair.

"Mister," she said, "doesn't anybody look at anybody or listen to them anymore?"

I realized that my answer needed to be concise otherwise I would surely miss the elevator. "No, honey, I'm afraid they don't. Nobody looks at anybody or listens to them anymore."

Perhaps that is part of the problem in society today. Maybe we've even become too wrapped up in doing our own thing and not paying enough attention to others.

In a sense we have forgotten how to value each other. A line in a song sung by rock star Madonna comes to mind which implies a material person within a material world.

We no longer say he's charitable or she's a nice girl. The lingo of our times is that "he drives a 911 Porsche" and "she carries a Gucci bag."

Apparently the days of the smiling salesman and the uncritical politeness advocated in the Dale Carnegie era have been replaced by courses in mental judo, fighting fair in marriage, and training to procure a psychological black belt in verbal self-defense.

Assertiveness may help the suicidal, but aggression and rampant self-centered behavior do nothing of the sort.

A lot of clichés are floating around about how we can eliminate the scourge of suicide around the globe. Things like improving communication, solving the identity crisis, or saving the traditional family structure are cases in point. And though each of these factors is an oversimplification and does not really explain why people choose to shorten their own lives, perhaps we can begin to break the trend by being considerate, concerned, and truly interested in our fellow human beings.

Let us start by looking, listening, and trying to understand one another. To know somebody cares is certainly nice.

In the late 1940s Frank Capra made a movie with James Stewart and Donna Reed entitled *It's a Wonderful Life*. In this classic, Stewart becomes extremely unhappy and decides to jump from a bridge in order to end it all. He is convinced others would be better off without him and that the world would be better place had he never been born. Fortunately, Stewart's guardian angel appears on the scene and shows him how awful things would have really been without his presence.

When Stewart realizes the tremendous positive impact he has on the environment then he vehemently wants to live.

When I give seminars and workshops on suicide prevention, I often have participants view a short movie called *Amy and the Angel* which has a plot similar to *It's a Wonderful Life except that Amy*, the girl who wishes to kill herself, is a teenager. Like Stewart, a tour by her guardian angel leaves her screaming, "I want to live, I want to live," because for the first time she sees how her own existence has brightened the lives around her. Prior to the visit from her angel she saw herself as a burden to others and fantasized that everyone would have been better off if she wasn't around.

The exercise I give my participants, as well as the one I would suggest to you (whether you are personally suicidal or merely wish to help others who are), is to *sit down and think about all the people who have benefited from your life.* You can even discuss it with a trusted friend. I absolutely guarantee you that if you really think about it, you will be truly amazed at how many people you have touched and you too will come to the conclusion that your life really does matter.

From this day on your life will appear happier and brighter.

From time to time when the tide gets a little rough you will say, "Not with my life I don't." And by golly, you know, you'll be right.

14

HELPFUL HAVENS

If you are feeling suicidal yourself, or know someone else who is, then you will discover that this chapter is a veritable treasure chest of resource possibilities.

The first list consists of major suicide/crisis intervention hotlines. The list is supplied through the courtesy of the American Association of Suicidology. If you are unable to locate a hotline or a survivors group in your area, you are urged to contact the American Association of Suicidology by writing them at 2459 S. Ash, Denver, Colorado 80222, or by Telephoning (303) 692-0985.

The next list, pages 211 through 217, consists of telephone numbers for contacting major survivors of suicide support groups. These are listed by state and then city within the state.

The third list, pages 218 and 219, contains names and addresses of mental health organization with the area designed in which each organization specializes. For more information on a specific issue write the mental health organization

The fourth list, pages 220 through 222, is an annotated bibliography of film and video resources on suicide prevention. These seven resources are excellent and are identified as to the groups for which each is most appropriate.

The fifth list, page 223, contains three national organizations that have brochures, pamphlets, and other suicide information. If you have need for that kind of material, the address and the telephone number of each organization are provided.

The sixth list, page 223, contains three books for survivors of suicide. These books may be in your local library or, if not, your local bookstore could order them for you.

The seventh list, page 223, has the name, address, and price for two newsletters for survivors. If interested, contact either or both.

The eighth list, page 224, contains three pamphlets for survivors. The name and address is supplied so that you can contact the source.

The nineth list, page 224, is a source of general counseling and therapy materials for professionals and peer counselors.

The tenth list, page 224, is my mailing address. If you have information to share, please contact me.

SUICIDE PREVENTION & CRISIS INTERVENTION AGENCIES IN THE UNITED STATES

*   Member, American Association of Suicidology
\#   AAS Certified

ALASKA

ANCHORAGE

* ANCHORAGE COMM. MENTAL
   HEALTH SERVICES, INC.
4020 FOLKER
ANCHORAGE, AK 99508
Crisis Phone 1:(907)563-1000
Business Phone: (907)563-1000
Hrs. Avail: 24

ANCHORAGE

*\# C.R.I.S.I.S. INC.
2611 FAIRBANKS ST, SUITE A
ANCHORAGE, AK 99503
Crisis Phone 1:(907)276-1600
Business Phone:(907)272-2496
Hrs Avail: 24

FAIRBANKS

*\#FAIRBANKS CRISIS CLINIC
   FOUNDATION
P.O. Box 81804
FAIRBANKS, AK 99708
Crisis Phone 1:(907)452-4403
Business Phone:(907)479-0166
Hrs Avail: 24

KENAI

CENTRAL PENINSULA MH CENTER
215 FIDALGO ST., SUITE 102
KENAI, AK 99611
Crisis Phone 1:(907)283-7501
Business Phone:(907)283-7501
Hrs Avail: 24

ALASKA (Con't.)

KETCHIKAN
GATEWAY CENTER FOR HUMAN
  SERVICES
3052 5TH AVENUE
KETCHIKAN, AK 99901
Crisis Phone 1:(907)225-4135
Business Phone:(907)225-4135
Hrs. Avail: 24

ALABAMA

ANDALUSIA
SOUTH CENTRAL MENTAL HEALTH
  BOARD HELPLINE
P.O. Box 1028
ANDALUSIA AL 36420
Crisis Phone 1:(205)222-7794
Business Phone:(205)222-2523
Hrs Avail: 24

AUBURN
CRISIS CENTER OF E. ALABAMA, INC.
P.O. Box 1949
AUBURN AL 36830
Crisis Phone 1:(205)821-8600
Business Phone:(205)821-8600
Hrs Avail: 24

BIRMINGHAM
*#CRISIS CENTER OF JEFFERSON
  COUNTY
3600 8TH AVE. S., STE. 501
BIRMINGHAM, AL 35222
Crisis Phone 1:(205)323-7777
Business Phone:(205)547-7782
Hrs Avail: 24

DECATUR
CRISIS CALL CENTER NORTH-
  CENTRAL ALABAMA MH CENTER
P.O. Box 637
DECATUR AL 35601
Crisis Phone 1:(205)355-6091
Business Phone:(205)355-6091
Hrs Avail: 24

GADSDEN
13TH PLACE
1525 CHESTNUT
GADSDEN AL 35901
Crisis Phone 1:(205)547-9505
Business Phone:(205)547-8971
Hrs Avail: 24

HUNTSVILLE
HUNTSVILLE, HELPLINE
P.O. Box 92
HUNTSVILLE, AL 35804
Crisis Phone 1:(205)539-1000
Business Phone:(205)534-1779
Hrs Avail: 24

MOBILE
*CONTACT MOBILE
P.O. Box 66608
MOBILE AL 36660-1608
Crisis Phone 1:(205)432-1222
TDD (205)433-9999
Business Phone:(205)438-4200
Hrs Avail: 24

MOBILE
MOBILE MENTAL HEALTH CENTER
  CRISIS INTERVENTION SERVICES
2400 GORDON SMITH DRIVE
MOBILE, AL 36617
Crisis Phone 1:(205)473-4423
Business Phone:(205)473-4423
Hrs Avail:24

MONTGOMERY

HELP A CRISIS
101 COLISEUM BOULEVARD
MONTGOMERY AL 36109
Crisis Phone 1:(205)279-7837
Business Phone:(205)279-7830
Hrs Avail: 24

TUSCALOOSA

* CRISIS LINE/TUSCALOOSA
P.O. Box 2190
TUSCALOOSA, AL 35403
Crisis Phone 1:(205)345-1600
Business Phone:(205)345-1600
Hrs Avail: 24, 7 DAYS/WK

ARKANSAS

HOT SPRINGS

COMMUNITY COUNSELING
    SERVICES, INC.
700 SOUTH AVENUE
P.O. Box 6399
HOT SPRINGS, AR 71913
Crisis Phone 1:(501)624-7111
Business Phone:(501)624-7111
Hrs Avail: 24

LITTLE ROCK

CRISIS CENTER OF ARKANSAS, INC.
1616 W 14TH ST.
LITTLE ROCK, AR 72202
Crisis Phone 1:(501)375-5151
Business Phone:(501)664-8834
Hrs Avail: 12:00PM-12:00AM

PINE BLUFF

CONTACT PINE BLUFF
P.O. Box 8734
PINE BLUFF, AR 71601
Crisis Phone 1:(501)536-4226
Business Phone:(501)536-4228
Hrs Avail: 24

SPRINGDALE

*NORTHWEST ARKANSAS CRISIS
    INTERV CNTR.
P.O. Box 1618
SPRINGDALE, AR 72765
Crisis Phone 1:(501)756-2337
Crisis Phone 2:(501)631-0060
Business Phone:(501)756-1995
Hrs Avail: 2P-2A

ARIZONA

CLIFTON

GRAHAM-GREENLEE COMM.
    SERVICE CENTER
169 FRISCO AVE.
P.O. Box 987
CLIFTON AZ 85533
Crisis Phone 1:(602)865-4531
Business Phone:(602)865-4531
Hrs Avail: 24

MESA

SPC OF MARICOPA COUNTY
2024 E. UNIVERSITY DRIVE, B-5
MESA, AZ 85203
Crisis Phone 1:(602)249-2915
Business Phone:(602)844-7320
Hrs Avail: 24

PHOENIX

PHOENIX CRISIS INTERVENTION
    PROGRAM
1250 S. 7TH AVE
PHOENIX, AZ 85007
Crisis Phone 1:(602)258-8011
Business Phone:(602)258-8011
Hrs Avail: 24

PHOENIX

PSYCHIATRIC CRISIS CENTER
MARICOPA COUNTY HOSPITAL
2601 E. ROOSEVELT
PHOENIX, AZ 85008
Crisis Phone 1:(602)267-5881
Business Phone:(602)267-5881
Hrs Avail: 24

ARIZONA (Con't)

PHOENIX
TERROS AGENCY
4545 N. 27th AVE.
PHOENIX, AZ 85017
Crisis Phone 1:(602)249-6314
Crisis Phone 2:(602)249-1749
Business Phone:(602)251-6314
Hrs Avail:24

SCOTTSDALE
*INTERFAITH COUNSELING
  SERVICE SUICIDE PREVENTION
  CENTER
7835 REDFIELD ROAD
SCOTTSDALE, AZ 85260
Crisis Phone 1:(602)249-2915
Business Phone:(602)948-1860
Hrs Avail: 24/7 DAYS

SAFFORD
* GRAHAM-GREENLEE
  COUNSELING CENTER, INC
P.O. Box 956
SAFFORD, AZ 85548
Crisis Phone 1:(602)428-5711
Business Phone:(602)428-4550
Hrs Avail: 24/7 DAYS

TUCSON
HELP ON CALL CRISIS LINE
  INFORMATION AND REFERRAL
  SERVICE
P.O. Box 43696
TUCSON, AZ 85733
Crisis Phone 1:(602)323-9373
Business Phone:(602)881-8045
Hrs Avail: 24

YUMA
* CASA DE YUMA SUICIDE
  PREVENTION HOTLINE CENTER
  AGAINST SEXUAL ASSAULT
P.O. Box 4201
YUMA, AZ 85364
Crisis Phone 1:(602)782-7273
Business Phone:(602)783-1860
Hrs Avail:24/7 DAYS

CALIFORNIA

ANAHEIM
*HOTLINE HELP CENTER
P.O. Box 999
ANAHEIM, CA 92805
Crisis Phone 1:(714)778-1000
Business Phone:(714)778-1000
Hrs Avail: 24

BERKELEY
* #SUICIDE PREV/CRISIS INTERV OF
  ALAMEDA COUNTY
P.O. Box 9102
BERKELEY, CA 94709
Crisis Phone 1:(415)849-2212
Crisis Phone 2:(415)889-1333
Crisis Phone 3:(415)794-5211
Crisis Phone 4:(415)449-5566
Business Phone:(415)848-1515
Hrs Avail: 24

SAN MATEO COUNTY
BURLINGAME
*#SUICIDE PREV/CC OF SAN MATEO
 COUNTY
1811 TROUSDALE DR
BURLINGAME, CA 94010
Crisis Phone 1:(415) 877-5600
Business Phone:(415)877-5604
Hrs Avail: 24

SANTA CRUZ COUNTY
CAPITOLA
*SPS OF SANTA CRUZ COUNTY
P.O. Box 734
CAPITOLA, CA 95010
Crisis Phone 1:(408)458-5300
Crisis Phone 2:(408)688-1818
Hrs Avail: 24

DAVIS
* SUICIDE PREVENTION OF YOLO
 COUNTY
P.O. Box 622
DAVIS, CA 95617
Crisis Phone 1:(916)756-5000
Crisis Phone 2:(916)666-7778
Crisis Phone 3:(916)372-6565
Business Phone:(916)756-7542
Hrs Avail: 24

EL CAJON
CRISIS HOUSE
125 W. MAIN ST
EL CAJON, CA 92020
Crisis Phone 1:(619)444-1194
Business Phone:(619)444-6506
Hrs Avail: 24

FRESNO
* HELP IN EMOTIONAL TROUBLE
P.O. Box 4282
FRESNO, CA 93744
Crisis Phone 1:(209)485-1432
Business Phone:(209)486-4703
Hrs Avail: 24

FRESNO
CONTACT FRESNO
7172 N. CEDAR
FRESNO, CA 93710
Crisis Phone 1:(209)298-2022
Business Phone:(209)298-8001
Hrs Avail: 24

FT. BRAGG
CRISIS LINE CARE PROJECT
461 N. FRANKLIN ST
P.O. Box 764
FT. BRAGG, CA 95437
Crisis Phone 1:(707)964-4357
Business Phone:(707)964-4055
Hrs Avail: 24

GARDEN GROVE
NEW HOPE COUNSELING CENTER
12141 LEWIS ST
GARDEN GROVE, CA 92640
Crisis Phone 1:(714)639-4673
Business Phone:(714)971-4123
Hrs Avail: 24

LAFAYETTE
* CONTACT-CARE CENTER
P.O. Box 901
LAFAYETTE, CA 94549
Crisis Phone 1:(415)284-2273
Business Phone:(415)284-2207
Hrs Avail: 24/7 DAYS

LAKEPORT
LAKE CO. MENTAL HEALTH
 EMERG. SERV
922 BEVINS COURT
LAKEPORT, CA 95453
Crisis Phone 1:(707)263-0160
Business Phone:(707)263-2258
Hrs Avail:24

LOS ALAMITOS
WEST ORANGE COUNTY HOTLINE
P.O. Box 32
LOS ALAMITOS, CA 90720
Crisis Phone 1:(714)761-4575
Crisis Phone 2:(213)596-5548
Crisis Phone 3:(714)894-4242
Business Phone:(213)594-0969
Hrs Avail:24

LOS ANGELES
*#LOS ANGELES SPC
1041 S. MENLO
LOS ANGELES, CA 90006
Crisis Phone 1:(213)381-5111
Business Phone:(213)386-5111
Hrs Avail:24

NAPA
*NORTH BAY SUICIDE
  PREVENTION, INC.
P.O. Box 2444
NAPA, CA 94558
Fairfield (707)422-2555
NAPA (707)255-2555
VALLEGO (707)643-2555
Business Phone:(707)257-3470
Hrs Avail:24

NEWARK
SECOND CHANCE, INC.
P.O. Box 643
NEWARK, CA 94560
Crisis Phone 1:(415)792-4357
Business Phone:(415)792-4357
Hrs Avail:24

PACIFIC GROVE
*SUICIDE PREVEN. CENT./
  MONTEREY CO
P.O. Box 52078
PACIFIC GROVE, CA 93950-7078
Crisis Phone 1:(408)649-8008
SALINAS (408)424-1485
Business Phone:(408)375-6966
Hrs Avail: 24

PASADENA
CONTACT PASADENA
73 N. HILL AVE
PASADENA CA 91106
Crisis Phone 1:(818)449-4500
Business Phone:(818)449-4502
Hrs Avail:24

RANCHO CUCAMONG
SUICIDE & CRISIS INTERV.
  SERVICES INC
7425 HELLMAN AVE
RANCHO CUCAMONG, CA 91730
Crisis Phone 1:(714)945-1066
Business Phone:(714)945-1066
Hrs Avail:24

REDDING
*HELP, INC.
P.O. Box 2498
REDDING, CA 96099
Crisis Phone 1:(916)225-5252
Business Phone:(916)255-5255
Hrs Avail: 24/7 DAYS

REDLANDS
EAST VALLEY CHAPTER OF
  MH ASSOC.
555 CAJON ST.
REDLANDS, CA 92373
Crisis Phone 1:(714)792-8255
Business Phone:(714)793-9405
Hrs Avail:24

SACRAMENTO
* SUICIDE PREV. SERV. OF
  SACRAMENTO
P.O. Box 449
SACRAMENTO, CA 95802
Crisis Phone 1:(916)441-1135
Business Phone:(916)441-1138
Hrs Avail:24

CALIFORNIA (CON'T)

SAN ANSELMO
MARIN SUICIDE PREVENTION
  CENTER
P.O. Box 792
SAN ANSELMO, CA 94960
Crisis Phone 1:(415)454-4524
Business Phone:(415)454-4566
Hrs Avail: 24

SAN BERNADINO
* SUICIDE & CRISIS INTERV.
  SERVICE
1669 N. "E" ST.
SAN BERNADINO, CA 92405
Crisis Phone 1:(714)886-4889
Hrs Avail: 24

SAN DIEGO
*#THE CRISIS TEAM
P.O. Box 85524
SAN DIEGO, CA 92138-5524
Crisis Phone 1:(619)236-3339
SAN DIEGO CO. ONLY (800)351-0757
Business Phone:(619)236-4576
Hrs Avail: 24

SAN DIEGO
* CRISIS LINE
FAMILY CRISIS INTERV. CENTER
5255 MT.ETNA DRIVE
SAN DIEGO, CA 92117
Crisis Phone 1:(619)268-7777
TTY (619)268-7778
Business Phone:(619)278-1211
Hrs Avail: 24

SAN FRANCISCO
*#SAN FRANCISCO SUICIDE
  PREVENTION
3940 GEARY BLVD.
SAN FRANCISCO, CA 94118
Crisis Phone 1:(415)221-1423
Crisis Phone 2:(415)221-1424
Crisis Phone 3:(415)221-1428
Business Phone:(415)752-4866
Hrs Avail:24/7 DAYS

SAN JOSE
CONTACT SANTA CLARA CO.
P.O. Box 24978
SAN JOSE, CA 95154
Crisis Phone 1:(408)266-8228
Business Phone:(408)266-1020
Hrs Avail:24

SAN JOSE
*#SANTA CLARA SUICIDE & CRISIS
  SERVICE
2220 MOORPARK
SAN JOSE, CA 95128
Crisis Phone 1:(408)279-3312
Crisis Phone 2:(408)683-2482
Business Phone:(408)299-6250
Hrs Avail: 24 HRS/7 DAYS

SAN LUIS OBISPO
HOTLINE OF SAN LUIS OBISPO
  CO., INC
P.O. Box 654
SAN LUIS OBISPO, CA 93406
Crisis Phone 1:(805)544-6163
Business Phone:(805)544-6016
HRS AVAIL: 24

SANTA BARBARA
*CALL-LINE
P.O. Box 14567
SANTA BARBARA, CA 93107
Crisis Phone 1:(805)569-2255
Business Phone:(805)682-2727
HRS AVAIL: 24

SANTA BARBARA
SANTA BARBARA CRISIS
  INTERVENTION PSYCHIATRIC
  EMERGENCY TEAM
4444 CALLE REAL
SANTA BARBARA, CA 93110
DAYTIME HRS. EXT. (805)964-6713
Business Phone:(805)964-6713
HRS AVAIL: 24

CALIFORNIA (CON'T)

SANTA CRUZ
CRISIS INTERV. SERVICE
SANTA CRUZ MENTAL HEALTH
  SERVICES
1060 EMELINE AVE.
SANTA CRUZ, CA 95060
NORTH COUNTY (408)425-2237
SOUTH COUNTY (408)722-3577
Business Phone:(408)425-2237
HRS AVAIL: 24

SANTA MONICA
NEW START
2500 COLORADO AVE
SANTA MONICA, CA 90404
Crisis Phone 1:(213)828-5561
Business Phone:(213)828-5561
HRS AVAIL: 24

SONOMA
FAMILY CENTER CRISIS INTERN.
  PROG.
SONOMA VALLEY FAMILY CENTER
  CRISIS INTERVENTION PROGRAM
P.O. Box 128
SONOMA, CA 95476
Crisis Phone 1:(707)938-HELP
Business Phone:(707)996-7877
HRS AVAIL: 24

ST. HELENA
* CRISIS-HELP OF NAPA VALLEY, INC.
1360 ADAMS ST.
ST. HELENA, CA 94574
Crisis Phone 1:(707)963-2555
Crisis Phone 2:(707)944-2212
Business Phone:(707)942-4319
HRS AVAIL: 24

STOCKTON
SAN JOAQUIN CO. MENTAL HEALTH
1212 N. CALIFORNIA
STOCKTON, CA 95202
Crisis Phone 1:(209)948-4484
8A.M.-5P.M. MON-FRI (209)982-1818
Business Phone:(209)948-4484
HRS AVAIL: 24

VENTURA
CRISIS EVALUATION UNIT
VENTURA CO. MENTAL HEALTH DEPT
300 HILLMONT AVE
VENTURA, CA 93003
Crisis Phone 1:(805)652-6727
Business Phone:(805)652-6727
HRS AVAIL: 24

WALNUT CREEK
*CONTRA COSTA CRISIS/SUICIDE
  INTERVENTION
P.O. Box 4852
WALNUT CREEK, CA 94596
Crisis Phone 1:(415)939-3232
Business Phone:(415)939-1916
HRS AVAIL: 24

YUBA CITY
SUTTER-YUBA MH CRISIS CLINIC
1965 LIVE OAK BLVD.
YUBA CITY, CA 95991
Crisis Phone 1:(916)673-8255
Business Phone:(916)674-8500
HRS AVAIL: 24

COLORADO

ARVADA
LIFE LINE OF COLORADO, INC.
5742 FIELD STREET
ARVADA, CO 80002
Crisis Phone 1:(303)458-7777
Business Phone:(303)421-6453
HRS AVAIL: 24

ARVADA
*JEFFERSON CO. MHC, INC.
5265 VANCE STREET
ARVADA, CO 80002
Crisis Phone 1:(303)425-0300
Business Phone:(303)425-0300
HRS AVAIL: 24

COLORADO (Con't)

AURORA

COMITIS CRISIS CENTER
9840 E. 17th AVE.
P.O. Box 913
AURORA, CO 80040
Crisis Phone 1:(303)343-9890
Business Phone:(303)341-9160
HRS AVAIL: 24

BOULDER

EMERG. PSYCH. SERVICES
1333 IRIS AVE
BOULDER, CO 80302
Crisis Phone 1:(303)447-1665
Business Phone:(303)443-8500
HRS AVAIL: 24

COLO. SPRINGS

COLORADO SPRINGS CRISIS
   SERVICES
PIKES PEAK MENTAL HEALTH
   CENTER, INC.
875 W. MORENO
COLORADO SPRINGS, CO 80905
Crisis Phone 1:(303)471-8300
Business Phone:(303)471-8300
HRS AVAIL: 24

COLO. SPRINGS

TERROS
P.O. Box 2642
COLORADO SPRINGS, CO 80901
Crisis Phone 1:(303)471-4127
Business Phone:(303)471-4128
HRS AVAIL: 24

DENVER

*SUICIDE AND CRISIS CONTROL
2459 SOUTH ASH
DENVER, CO 80222
Crisis Phone 1:(303)757-0988
Crisis Phone 2:(303)789-3073
Business Phone:(303)756-8485
HRS AVAIL: 24

FT. MORGAN

FT. MORGAN HELPLINE
330 MEAKER STREET
FT. MORGAN, CO 80701
Crisis Phone 1:(303)867-3411
Crisis Phone 2:(303)867-2451
Business Phone:(303)867-3411
HRS AVAIL: 24

GRAND JUNCTION

CRISIS LINE-A SERVICE OF INDIV &
   FAMILY COUNSELING
P.O. Box 644
GRAND JUNCTION, CO 81502
Crisis Phone 1:(303)242-HELP
Business Phone:(303)243-4414
HRS AVAIL: 24

PUEBLO

*#PUEBLO SUICIDE PREVENTION,
   INC.
229 COLORADO AVE
PUEBLO, CO 81004
Crisis Phone 1:(303)544-1133
Business Phone:(303)545-2477
HRS AVAIL: 24

CONNECTICUT

GREENWICH

* HOTLINE OF GREENWICH, INC.
189 MASON ST.
GREENWICH, CT 06830
Crisis Phone 1:(203)661-HELP
Business Phone:(203)661-4378
HRS AVAIL: 24

HARTFORD

INFOLINE
999 ASYLUM AVE.
HARTFORD, CT 06105
Crisis Phone 1:(203)522-4636
Business Phone:(203)522-4636
HRS AVAIL: 24

NORWALK

INFO LINE OF SOUTHWESTERN CT
7 ACADEMY ST
NORWALK, CT 06850
BRIDGEPORT (203)333-7555
NORWALK (203)853-2525
STAMFORD (203)324-1010
Business Phone:(203)853-9109
HRS AVAIL: 24

PLAINVILLE

*#THE WHEELER CLINIC, INC.
EMERGENCY SERVICES
91 NORTHWEST DR
PLAINVILLE, CT 06062
Crisis Phone 1:(203)747-3434
Crisis Phone 2:(203)524-1182
Business Phone:(203)747-6801
HRS AVAIL: 24

TRUMBULL

TRUMBULL COUNSELING CENTER
121 OLD MINE ROAD
TRUMBULL, CT 06107
Crisis Phone 1:(203)261-5110
Business Phone:(203)452-5082
HRS AVAIL: 24

WESTPORT

OPEN LINE, LTD
245 POST ROAD EAST
WESTPORT, CT 06880
Crisis Phone 1:(203)226-3546
Business Phone:(203)226-3546
HRS AVAIL: 12:00PM-12:00AM

WASHINGTON DC

WASHINGTON

* FACT HOTLINE
(FAMILIES AND CHILDREN IN
  TROUBLE)
FAMILY STRESS SERVICES OF
  DC/NCPCA
2001 "O" ST., NW, SUITE G-100
WASHINGTON DC 20036
Crisis Phone 1:(202)628-3228
Business Phone:(202)965-1900
HRS AVAIL: 24

WASHINGTON

* THE SAMARITANS OF
  WASHINGTON, INC
4115 WISCONSIN AVE. NW
WASHINGTON DC 20016
Crisis Phone 1:(202)362-8100
Crisis Phone 2:(202)362-8661
Crisis Phone 3:(202)362-8665
Business Phone:(202)362-8858 or 67
HRS AVAIL: 24

WASHINGTON

EMERGENCY PSYCH. RESPONSE
  DIV
D.C. DEPT. OF HUMAN SERVICES
1905 E ST. S.E. (SOUTH MHC)
WASHINGTON DC 20005
Crisis Phone 1:(202)561-7000
Business Phone:(202)727-0700
HRS AVAIL: 24

WASHINGTON

D.C. HOTLINE
P.O. Box 57194
WASHINGTON DC 20037
Crisis Phone 1:(202)223-2255
Business Phone:(202)223-0020
HRS AVAIL: M-F 1PM-1AM,
  SA,SU 9AM-1AM

WASHINGTON
* ANDROMEDA TRANSCULTURAL
  HISPANO MENTAL HEALTH
  CENTER
  1823 18TH STREET, N.W.
  WASHINGTON DC 20009
  Crisis Phone 1:(202)677-6766
  Business Phone:(202)387-8926
  HRS AVAIL: 24 HRS/7 DAYS

DELAWARE

DOVER
* KENT/SUSSEX MOBILE CRISIS
  UNIT
  KENT/SUSSEX COMM. MHC
  805 RIVER ROAD
  DOVER, DE 19901
  IN DELAWARE (800)345-6785
  Business Phone:(302)736-4275
  HRS AVAIL: 24 HRS/7 DAYS

NEW CASTLE
* GRTR WILMINGTON-NEW CASTLE
  CO. CMHC PSYCHIATRIC
  EMERGENCY SERVICE
  14 CENTRAL AVENUE
  NEW CASTLE, DE 19720
  Crisis Phone 1:(302)421-6711
  Crisis Phone 2:(302)421-6712
  Crisis Phone 3:(302)421-6713
  Business Phone:(302)421-6714,6715
  HRS AVAIL: 24 HRS/7 DAYS

GEORGETOWN
GEORGETOWN HELPLINE
SUSSEX COUNTY COMMUNITY MHC
GEORGETOWN, DE 19947
Crisis Phone 1:(302)856-6626
Business Phone:(302)856-2151
HRS AVAIL: 24

WILMINGTON
*CONTACT-DELAWARE, INC
P.O. Box 2939
WILMINGTON, DE 19805
Crisis Phone 1:(302)656-6660
Crisis Phone 2:(302)575-1112
Business Phone:(302)656-6222
HRS AVAIL: 24 HRS/7 DAYS

FLORIDA

BRADENTON
MANATEE GLENS CORPORATION
  CRISIS SERVICES
P.O. Box 9478
BRADENTON, FL 34206
Crisis Phone 1:(813)748-8585
Business Phone:(813)747-8648
HRS AVAIL: 24

DE FUNIAK SPRINGS
* C.O.P.E. CENTER
  SHAUTAUQUA OFF. OF
  PSYCHOTHERAPY
  112 A WEST NELSON AVENUE
  P.O. Box 607
  DE FUNIAK SPRGS, FL 32433
  Crisis Phone 1:(904)892-4357
  Business Phone:(904)892-2167
  HRS AVAIL: 24 HRS/7 DAYS

FLORIDA (Con't)

FORT LAUDERDALE

* CRISIS LINE/INFO. & REFERRAL OF
  COMM. SERV. COUNCIL OF
  BROWARD CO
1300 SO. ANDREWS AVE
P.O. Box 22877
FORT LAUDERDALE, FL 33335
Crisis Phone 1:(305)467-6333
Business Phone:(305)524-8371
HRS AVAIL: 24

FT. MYERS

LEE MENTAL HEALTH CENTER, INC.
  CRISIS STABILIZATION UNIT
P.O. Box 06137
FT. MYERS, FL 33906
HOTLINE (813)275-4242
Business Phone:(813)275-3222 x388
HRS AVAIL: 24

FT. PIERCE

INDIAN RIVER COMM. MHC
800 AVE. H
FT. PIERCE, FL 33450
Crisis Phone 1:(305)464-8111
Business Phone:(305)464-8111
HRS AVAIL: 24

FT. WALTON BEACH

CRISIS LINE/FT. WALTON BEACH
105 LEWIS ST.
FT. WALTON BEACH, FL 32548
Crisis Phone 1:(904)244-9191
CRESTVIEW, TOLL FREE
  (904)682-0101
Business Phone:(904)244-0151 x35
HRS AVAIL: 24

GAINESVILLE

*#ALACHUA COUNTY CRISIS
  CENTER
730 N. WALDO RD., SUITE #100
GAINESVILLE, FL 32601
Crisis Phone 1:(904)376-4444
Crisis Phone 2:(904)376-4445
Business Phone:(904)372-3659
HRS AVAIL: 24

HIALEAH

* NORTHWEST DADE COMM. MHC
  CHILDREN/ADOLESCENTS CRISIS
  SERV
1840 W. 49TH ST., PENTHOUSE
HIALEAH, FL 33012
Crisis Phone 1:(305)825-0300
Business Phone:(305)825-0300
HRS AVAIL: 24/7 DAYS

JACKSONVILLE

* SUICIDE PREVENTION SERVICE/
  JACKS
2218 PARK ST
JACKSONVILLE, FL 32204
Crisis Phone 1:(904)384-5641
Business Phone:(904)387-5643
HRS AVAIL: 24

KEY WEST/MONROE COUNTY

* HELPLINE, INC.
P.O. Box 2186
KEY WEST, FL 33045-2186
Crisis Phone 1:(305)296-HELP
Crisis Phone 2:(305)294-LINE
MIDDLE & UPPER KEYS
  (800)341-4343
HRS AVAIL: 24

KISSIMMEE

HELP NOW IN OSCEOLA, INC
917 EMMETT ST
KISSIMMEE, FL 32741
Crisis Phone 1:(305)847-8811
Business Phone:(305)847-8562
HRS AVAIL: 24

LAKE CITY

COLUMBIA COUNSELING CENTER
P.O. Box 2818
LAKE CITY, FL 32056
Crisis Phone 1:(904)752-1045
AFTER 5:00 P.M. (904)752-2140
Business Phone:(904)752-1045
HRS AVAIL: 24

FLORIDA (Con't)

MIAMI

*#SWITCHBOARD OF MIAMI, INC.
35 S.W. 8TH ST
MIAMI, FL 33130
Crisis Phone 1:(305)358-4357
Business Phone:(305)358-1640
HRS AVAIL: 24

MILTON

AVALON CENTER CRISIS LINE
1101 OLD BAGDAD HWY
P.O. Box 769
MILTON, FL 32572
Crisis Phone 1:(904)623-6363
Business Phone:(904)623-9434
HRS AVAIL: 24

ORLANDO

WE CARE, INC
112 PASADENA PLACE
ORLANDO, FL 32803
Crisis Phone 1:(305)628-1227
TEEN/KID (305)644-2027
Business Phone:(305)425-2624
HRS AVAIL: 24

ORLANDO

* MENTAL HEALTH SERVICE OF
   ORANGE
2520 NORTH ORANGE AVE.
ORLANDO, FL 32804
Crisis Phone 1:(305)896-9306
Business Phone:(305)896-9306
HRS AVAIL: 24

PANAMA CITY

PANAMA CITY CRISIS LINE
NORTHWEST MENTAL HEALTH
   CENTER
615 N. MCARTHUR AVE
PANAMA CITY, FL 32401
Crisis Phone 1:(904)769-9481
Business Phone:(904)769-9481
HRS AVAIL: 24

PENSACOLA

PENSACOLA HELP LINE
LAKEVIEW CENTER, INC.
1221 W. LAKEVIEW ST
PENSCOLA, FL 32501
Crisis Phone 1:(904)438-1617
Business Phone:(904)432-1222 x300
HRS AVAIL: 24

PINELLAS

*#PINELLAS EMERGENCY MHS, INC
11254 58TH STREET NORTH
PINELLAS FL 33565-2606
Crisis Phone 1:(813)791-3131
Crisis Phone 2:(813)791-1117
Business Phone:(813)545-5636,7
HRS AVAIL: 24/7 DAYS

ROCKLEDGE

* SUICIDE/CRISIS HOTLINE
BREVARD CNTY M.H. ASSOCIATION
566 BARTON BLVD. #304
ROCKLEDGE, FL 32955
Crisis Phone 1:(305)631-8944
Business Phone:(305)631-9290
HRS AVAIL: 24

ROCKLEDGE

TEEN & PARENT STRESS LINE
1770 CEDAR ST
P.O. Box 69
ROCKLEDGE, FL 32955
Crisis Phone 1:(305)631-8944
Business Phone:(305)631-9290
HRS AVAIL: 24

SARASOTA

SUNCOAST CRISIS UNIT
1700 S. TAMIAMI TRAIL 5 NW
SARASOTA, FL 34239
LIFE LINE (813)955-8702
UNIT LINE (813)955-9913
Business Phone:(813)966-7471
HRS AVAIL: 24

FLORIDA (Con't)

ST. PETERSBURG
* HOTLINE/INFORMATION &
  REFERRAL ALTERNATIVE HUMAN
  SERVICES, INC.
P.O. Box 13087
ST. PETERSBURG, FL 33733
Crisis Phone 1:(813)531-4664
Crisis Phone 2:(813)848-5555
Crisis Phone 3:(904)567-1111
BUSINESS LINE: (813)526-1100
Business Phone:(813)526-5351
HRS AVAIL: 24/7 DAYS

TALLAHASSEE
* TELEPHONE COUNSEL &
  REFERRAL SERV
P.O. Box 20169
TALLAHASSEE, FL 32316
Crisis Phone 1:(904)224-6333
Business Phone:(904)575-8111
HRS AVAIL: 24

TAMPA
* #SUICIDE & CRISIS CENTER OF
  HILLSBOROUGH COUNTY
2214 E. HENRY AVE.
TAMPA, FL 33610-4497
Crisis Phone 1:(813)238-8821
Business Phone:(813)238-8411
HRS AVAIL: 24

TAMPA
CONTACT TAMPA HELP LINE
P.O. Box 10117
TAMPA, FL 33679
Crisis Phone 1:(813)251-4000
Business Phone:(813)251-4040
HRS AVAIL: 24

W. PALM BEACH
* CRISIS LINE INFO. & REF
  SERVICES, INC
P.O. Box 15456
W. PALM BEACH, FL 33416
NORTH AND CENTRAL
  (305)686-4000
SOUTH (305)272-1121
WEST (GLADES) (305)996-1121
Business Phone:(305)689-3334
HRS AVAIL: 24

WINTER HAVEN
HELP AND RESOURCELINE
COMMUNITY MENTAL HEALTH
  CENTER
WINTER HAVEN HOSPITAL
WINTER HAVEN, FL 33881
Crisis Phone 1:(813)299-5858
Business Phone:(813)293-1121
  x1158
HRS AVAIL: 24

GEORGIA

ATLANTA
* EMERGENCY MENTAL HEALTH
  SERVICE
FULTON COUNTY HEALTH
  DEPARTMENT
99 BUTLER ST., S.E.
ATLANTA, GA 30303
Crisis Phone 1:(404)522-9222
Business Phone:(404)522-9222
HRS AVAIL: 24

ATLANTA
DE KALB EMERG./CRISIS INTERV
  SERV
GEORGIA MENTAL HEALTH
  INSTITUTE
1256 BRIARCLIFF RD. N.E.
ATLANTA, GA 30306
Crisis Phone 1:(404)892-4646
Business Phone:(404)892-4646
HRS AVAIL: 24

AUGUSTA

HELP LINE
P.O. Box 1724
AUGUSTA, GA 30903
Crisis Phone 1:(404)724-4357
Business Phone:(404)724-4357
HRS AVAIL: 24

AUSTELL

EMERGENCY SERVICES
COBB/DOUGLAS COMM MH
  SERVICE AREA
6133 LOVE ST
AUSTELL, GA 30001
Crisis Phone 1:(404)422-0202
Business Phone:(404)941-2416
HRS AVAIL: 24

COLUMBUS

CONTACT CHATTAHOOCHEE
  VALLEY
P.O. Box 12002
COLUMBUS, GA 31907
Crisis Phone 1:(404)327-3999
Business Phone:(404)327-0199
HRS AVAIL: 24

GAINESVILLE

CONTACT HALL COUNTY
P.O. Box 1616
GAINESVILLE, GA 30503
Crisis Phone 1:(404)534-0617
Business Phone:(404)536-7145
HRS AVAIL: 24

LAWRENCEVILLE

GWINNETT/ROCKALE/NEWTON
  MH-MR & ALCOHOL & DRUG
  SERVICES
P.O. Box 687
LAWRENCEVILLE, GA 30246-0687
Crisis Phone 1:(404)963-8141
EVENING, WEEK-ENDS
  (404)963-3223
Business Phone: (404) 963-8141
HRS AVAIL: 24

MACON

CRISIS LINE OF MACON AND BIBB CO.
MERCER UNIVERSITY
P.O. Box 56
MACON, GA 31207
Crisis Phone 1:(912)745-9292
Business Phone:(912)745-9292
HRS AVAIL: 24

MARIETTA

COBB-DOUGLAS MENTAL HEALTH
EMERGENCY MENTAL HEALTH
  SERVICES
COMMUNITY SERVICES BUILDING
737 CHURCH ST., SUITE #420
MARIETTA, GA 30060
Crisis Phone 1:(404)422-0202
Business Phone:(404)424-0870
HRS AVAIL: 24

RIVERDALE

CLAYTON CRISIS LINE
CLAYTON GENERAL HOSPITAL
11 S.W. UPPER RIVERDALE RD.
RIVERDALE, GA 30274
Crisis Phone 1:(404)996-4357
Business Phone:(404)996-4361
HRS AVAIL: 24

SAVANNAH

FIRST CALL FOR HELP
P.O. Box 9119
SAVANNAH, GA 31412
Crisis Phone 1:(912)232-3383
Business Phone:(912)232-3383
HRS AVAIL: 24

HAWAII

HONOLULU/OAHU
* SUICIDE AND CRISIS CENTER
200 N. VINEYARD BLVD., RM. #603
HONOLULU, HI 96817
Crisis Phone 1:(808)521-4555
Business Phone:(808)536-7234
HRS AVAIL: 24

KAILUA-KONA
KONA CRISIS CENTER, INC.
P.O. Box 4363
KAILUA-KONA, HI 96740
Crisis Phone 1:(808)329-9111
Business Phone:(808)329-6744
HRS AVAIL: 24

IOWA

AMES
OPEN LINE
WELCH AVE. STATION
P.O. Box 1138
AMES, IA 50010
Crisis Phone 1:(515)292-7000
Business Phone:(515)292-4983
HRS AVAIL: SU-TH 9A-12MN,
    F&S 9A-3A

CEDAR RAPIDS
* FOUNDATION 2, INC.
1251 THIRD AVE. SE
CEDAR RAPIDS, IA 52403
Crisis Phone 1:(319)362-2174
IN IOWA (800) 332-4224
Business Phone:(319)362-1170
HRS AVAIL: 24

DAVENPORT
VERA FRENCH COMM. HEALTH
    CENTER
SUICIDE LINE AT MERCY HOSPITAL
1441 W. CENTRAL PARK AVE.
DAVENPORT, IA 52804
Crisis Phone 1:(319)383-1900
Business Phone:(319)383-1900
HRS AVAIL: 24

DES MOINES
* COMMUNITY TELEPHONE
    SERVICES
CRISIS LINE
SERVICE OF THE AMER. RED CROSS
2116 GRAND AVENUE
DES MOINES, IA 50312
CRISIS (515)244-1000

Des Moines—Com Tel Serv Con't
COUNSELING (515)244-1010
Business Phone:(515)244-6700
HRS AVAIL: M-TH 3PM-8AM
    ALL OTHER 24

DES MOINES
FIRST CALL FOR
    HELP/DES MOINES
700 SIXTH AVENUE
DES MOINES, IA 50309
WATS IN IOWA (800)532-1194
Business Phone:(515)244-8646
HRS AVAIL: 24

DUBUQUE
PHONE A FRIEND CRISIS LINE
XAVIER PARK
DUBUQUE, IA 52001
Crisis Phone 1:(319)588-4016
Business Phone:(319)557-8331
HRS AVAIL: 24

IOWA CITY
IOWA CITY CRISIS INTERVENTION
    CENTER
321 EAST FIRST STREET
IOWA CITY, IA 52240
Crisis Phone 1:(319)351-0140
Business Phone:(319)351-2726
HRS AVAIL: 24

IOWA (Con't)

SIOUX CITY

AID CENTER
406 5TH ST.
SIOUX CITY, IA 51101
Crisis Phone 1:(712)252-5000
Business Phone:(712)252-1861
HRS AVAIL: 24

WATERLOO

* CRISIS SERVICES OF WATERLOO
2530 UNIVERSITY AVENUE
WATERLOO, IA 50701
Crisis Phone 1:(319)233-9270
Business Phone:(319)233-9270
HRS AVAIL: 24/7 DAYS

IDAHO

BOISE

EMERGENCY LINE
REGION IV SERVICES/
  MENTAL HEALTH
1105 S. ORCHARD
BOISE, ID 83705
Crisis Phone 1:(208)338-7044
Business Phone:(208)338-7020
HRS AVAIL:24

COEUR D'ALENE

COEUR D'ALENE EMERGENCY LINE
W. GEORGE MOODY HEALTH
  CENTER
2195 IRONWOOD COURT
COEUR D' ALENE, ID 83814
Crisis Phone 1:(208)667-6406
Business Phone:(208)667-6406
HRS AVAIL: 24

IDAHO FALLS

IDAHO FALLS EMERGENCY
  SERVICES
REGION VII MENTAL HEALTH
150 SHOUP
IDAHO FALLS, ID 83402
Crisis Phone 1:(208)525-7129
Business Phone:(208)525-7129
HRS AVAIL: 24

KELLOGG

KELLOGG EMERGENCY LINE
HEALTH AND WELFARE SERVICE
  CENTER
140 RAIL RD. AVE
KELLOGG, ID 83837
Crisis Phone 1:(208)667-6406
Crisis Phone 2:(208)786-2781
Business Phone:(208)784-1351
HRS AVAIL: 24

LEWISTON

YWCA CRISIS SERVICES
300 MAIN ST
LEWISTON, ID 83501
Crisis Phone 1:(208)746-9655
Business Phone:(208)746-9655
HRS AVAIL: 24

ST. MARIES

ST. MARIES EMERGENCY LINE
HEALTH AND WELFARE SERVICE
  CENTER
128 S. 7TH STREET
ST. MARIES, ID 83861
Crisis Phone 1:(208)245-2527
Business Phone:(208)245-2541
HRS AVAIL: 8:00 AM-5:00 PM

TWIN FALLS

TWIN FALLS EMERGENCY
  SERVICES
REGION 5 MENTAL HEALTH
823 HARRISON
TWIN FALLS, ID 83301
Crisis Phone 1:(208)734-4000
Business Phone:(208)734-9770
HRS AVAIL: 24

ALTON

MADISON CO. MENTAL HEALTH
  CENTER
2615 EDWARDS ST
P.O. Box 1054
ALTON, IL 62002
Crisis Phone 1:(618)463-1058
Business Phone:(618)462-2331
HRS AVAIL: 24

ANNA

UNION COUNTY COUNSELING
  SERVICE
204 SOUTH ST
ANNA, IL 62906
Crisis Phone 1:(618)833-8551
Business Phone:(618)833-8551
HRS AVAIL: 24

AURORA

* #CRISIS LINE OF THE FOX VALLEY
309 W. NEW INDIAN TRAIL CT.
AURORA, IL 60506
Crisis Phone 1:(312)897-5522
Business Phone:(312)897-5531
HRS AVAIL: 24

BEARDSTOWN

CASS COUNTY MENTAL HEALTH
  CENTER
101 W. 15TH STREET
BEARDSTOWN, IL 62618
Crisis Phone 1:(217)323-2980
Business Phone:(217)323-2980
HRS AVAIL: 24

BELLEVILLE

* #CALL FOR HELP
SUICIDE & CRISIS INTERV. SERVICE
500 WILSHIRE DR
BELLEVILLE, IL 62223
Crisis Phone 1:(618)397-0963
Business Phone:(618)397-0968
HRS AVAIL: 24

BLOOMINGTON

* EMERGENCY CRISIS
  INTERVENTION TEAM
MC LEAN CO. CENTER FOR HUMAN
  SERV
108 W. MARKET
BLOOMINGTON, IL 61701
Crisis Phone 1:(309)827-4005
Business Phone:(309)827-5351
HRS AVAIL: 24

BLOOMINGTON

PATH (PERSONAL ASSISTANCE
  TELEPHONE HELP)
201 E GROVE
BLOOMINGTON, IL 61701
Crisis Phone 1:(309)827-4005
TOLL FREE NUMBER (800)322-5015
Business Phone:(309)828-1922
HRS AVAIL: 24

CAIRO

CAIRO CRISIS LINE
MENTAL HEALTH CENTER
1001 WASHINGTON AVENUE
CAIRO, IL 62914
Crisis Phone 1:(618)734-2665
Business Phone:(618)734-2665
HRS AVAIL: 24

CHAMPAIGN

* CHAMPAIGN COUNTY MENTAL
  HEALTH CENTER
CRISIS LINE
P.O. Box 429
CHAMPAIGN, IL 61820
Crisis Phone 1:(217)398-8080
Crisis Phone 2:(217)359-4141
Business Phone:(217)398-8080
HRS AVAIL: 24/7 DAYS

ILLINOIS (Con't)

CHICAGO

* SOCIETY OF SAMARITANS—
  CHICAGO
5638 S. WOODLAWN AVE
CHICAGO, IL 60637
Crisis Phone 1:(312)947-8300
Business Phone:(312)947-8844
HRS AVAIL: 24

CHICAGO

IN-TOUCH HOTLINE
STUDENT COUNSELING SERVICE
UNIVERSITY OF ILLINOIS AT
  CHICAGO
P.O. Box 4348
CHICAGO, IL 60680
Crisis Phone 1:(312)996-5535
Business Phone:(312)996-3490
HRS AVAIL: 6PM-3AM/7 DAYS

CLINTON

DEWITT COUNTY HUMAN
  RESOURCE CENTER
P.O. Box 616
CLINTON, IL 61727
Crisis Phone 1:(217)935-9496
Business Phone:(217)935-9496
HRS AVAIL: 24

COLLINSVILLE

COMMUNITY COUNSELING
  SERVICES
1315 VANDALIA
COLLINSVILLE, IL 62234
Crisis Phone 1:(618)877-4420
Business Phone:(618)344-0393
HRS AVAIL: 24

DANVILLE

CONTACT DANVILLE
504 N. VERMILION
DANVILLE, IL 61832
Crisis Phone 1:(217)443-2273
Business Phone:(217)446-8212
HRS AVAIL: 24

DU QUOIN

PERRY COUNTY HELP LINE
R.R. #1
P.O. Box 106
DU QUOIN, IL 62832
Crisis Phone 1:(618)542-4357
Business Phone:(618)542-4357
HRS AVAIL: 24

EDWARDSVILLE

EDWARDSVILLE COMM.
  COUNSELING SERV
1507 TROY RD., SUITE #3
EDWARDSVILLE, IL 62025
Crisis Phone 1:(618)877-4420
Business Phone:(618)656-8721
HRS AVAIL: 24

ELGIN

*COMMUNITY CRISIS CENTER
P.O. Box 1390
ELGIN, IL 60121
Crisis Phone 1:(312)697-2380
Business Phone:(312)742-4031
HRS AVAIL: 24

ELK GROVE

TALK LINE/KIDS LINE, INC.
P.O. Box 1321
ELK GROVE, IL 60007
TALK LINE (312)228-6400
KIDS LINE (312)228-KIDS
Business Phone:(312)981-1271
HRS AVAIL: 24

EVANSTON

EVANSTON HOSPITAL CRISIS INTERV
2650 RIDGE AVE.
EVANSTON, IL 60201
Crisis Phone 1:(312)492-6500
Business Phone:(312)492-6500
HRS AVAIL: 24

FREEPORT

CONTACT STEPHENSON CO.
P.O. Box 83
FREEPORT, IL 61032
Crisis Phone 1:(815)233-4357
Business Phone:(815)233-4357
HRS AVAIL: 24

GALESBURG

* SPOON RIVER CENTER
2323 WINDISH DRIVE
P.O. Box 1447
GALESBURG, IL 61402-1447
Crisis Phone 1:(800)322-7143
Business Phone:(309)344-2323
HRS AVAIL: 24

GRANITE CITY

MENTAL HEALTH CENTER
2024 STATE ST.
GRANITE CITY, IL 62040
Crisis Phone 1:(618)877-4420
Business Phone:(618)877-4420
HRS AVAIL: 24

HIGHLAND

HIGHLAND COMM. COUNSELING
    SERVICES
508 BROADWAY
HIGHLAND, IL 62249
Crisis Phone 1:(618)877-4420
Business Phone:(618)654-7232
HRS AVAIL: 24

HILLSBORO

MONTGOMERY CO. HELPLINE
MONTGOMERY CO. COUNSELING
    CENTER
200 S. MAIN ST
HILLSBORO, IL 62049
Crisis Phone 1:(217)532-9581
Crisis Phone 2:(217)324-5052
Business Phone:(217)532-9581
HRS AVAIL: 24

JOLIET

* CRISIS LINE OF WILL COUNTY
P.O. Box 2354
JOLIET, IL 60435
JOLIET (815)722-3344
FRANKFORT (815)469-6166
BOLINGBROOK (312)759-4555
PEOTONE (312)258-3333
WILMINGTON (815)476-6969
Business Phone:(815)744-5280
HRS AVAIL: 24/7 DAYS

LIBERTYVILLE

CONNECTION TELEPHONE CRISIS
INTERV. & REFERRAL SERVICE
P.O. Box 906
LIBERTYVILLE, IL 60048
Crisis Phone 1:(312)367-1080
Business Phone:(312)362-3381
HRS AVAIL: 24

LINCOLN

LINCOLN CRISIS CLINIC
LOGAN-MASON MENTAL HEALTH
315 8TH
LINCOLN, IL 62656
Crisis Phone 1:(217)732-3500
Business Phone:(217)732-2161
HRS AVAIL: 24

MT. VERNON

MT. VERNON CRISIS LINE
COMPREHENSIVE SERVICES
601 N. 18TH
P.O. BOX 428
MT. VERNON, IL 62864
Crisis Phone 1:(618)242-1512
Business Phone:(618)242-1510
HRS AVAIL: 24

PARIS
HUMAN RESOURCES CENTER
P.O. Box 1118
PARIS, IL 61944
DAYS (217)465-4118
EVENINGS, WEEK-ENDS
    (217)465-4141
Business Phone:(217)465-4118
HRS AVAIL: 24

PEORIA
PEORIA CALL FOR HELP
5407 N. UNIVERSITY
PEORIA, IL 61614
Crisis Phone 1:(309)673-7373
Business Phone:(309)692-1766
HRS AVAIL: 24

QUINCY
QUINCY SUICIDE PREV. & CRISIS
    SERV
4409 MAINE
QUINCY, IL 62301
Crisis Phone 1:(217)222-1166
Business Phone:(217)223-0413
HRS AVAIL: 24

ROCKFORD
* CONTACT ROCKFORD
P.O. Box 1976
ROCKFORD, IL 61110
Crisis Phone 1:(815)964-4044
Business Phone:(815)964-0400
HRS AVAIL: 24

SULLIVAN
SULLIVAN CRISIS LINE
MOULTREE CO. COUNSELING
    CENTER
2 W. ADAMS
SULLIVAN, IL 61951
Crisis Phone 1:(217)728-7611
Business Phone:(217)728-4358
HRS AVAIL: 24

TAYLORVILLE
TAYLORVILLE HELPLINE
CHRISTIAN CO. MENTAL HEALTH
    CENTER
421 W. MARKET
P.O. Box 438
TAYLORVILLE, IL 62568
DAYS (217)824-4905
EVENINGS, WEEK-ENDS
    (217)824-3335
Business Phone:(217)824-4905
HRS AVAIL: 24

WOOD RIVER
* CRISIS SERVICES OF MADISON
    COUNTY
P.O. Box 570
WOOD RIVER, IL 62095
Crisis Phone 1:(618)877-4420
Crisis Phone 2:(618)463-1058
Business Phone:(618)251-4073
HRS AVAIL: 24

INDIANA

ANDERSON
CONTACT/HELP
P.O. Box 303
ANDERSON, IN 46015
Crisis Phone 1:(317)649-5211
Business Phone:(317)649-4939
HRS AVAIL: 24

EVANSVILLE
* SOUTHWESTERN INDIANA MHC, INC
415 MULBERRY
EVANSVILLE, IN 47713
Crisis Phone 1:(812)423-7791
Business Phone:(812)423-7791
HRS AVAIL: 24

FT. WAYNE
SWITCHBOARD, INC
316 W. CREIGHTON
FT. WAYNE, IN 46807
Crisis Phone 1:(219)456-4561
Business Phone:(219)745-7914
HRS AVAIL: 24

GARY
RAP LINE—CRISIS CENTER
215 N. GRAND BLVD
GARY, IN 46403
Crisis Phone 1:(219)980-9243
Business Phone:)219)980-4207
HRS AVAIL: 24

GREENCASTLE
CONTACT PUTNAM COUNTY
P.O. Box 15
GREENCASTLE, IN 46135
Crisis Phone 1:(317)653-2645
Business Phone:(317)653-5040
HRS AVAIL: 24

INDIANAPOLIS
* MENTAL HEALTH ASSOC. IN
  MARION CO.
CRISIS & SUICIDE INTERVENTION
  SERVICE
1433 N. MERIDIAN ST., RM #202
INDIANAPOLIS, IN 46202
Crisis Phone 1:(317)632-7575
Business Phone:(317)269-1569
HRS AVAIL: 24

LAFAYETTE
LAFAYETTE CRISIS CENTER
803 N. 8TH ST
LAFAYETTE, IN 47904
Crisis Phone 1:(317)742-0244
Business Phone:(317)742-0247
HRS AVAIL: 24

LAWRENCEBURG
LAWRENCEBURG CRISIS LINE
COMMUNITY MENTAL HEALTH
  CENTER
285 BIELBY RD
LAWRENCEBURG, IN 47025
Crisis Phone 1:(812)537-1302
TOLL FREE NUMBER (800)832-5387
Business Phone:(812)537-1302
HRS AVAIL: 24

LEBANON
PROJECT HELP
CRISIS INTERVENTION SERVICE
ST. PETER'S EPISCOPAL CHURCH
950 E. WASHINGTON ST
LEBANON, IN 46052
Crisis Phone 1:(317)482-1599
Business Phone:(317)482-1599
HRS AVAIL: 24

MARYVILLE
CONTACT TELE. OF BLOUNT CO
P.O. Box 0382
MARYVILLE, IN 37803
Crisis Phone 1:(615)984-7689
Business Phone:(615)984-7686
HRS AVAIL: 24

MERRILLVILLE
CONTACT—CARES OF NW INDIANA
P.O. Box 10247
MERRILLVILLE, IN 46411
Crisis Phone 1:(219)769-3141
Crisis Phone 2:(219)374-7660
Crisis Phone 3:(219)462-9880
Business Phone:(219)769-3278
HRS AVAIL: 24

MONTICELLO
TWIN LAKES CONTACT—HELP
P.O. Box 67
MONTICELLO, IN 47960
Crisis Phone 1:(219)583-4357
Business Phone:(219)583-4357
HRS AVAIL: 24

KANSAS

EMPORIA

EMPORIA EMERGENCY SERVICES
MH CENTER OF E. CENTRAL
  KANSAS
705 S. COMMERCIAL
EMPORIA, KS 66801
Crisis Phone 1:(316)343-2626
Business Phone:(316)342-6116
HRS AVAIL: 24

FT. SCOTT

FT. SCOTT HELPLINE
MENTAL HEALTH ASSOCIATION
1ST TO SCOTT AVE.
FT. SCOTT, KS 66701
Crisis Phone 1:(316)223-2420
Business Phone:(316)223-5030
HRS AVAIL:24

GARDEN CITY

GARDEN CITY AREA MHC
156 GARDENDALE
GARDEN CITY, KS 67846
Crisis Phone 1:(316)276-7689
Business Phone:(316)276-7689
HRS AVAIL:24

HUMBOLDT

SOUTHEAST KANSAS MHS
  EMERGENCY LINE
1106 SOUTH 9TH STREET
HUMBOLDT, KS 66748
Crisis Phone 1:(316)473-2241
Business Phone:(316)473-2241
HRS AVAIL:24

KANSAS CITY

WYANDOT MENTAL HEALTH
  CENTER
WYANDOTTE COUNTY CRISIS LINE
36TH AND EATON
KANSAS CITY, KS 66103
Crisis Phone 1:(913)831-1773
Business Phone:(913)831-9500
HRS AVAIL:24

LAWRENCE

*HEADQUARTERS, INC.
1419 MASSACHUSETTS
P.O. Box 999
LAWRENCE, KS 66044
Crisis Phone 1:(913)841-2345
Business Phone:(913)841-2345
HRS AVAIL:24

MANHATTAN

REGIONAL CRISIS CENTER
P.O. Box 164
MANHATTAN, KS 66502
Crisis Phone 1:(913)539-2785
Business Phone:(913)539-2785
HRS AVAIL:24

SALINA

HOTLINE CRISIS INFO. & REFERRAL
P.O. Box 1982
SALINA, KS 67402-1878
Crisis Phone 1:(913)827-4747
Business Phone:(913)827-4803
HRS AVAIL:24

SCOTT CITY

S.CITY AREA MENTAL HEALTH
  CENTER
210 W. 4TH
SCOTT CITY, KS 67871
Crisis Phone 1:(316)872-5338
Business Phone:(316)872-5338
HRS AVAIL:24

ULYSSES

ULYSSES AREA MENTAL HEALTH
  CENTER
102 W. FLOWER
ULYSSES, KS 76880
Crisis Phone 1:(316)356-3198
Crisis Phone 2:(316)356-1226
Business Phone:(316)356-3198
HRS AVAIL: 24

KANSAS (Con't)

WICHITA
*SEDGWICK CO. DEPT. OF MENTAL
  HEALTH
1801 E. TENTH STREET
WICHITA, KS 67214-3197
Crisis Phone 1:(316)686-7465
Business Phone:(316)268-2851
HRS AVAIL:24

KENTUCKY

ASHLAND
*PATHWAYS, INC. OF ASHLAND
CRISIS SERVICE
2162 GREENUP AVE
P.O. Box 790
ASHLAND, KY 41105-0790
Crisis Phone 1:(606)324-1141
Crisis Phone 2:(800)562-8909
Business Phone:(606)324-1141
HRS AVAIL:24/7 DAYS

BOWLING GREEN
BOWLING GREEN HELPLINE
BARREN RIVER MENTAL HEALTH
822 WOODWAY DR.
BOWLING GREEN, KY 42101
Crisis Phone 1:(502)842-5642
Business Phone:(502)843-4382
HRS AVAIL:24

CORBIN
CORBIN EMERGENCY SERVICES
CUMBERLAND RIVER COMPREH.
  CARE CTR.
AMERICAN GREETING ROAD
P.O. Box 568
CORBIN, KY 40701
Crisis Phone 1:(606)528-7010
Business Phone:(606)528-7010
HRS AVAIL:24

ELIZABETH
ELIZABETHTOWN CRISIS LINE
N. CENTRAL COMPREHENSIVE
  CARE CTR
907 N. DIXIE AVE
ELIZABETH, KY 42701
Crisis Phone 1:(502)769-1304
Business Phone:(502)769-1304
HRS AVAIL:24

HOPKINSVILLE
HOPKINSVILLE CRISIS LINE
PENNYROYAL REGIONAL MENTAL
  HEALTH
735 NORTH DRIVE
HOPKINSVILLE, KY 42240
Crisis Phone 1:(502)886-5163
Business Phone:(502)886-5163
HRS AVAIL:24

JACKSON
HAZARD/JACKSON CRISIS LINE
KENTUCKY RIVER COMMUNITY
  CARE
P.O. Box 603
JACKSON, KY 41339
TOLL FREE NUMBER (800)262-7491
Business Phone:(606)666-4904
HRS AVAIL:24

LEXINGTON

COMPREHENSIVE CARE CENTER
CRISIS INTERVENTION MENTAL
  HEALTH
BLUEGRASS REGIONAL MENTAL
HEALTH
201 MECHANIC STREET
LEXINGTON, KY 40507-1096
Crisis Phone 1:(606)254-3844
Business Phone:(606)233-0444
HRS AVAIL:24

LOUISVILLE

*#CRISIS AND INFORMATION
  CENTER
SEVEN COUNTIES SERVICES, INC.
101 W. MUHAMMAD ALI BLVD
LOUISVILLE, KY 40202
Crisis Phone 1:(502)589-4313
TDD (502)589-4259
KY WATTS: (800)221-0446
Business Phone:(502)589-8630
HRS AVAIL:24

MAYSVILLE

MAYSVILLE CRISIS LINE
COMPREHEND, INC. DISTRICT MH
P.O. Box G
MAYSVILLE, KY 51056
Crisis Phone 1:(606)564-4016
Business Phone:(606)564-4016
HRS AVAIL:24

MOREHEAD

PATHWAYS, INC. OF MOREHEAD
325 E. MAIN STREET
MOREHEAD, KY 40351
Crisis Phone 1:(800)562-8909
Business Phone:(606)784-4161
Hrs. Avail:24

OWENSBORO

GREEN RIVER COMPREHENSIVE
  CARE CNTR.
CRISIS LINE
1001 FREDERICA ST.
OWENSBORO KY 42301
Crisis Phone 1:(502)684-9466
Business Phone:(502)683-0277
HRS AVAIL:24

PADUCAH

PADUCAH CRISIS LINE
WESTERN KENTUCKY REGIONAL
  MH/MR.BD.
1530 LONE OAK RD.
PADUCAH, KY 42001
Crisis Phone 1:(800)592-3980
Business Phone:(502)442-7121
HRS AVAIL:24

PRESTONSBURG

PRESTONSBURG HELPLINE
  MOUNTAIN COMPREHENSIVE
  CARE CENTER
18 S. FRONT AVE.
PRESTONSBURG, KY 41653
Crisis Phone 1:(800)422-1060
Business Phone:(606)886-8572
HRS AVAIL:24

SOMERSET

*LAKE CUMBERLAND CLINICAL
  SERVICES
SOMERSET CLINIC, PROF.PLAZA BLVD.
401 BOGLE ST. SUITE 204
SOMERSET, KY 42501
Crisis Phone 1:(800)632-8581
Business Phone:(606)679-7348
HRS AVAIL:24

LOUISIANA

ALEXANDRIA

ALEXANDRIA HELPLINE
P.O. Box 749
ALEXANDRIA, LA 71301
Crisis Phone 1:(318)445-4357
Business Phone:(318)445-4357
HRS AVAIL:24

BATON ROUGE

*#BATON ROUGE CRISIS INTERV.
  CENTER
2424 BUNKER HILL DR., #1000
BATON ROUGE, LA 70808
Crisis Phone 1:(504)924-3900
Business Phone:(504)928-6482
HRS AVAIL:24

DE RIDDER

*BEAUREGARD DE RIDDER COMM.
HELP-LINE
P.O. Box 815
DE RIDDER, LA 70634
Crisis Phone 1:(318)462-0609
Business Phone:(318)462-1452
HRS AVAIL:24

HOUMA

HOUMA-TERREBONNE CRISIS LINE
735 SCHOOL
HOUMA, LA 70360
Crisis Phone 1:(504)872-1111
Business Phone:(504)851-5950
HRS AVAIL:24

LAFAYETTE

SW LOUISIANA EDUC. & REFERRAL
  CENTER
P.O. Box 52763
LAFAYETTE, LA 70505
Crisis Phone 1:(318)232-HELP
Business Phone:(318)232-4357
HRS AVAIL:24

LAKE CHARLES

*CRISIS PHONE (439-CARE)
ETC COUNSELING CENTER
1146 HODGES
LAKE CHARLES, LA 70601
Crisis Phone 1:(318)439-2273
Business Phone:(318)433-1062
HRS AVAIL:24

MONROE

MAIN LINE
P.O. Box 1322
MONROE, LA 71201
Crisis Phone 1: (318) 387-5683
Business Phone: (318) 387-5690
HRS AVAIL: 24

NEW ORLEANS

*#MHA OF GREATER NEW ORLEANS
CRISIS LINE PROGRAM
8200 Hampson St., Suite 300
NEW ORLEANS, LA 70118
Crisis Phone 1: (504) 523-2673
Business Phone: (504) 866-1901
HRS AVAIL: 24

NEW ORLEANS

*RIVER OAKS CRISIS CENTER
1525 RIVER OAKS ROAD W.
NEW ORLEANS, LA 70123
Crisis Phone 1:(504)733-2273
Business Phone:(504)734-1740
HRS AVAIL:24

OPELOUSAS

*ST. LANDRY PARISH SUICIDE
  PREV. PRG.
P.O. Box 1361
OPELOUSAS, LA 70571-1361
Crisis Phone 1:(318)942-4673
Business Phone:(318)948-7236
HRS AVAIL:6-12 PM/7 DAYS

LOUISIANA (Con't)

SLIDELL
SLIDELL CRISIS LINE, INC.
360 ROBERT RD.
SLIDELL, LA 70458
Crisis Phone 1:(504)643-6832
Business Phone:(504)643-6832
HRS AVAIL:24

VILLE PLATTE
VILLE PLATTE M.H.C.I.C.
520 DE MONCHERVEAUX BLVD
VILLE PLATTE, LA 70586
Crisis Phone 1:(318)363-5579
Business Phone:(318)363-5525
HRS AVAIL:24

MASSACHUSETTS

ACTON
CODE HOTLINE
481 GREAT RD
ACTON, MA 01720
Crisis Phone 1:(617)263-8777
Crisis Phone 2:(617)486-3130
Business Phone:(617)263-8777
HRS AVAIL:24

ATTLEBORO
NEW HOPE/ATTLEBORO
P.O. Box 48
ATTLEBORO, MA 02703
Crisis Phone 1:(617)695-2113
Crisis Phone 2:(617)762-1530
Crisis Phone 3:(617)824-4757
Business Phone:(617)226-4015
HRS AVAIL:24

BEVERLY
PROJECT RAP, INC.
3 BROADWAY
BEVERLY, MA 01915
Crisis Phone 1:(617)922-0000
Business Phone:(617)927-4506
HRS AVAIL:24

BOSTON
*#THE SAMARITANS
500 COMMONWEALTH AVE
BOSTON, MA 02215
Crisis Phone 1:(617)247-0220
SAMARITEEN LINE (617)247-8050
Business Phone:(617)536-2460
Hrs. Avail:24

BROCKTON
BROCKTON, CANTON HELPLINE
837 N. MAIN ST
BROCKTON, MA 02401
Crisis Phone 1:(617)828-6666
Business Phone:(617)584-4357
HRS AVAIL:2:30-4:00

FALL RIVER
*SAMARITANS OF FALL RIVER—
 NEW BEDFORD
386 STANLEY ST.
FALL RIVER, MA 02720
Crisis Phone 1:(617)636-1111
Business Phone:(617)636-1111
HRS AVAIL:24

FALMOUTH
*SAMARITANS ON CAPE COD
P.O. Box 65
FALMOUTH, MA 02540
Crisis Phone 1:(617)548-8900
Crisis Phone 2:(617)548-8901
Business Phone:(617)548-8900
HRS AVAIL:24

FITCHBURG
LUK CRISIS CENTER, INC.
9 DAY ST.
FITCHBURG, MA 01420
Crisis Phone 1:(617)345-7353
Crisis Phone 2:(617)632-7374
Crisis Phone 3:(617)772-2203
Crisis Phone 4:(617)365-6750
Business Phone:(617)345-0685
HRS AVAIL:24

FRAMINGHAM

*SAMARITANS OF SOUTH
  MIDDLESEX, INC.
73 UNION AVE
FRAMINGHAM, MA 01701
Crisis Phone 1:(617)875-4500
Crisis Phone 1:(617)478-7877
Business Phone:(617)875-4500
HRS AVAIL:24

GREENFIELD

GREENFIELD EMERGENCY
  SERVICES
60 WELLS ST.
GREENFIELD, MA 01301
Crisis Phone 1:(413)774-2758
HRS AVAIL:24

HAVERHILL

*NORTH ESSEX HEALTH
  RESOURCE CENTER INTAKE,
  EVALUATION AND CRISIS
  SERVICES
100 WINTER ST
HAVERHILL, MA 01830
Crisis Phone 1:(800)892-0818
Business Phone:(617)373-6624
HRS AVAIL:24

HOPEDALE

COMM. COUNS. CENT. OF
  BLACKSTONE VALLEY
101 MILL STREET
HOPEDALE, MA 01747
Crisis Phone 1:(617)473-6723
Business Phone:(617)473-6723
HRS AVAIL:24

LAWRENCE

*GREATER LAWRENCE MHC
351 ESSEX ST.
LAWRENCE, MA 01840
Crisis Phone 1:(617)683-3128
Business Phone:(617)683-6303
Hrs. Avail:24

LAWRENCE

*SAMARITANS OF THE MERRIMACK
  VALLEY
55 JACKSON ST
LAWRENCE, MA 01840
Crisis Phone 1:(617)688-6607
Crisis Phone 2:(617)452-6733
Crisis Phone 3:(617)372-7200
Crisis Phone 4:(617)465-6100
Business Phone:(617)688-0030
HRS AVAIL:24

MELROSE

EASTERN MIDDLESEX CIS
150 GREEN ST.
MELROSE, MA 01880
Crisis Phone 1:(617)662-6623
Business Phone:(617)662-6623
HRS AVAIL:24

NEW BEDFORD

*NEW BEDFORD CRISIS CENTER
378 COUNTY STREET
NEW BEDFORD, MA 02740
Crisis Phone 1:(617)996-3154
Business Phone:(617)996-3154
HRS AVAIL:24/7DAYS

NEWBURYPORT

TURNING POINT HOT LINE
5 MIDDLE ST.
NEWBURYPORT, MA 01950
Crisis Phone 1:(617)465-8800
Business Phone:(617)462-8251
HRS AVAIL:24

NEWTONVILLE/
BOSTON AREA

CONTACT BOSTON
P.O. Box 287
NEWTONVILLE, MA 02160
Crisis Phone 1:(617)244-4350
Business Phone:(617)244-4353
HRS AVAIL:24

NORTH ADAMS

HELP LINE, INC.
111 MAIN ST.
NORTH ADAMS, MA 01247
Crisis Phone 1:(413)663-6555
Business Phone:(413)663-5244
HRS AVAIL:24

NORTHAMPTON

NORTHAMPTON EMERGENCY
  SERVICES
48 PLEASANT ST.
NORTHAMPTON, MA 01060
Crisis Phone 1:(413)586-5555
Business Phone:(413)586-5555
HRS AVAIL:24

NORWOOD

*SO. NORFOLD SCREENING &
  EMERG. TEAM
190 LENOX ST.
NORWOOD, MA 02062
Crisis Phone 1:(617)769-6060
Business Phone:(617)769-6060
HRS AVAIL:24

NORWOOD

PULSE HOTLINE
P.O. Box 273
NORWOOD, MA 02062
Crisis Phone 1:(617)762-5144
Business Phone:(617)762-5145
HRS AVAIL:7 PM-11PM

SOUTHBRIDGE

*TRI-LINK, INC
51 EVERETT STREET
SOUTHBRIDGE, MA 01550
Crisis Phone 1:(617)765-9101
Business Phone:(617)765-9101
HRS AVAIL:24

WARE

WARE HELPLINE
VALLEY HUMAN SERVICES
96 SOUTH ST
WARE, MA 01082
Crisis Phone 1:(413)283-3473
Business Phone:(413)967-6241
HRS AVAIL:24

WORCESTER

* CRISIS CENTER, INC.
P.O. Box 652
WORCESTER, MA 01602
Crisis Phone 1:(617)791-6562
Business Phone:(617)791-7205
Hrs. Avail:24

MARYLAND

BALTIMORE

BALTIMORE CRISIS CENTER
WALTER P. CARTER MHC
630 W. FAYETTE ST.
BALTIMORE, MD 21201
Crisis Phone 1:(301)528-2200
Business Phone:(301)528-2200
HRS AVAIL:24

BALTIMORE

BALTIMORE CRISIS LINE
SINAI HOSPITAL
BELVEDERE AND GREENSPRING AVE
BALTIMORE, MD 21215
WEEKDAYS:(301)578-5457
EVENINGS & WEEKENDS
  (301)578-5000
Business Phone:(301)578-5457
HRS AVAIL:24

BOWIE

BOWIE HOTLINE
P.O. Box 535
BOWIE, MD 20715
Crisis Phone 1:(301)262-2433
Business Phone:(301)262-2433
HRS AVAIL:4:00PM-12:00AM

COLUMBIA

GRASS ROOTS
8045 GUILFORD RD
COLUMIA, MD 21044
Crisis Phone 1:(301)531-6677
Business Phone:(301)351-6006
HRS AVAIL:24

KENSINGTON

*#MONTGOMERY COUNTY HOTLINE
10920 CONNECTICUT AVE
KENSINGTON, MD 20795
Crisis Phone 1:(301)949-6603
Business Phone:(301)949-1255
HRS AVAIL:24

RIVERDALE

*#PRINCE GEORGE'S COUNTY
  HOTLINE & SUICIDE PREVENTION
  CENTER
6607 RIVERDALE RD
RIVERDALE, MD 20737
Crisis Phone 1:(301)577-4866
Crisis Phone 2:(301)731-0004
Business Phone:(301)577-3140
HRS AVAIL:24

SALISBURY

LIFE CRISIS CENTER, INC.
P.O. Box 387
SALISBURY, MD 21801
Crisis Phone 1:(301)749-HELP
HRS AVAIL:24

WALDORF

*COMMUNITY CRISIS AND
  REFERRAL CENTER
P.O. Box 1291
WALDORF, MD 20601
Crisis Phone 1:(301)645-3336
Crisis Phone 2:(301)843-1110
Crisis Phone 3:(301)645-3337
Business Phone:(301)645-3336
HRS AVAIL:24/7 DAYS

MAINE

BANGOR

DIAL HELP
43 ILLINOIS AVE
BANGOR, ME 04401
Crisis Phone 1:(207)947-6143
TOLL FREE NUMBER (800)431-7810
Business Phone:(207)947-6143
HRS AVAIL:24

PORTLAND

* INGRAHAM VOLUNTEERS, INC.
142 HIGH ST.
PORTLAND, ME 04101
Crisis Phone 1:(207)774-HELP
TTY/TDD (207)773-7321
Business Phone:(207)874-1055
HRS AVAIL:24

SKOWHEGAN

*#CRISIS STABILIZATION UNIT
147 WATER ST
SKOWHEGAN, ME 04976
AUGUSTA (207)626-3448
SKOWHEGAN (800)452-1933
Business Phone:(207)474-2506
HRS AVAIL:24

MICHIGAN

ADRIAN
CALL SOMEONE CONCERNED
227 N. WINTER #215
ADRIAN, MI 49221
Crisis Phone 1:(517)263-6737
TOLL FREE NUMBER (800)322-0044
Business Phone:(517)263-6739
HRS AVAIL:24

ANN ARBOR
WASHTENAW COUNTY COMMUNITY
   MHC
110 N FOURTH, SUITE 103
ANN ARBOR, MI 48104
Crisis Phone 1:(313)996-4747
Business Phone:(313)994-2285
HRS AVAIL:24

BIRMINGHAM
COMMON GROUND
1090 S. ADAMS
BIRMINGHAM, MI 48011
Crisis Phone 1:(313)645-9676
Business Phone:(313)645-1173
HRS AVAIL:24

DETROIT
*#NSO EMERGENCY TELEPHONE
   SERVICE
SUICIDE PREVENTION CENTER
220 BAGLEY SUITE 626
DETROIT, MI 48226
Crisis Phone 1:(313)224-7000
Business Phone:(313)963-7890
HRS AVAIL:24

DETROIT
CONTACT LIFE LINE
7430 2ND ST., RM. #428
DETROIT, MI 48202
Crisis Phone 1:(313)894-5555
Business Phone:(313)875-0426
HRS AVAIL:24

EAST LANSING
LISTENING EAR OF EAST LANSING
547 E. Grand River
EAST LANSING, MI 48823
Crisis Phone 1: (517) 337-1717
Business Phones: (517) 337-1717
HRS AVAIL: 24

FLINT
FLINT EMERGENCY SERVICE
GENESEE CO MENTAL HEALTH
420 W 5th Ave
FLINT MI 48503
Crisis Phone 1: (313) 257-3740
Business Phones: (313) 257-3742
HRS AVAIL: 24

GRAND HAVEN
GRAND HAVEN HELPLINE
OTTAWA COUNTY MENTAL HEALTH
   CENTER
1111 FULTON ST
GRAND HAVEN, MI 49417
Crisis Phone 1:(616)842-4357
Business Phone:(616)842-5350
HRS AVAIL:24

HART
* OCEANA CO. COMMUNITY MENTAL
   HEALTH
P.O. Box 127
HART, MI 49420
Crisis Phone 1:(616)873-2108
Business Phone:(616)873-2108
HRS AVAIL:24

HOLLAND
HOLLAND HELPLINE
12265 JAMES ST
HOLLAND, MI 49423
Crisis Phone 1:(616)396-4357
GRAND HAVEN (616)842-4357
GRAND RAPIDS (616)458-4357
Business Phone:(616)392-1873
HRS AVAIL:24

MICHIGAN (Con't)

JACKSON

AWARE, INC.—HELPLINE
P.O. Box 1526
JACKSON, MI 49204
Crisis Phone 1:(517)783-2671
Business Phone:(517)783-2861
HRS AVAIL:24

KALAMAZOO

* GRYPHON PLACE
1104 S. WESTNEDGE
KALAMAZOO, MI 49008
Crisis Phone 1:(616)381-4357
Business Phone:(616)381-1510
HRS AVAIL:24

LAPEER

* LAPEER CO. COMM. MHC
1575 SUNCREST DR.
LAPEER, MI 48446
Crisis Phone 1:(313)667-0500
Business Phone:(313)667-0500
HRS AVAIL:24

LIVONIA

TELEPHONE LISTENING CENTER
P.O. Box 9391
LIVONIA, MI 48150
Crisis Phone 1:(313)422-4852
Business Phone:(313)422-4854
HRS AVAIL:24

MT. CLEMENS

* MACOMB COUNTY CRISIS CENTER
5TH FLOOR, COUNTY BUILDING
MT. CLEMENS, MI 48043
Crisis Phone 1:(313)573-8700
Business Phone:(313)573-8700
HRS AVAIL:24

MT. PLEASANT

LISTENING EAR CRISIS CENTER, INC
P.O. Box 65
MT. PLEASANT, MI 48858
Crisis Phone 1:(517)772-2918
Business Phone:(517)772-2918
HRS AVAIL:24

MUSKEGON

* COMM. MH SERVICES OF
   MUSKEGON CO.
125 E. SOUTHERN
MUSKEGON, MI 49442
Crisis Phone 1:(616)722-4357
Business Phone:(616)726-5266
HRS AVAIL:24

PLYMOUTH

TURNING POINT CRISIS CENTER
P.O. Box 115
PLYMOUTH, MI 48170
Crisis Phone 1:(313)455-4900
Business Phone:(313)455-4902
HRS AVAIL:6:30 PM-10:30PM

PORT HURON

* BLUE WATER MH & CHILD
   GUIDANCE CLINIC
1501 KRAFFT RD
PORT HURON, MI 48060
Crisis Phone 1:(313)985-5125
Business Phone:(313)985-5125
HRS AVAIL:24

PORT HURON

* #CENTER FOR HUMAN
   RESOURCES
1003 MILITARY ST
PORT HURON, MI 48060
Crisis Phone 1:(313)985-7161
FREE IN 313 AREA (800)462-6350
Business Phone:(313)985-5168
HRS AVAIL:24

PORT HURON

* ST. CLAIR CO. COMM MH
   SERVICES
3415 28TH ST.
PORT HURON, MI 48060
Crisis Phone 1:(313)985-7161
Business Phone:(313)985-9618
HRS AVAIL:24

MICHIGAN

ROYAL OAK
THE SANCTUARY
1222 S. WASHINGTON
ROYAL OAK, MI 48067
Crisis Phone 1:(313)547-2260
Business Phone:(313)547-2260
HRS AVAIL:24

ST. JOSEPH
ST. JOSEPH HELPLINE
RIVERWOOD COMMUNITY MHC
MEMORIAL HOSPITAL
2681 MORTON AVE
ST. JOSEPH, MI 49085
Crisis Phone 1:(616)927-4447
TOLL FREE NUMBER (800)422-0757
Business Phone:(616)983-7781
HRS AVAIL:24

ST. JOSEPH
THE LINK CRISIS INTERVENTION
  CENTER
2002 S. STATE ST.
ST. JOSEPH, MI 49085
Crisis Phone 1:(616)983-6351
Business Phone:(616)983-6351
HRS AVAIL:24

TRAVERSE CITY
* THIRD LEVEL CRISIS INT. CENT. INC.
P.O. Box 1035
TRAVERSE CITY, MI 49685
Crisis Phone 1:(616)922-4800
TOLL FREE (800)442-7315
Crisis Phone 3:(616)922-4801
Business Phone:(616)922-4802
HRS AVAIL:24/7 DAYS

YPSILANTI
SOS CRISIS CENTER
114 NORTH RIVER ST.
YPSILANTI, MI 48198
Crisis Phone 1:(313)485-3222
Business Phone:(313)485-8730
HRS AVAIL:24

MINNESOTA

ALEXANDRIA
LISTENING EAR CRISIS CENTER
111 17TH AVE EAST
ALEXANDRIA, MN 56308
Crisis Phone 1:(612)763-6638
Business Phone:(612)762-1511 x283
HRS AVAIL:24

AUSTIN
VICTIMS CRISIS CENTER
908 N.W. 1ST DRIVE
AUSTIN, MN 55912
Crisis Phone 1:(507)437-6680
Business Phone:(507)437-6680
HRS AVAIL:24

GRAND RAPIDS
FIRST CALL FOR HELP/
  GRAND RAPIDS
P.O. Box 113
GRAND RAPIDS, MN 55744
Crisis Phone 1:(218)326-8565
Business Phone:(218)326-8565
HRS AVAIL:24

MINNEAPOLIS
*#CRISIS INTERV. CENTER
HENNEPIN COUNTY MEDICAL
  CENTER 701 PARK AVE. SOUTH
MINNEAPOLIS, MN 55415
CRISIS (612)347-3161
SUICIDE (612)347-2222

MINNESOTA

Minneapolis—Crisis Interv Ctr (Con't)
CRISIS HOME PROGRAM
(612)347-3170
SEXUAL ASSAULT SERV
(612)347-5838
BEHAV. EM. OUTREACH
(612)347-2011
Business Phone:(612)347-3164
HRS AVAIL:24

MINNEAPOLIS
CONTACT TWIN CITIES
83 S. 12TH ST
MINNEAPOLIS, MN 55403
Crisis Phone 1:(612)341-2896
Business Phone:(612)341-2212
HRS AVAIL:24

OWATONNA
OWATONNA—STEELE CO. CONTACT
P.O. Box 524
OWATONNA, MN 55060
Crisis Phone 1:(507)451-9100
Business Phone:(507)451-1897
HRS AVAIL:24

MISSOURI

JOPLIN
JOPLIN CRISIS INTERVENTION, INC
P.O. Box 582
JOPLIN, MO 64801
Crisis Phone 1:(417)781-2255
Business Phone:(417)781-2255
HRS AVAIL:24

KANSAS CITY
K.C. SUICIDE PREVENTION LINE
WESTERN MO. MENTAL HEALTH
  CENTER
600 E. 22ND ST.
KANSAS CITY, MO 64108
Crisis Phone 1:(816)471-3939
Crisis Phone 2:(816)471-3940
Business Phone:(816)471-3000
HRS AVAIL:24

KIRKSVILLE
* LAUGHLIN PAVILION
900 EAST LAHARPE
KIRKSVILLE, MO 63501
IN-STATE (800)223-5171
OUT-OF-STATE (800)223-5170
Business Phone:(816)665-5171
HRS AVAIL:24/7 DAYS

NEVADA
*HSA HEARTLAND HOSPITAL
1500 W. ASHLAND
NEVADA, MO 64772
Crisis Phone 1:(800)492-2139
Business Phone:(417)667-2666
HRS AVAIL:24/7 DAYS

ST. JOSEPH
CRISIS INTERVENTION/ST. JOSEPH
P.O. Box 263
ST. JOSEPH, MO 64502
Crisis Phone 1:(816)232-1655
Business Phone:(816)232-8431
HRS AVAIL:24

ST. LOUIS
* #LIFE CRISIS SERVICES, INC.
1423 S. BIG BEND BLVD
ST. LOUIS, MO 63117
Crisis Phone 1:(314)647-4357
Business Phone:(314)647-3100
HRS AVAIL:24

ST. LOUIS

CONTACT ST. LOUIS
P.O. Box 160070
ST. LOUIS, MO 63116
Crisis Phone 1:(314)771-0404
Business Phone:(314)771-8181
HRS AVAIL:24

MISSISSIPPI

COLUMBUS

* CONTACT HELPLINE
P.O. Box 1304
COLUMBUS, MS 39703-1304
Crisis Phone 1:(601)328-0200
Crisis Phone 2:(601)323-4357
Business Phone:(601)328-0200
HRS AVAIL:24

JACKSON

CONTACT JACKSON
P.O. Box 5192
JACKSON, MS 39216
Crisis Phone 1:(601)969-2077
Business Phone:(601)969-2077
HRS AVAIL:24

HATTIESBURG

HATTIESBURG HELP LINE, INC.
P.O. Box 183
HATTIESBURG, MS 39401
Crisis Phone 1:(601)544-HELP
Business Phone:(601)544-HELP
HRS AVAIL:24

MERIDIAN

WEEMS MENTAL HEALTH CENTER
P.O. Box 4376 WS
MERIDIAN, MS 39301
Crisis Phone 1:(601)483-4821
Business Phone:(601)483-4821
HRS AVAIL:24

MONTANA

BILLINGS

BILLINGS HELPLINE
YELLOWSTONE CO. WELFARE
3021 3RD AVENUE N
BILLINGS, MT 59191
Crisis Phone 1:(406)248-1691
Business Phone:(406)248-1691
HRS AVAIL:24

BOZEMAN

BOZEMAN HELP CENTER
323 S. WALLACE
BOZEMAN, MT 59715
Crisis Phone 1:(406)248-1691
Business Phone:(406)248-1691
HRS AVAIL:24

BILLINGS

HELPLINE—MENTAL HEALTH
   CENTER
1245 NORTH 29TH ST
BILLINGS, MT 59101
Crisis Phone 1:(406)252-1212
Business Phone:(406)252-5658
HRS AVAIL:24

GREAT FALLS

COMMUNITY HELP LINE OF
   GREAT FALLS
113 6TH ST. N.
GREAT FALLS, MT 59401
Crisis Phone 1:(406)453-4357
Business Phone:(406)761-6010
HRS AVAIL:24

MONTANA

HELENA

MENTAL HEALTH SERVICES, INC./
  HELENA
572 LOGAN
HELENA, MT 59601
Crisis Phone 1:(406)442-0640
Business Phone:(406)442-0310
HRS AVAIL:24

NORTH CAROLINA

ASHVILLE

CONTACT-ASHVILLE/BUNCOMBE
P.O. Box 6747
ASHVILLE, NC 28816
Crisis Phone 1:(704)253-4357
Business Phone:(704)252-7703
HRS AVAIL:24

BURLINGTON

*#SUICIDE & CRISIS SERV/
  ALAMANCE CO
P.O. Box 2573
BURLINGTON, NC 27215
Crisis Phone 1:(919)227-6220
Business Phone:(919)228-1720
HRS AVAIL: 24

CHAPEL HILL

HELPLINE/CHAPEL HILL
333 MC MASTERS ST.
CHAPEL HILL, NC 27514
Crisis Phone 1:(919)929-0479
Crisis Phone 2:(919)732-2796
Crisis Phone 3:(919)599-8366
Crisis Phone 4:(919)542-4422
Crisis Phone 5:(919)742-5612
Business Phone:(919)929-0479
HRS AVAIL:24

CHARLOTTE

REACHLINE
TELEPHONE COUNSELING
501 N. TYRON ST.
CHARLOTTE, NC 28202
Crisis Phone 1:(704)333-6121
Business Phone:(919)333-6121
HRS AVAIL:24

CHARLOTTE

THE RELATIVES, INC.
1100 E. BOULEVARD
CHARLOTTE, NC 28203
Crisis Phone 1:(704)377-0602
Business Phone:(704)335-0203
HRS AVAIL:24

DURHAM

CONTACT DURHAM
806 A CLARENDON ST
DURHAM NC 27705
Crisis Phone 1:(919)683-1595
Business Phone:(919)286-4175
HRS AVAIL:24

DURHAM

* HELPLINE OF DURHAM
414 E. MAIN ST
DURHAM, NC 27701
Crisis Phone 1:(919)683-8628
Business Phone:(919)683-2392
HRS AVAIL:24

FAYETTEVILLE

CONTACT OF FAYETTEVILLE, INC.
310 GREEN STREET
FAYETTEVILLE, NC 28301
Crisis Phone 1:(919)485-4134
Business Phone:(919)483-8970
HRS AVAIL:24

FRANKLYN

RESPECT, INC.
431 WIDE HORIZON DR
FRANKLYN, NC 28734
Crisis Phone 1:(704)369-6143
Business Phone:(704)369-7333
HRS AVAIL:24

GOLDSBORO

WAYNE CO. MHC HOTLINE
301 N. HERMAN ST
GOLDSBORO, NC 27514
Crisis Phone 1:(919)735-4357
Business Phone:(919)731-1133
HRS AVAIL:24

GREENSBORO

CRISIS CONTROL CENTER, INC.
P.O. Box 8663
GREENSBORO, NC 27419
Crisis Phone 1:(919)852-4444
Business Phone:(919)852-6366
HRS AVAIL:24

GREENSBORO

SWITCHBOARD CRISIS CENTER
101 W. SYCAMORE ST., SUITE 410
GREENSBORO, NC 27401
Crisis Phone 1:(919)275-0896
Business Phone:(919)275-0896
HRS AVAIL:24

GREENVILLE

REAL CRISIS INTERV., INC.
312 E. 10TH ST.
GREENVILLE, NC 28203
Crisis Phone 1:(919)758-HELP
Crisis Phone 2:(919)758-0787
Business Phone:(704)377-0602
HRS AVAIL:24

HARRELLSVILLE

ROANOKE-CHOWAN
HUMAN SERVICES CENTER
WICCACON CENTER
P.O. Box 407
HARRELLSVILLE, NC 27942
Crisis Phone 1:(919)332-4442
Business Phone:(919)356-2938
HRS AVAIL:24

HIGH POINT

CONTACT HIGH POINT
463 S. MAIN ST
HIGH POINT, NC 27260
Crisis Phone 1:(919)882-1184
Business Phone:(919)885-0191
HRS AVAIL:24

LEXINGTON

CONTACT LEXINGTON
P.O. Box 924
LEXINGTON, NC 27292
Crisis Phone 1:(704)249-8974
Business Phone:(704)249-8824
HRS AVAIL:24

MANTEO

OUTER BANKS HOTLINE
P.O. Box 1417
MANTEO, NC 27954
Crisis Phone 1:(919)473-3366
Crisis Phone 2:(919)995-5104
Crisis Phone 3:(919)338-2829
Business Phone:(919)473-5121
HRS AVAIL:24

MOREHEAD

HELPLINE OF MOREHEAD
P.O. Box 3537
MOREHEAD, NC 28557
Crisis Phone 1:(919)247-3023
Business Phone:(919)247-3023
HRS AVAIL:24

RALEIGH

HOPELINE, INC.
P.O. Box 6036
RALEIGH, NC 27628
Crisis Phone 1:(919)755-6555
TEEN HOPELINE (919)755-6777
Business Phone:(919)755-6588
HRS AVAIL:24/7 DAYS

ROANOKE RAPIDS

ROANOKE RAPIDS CRISIS LINE
HALIFAX CO. MENTAL HEALTH
P.O. Box 1199
ROANOKE RAPIDS, NC 27870
Crisis Phone 1:(919)537-2909
Business Phone:(919)537-2909
HRS AVAIL:24

SALISBURY

SALISBURY DIAL HELP
165 MAHALEY
SALISBURY, NC 28144
Crisis Phone 1:(704)636-9222
Business Phone:(704)633-3616
HRS AVAIL:24

SANFORD

LEE COUNTY MH CRISIS LINE
130 CARBONTON RD
SANFORD, 27330
Crisis Phone 1:(919)774-4520
Business Phone:(919)774-6521
HRS AVAIL:24

SMITHFIELD

CONTACT JOHNSTON CO.
140 MARKET ST.
SMITHFIELD, NC 27577
Crisis Phone 1:(919)934-6161
Business Phone:(919)934-6979
HRS AVAIL:24

STATESVILLE

THE CUP OF WATER, INC
125 W. BELL ST
STATESVILLE, NC 28677
Crisis Phone 1:(704)872-7638
Business Phone:(704)872-7638
HRS AVAIL:24

WILMINGTON

CRISIS LINE/OPEN HOUSE
415 GRACE ST
WILMINGTON, NC 28401
Crisis Phone 1:(919)763-3695
IN N.C. ONLY (800)672-2903
Business Phone:(919)762-4255
HRS AVAIL:24

WILSON

WILSON CRISIS CENTER
P.O. Box 593
WILSON, NC 27893
Crisis Phone 1:(919)237-5156
Business Phone:(919)237-5156
HRS AVAIL:24

WINSTON-SALEM

CONTACT: WINSTON-SALEM
1111 W. FIRST ST.
WINSTON-SALEM, NC 27101
Crisis Phone 1:(919)722-5153
Business Phone:(919)723-4338
HRS AVAIL:24

NORTH DAKOTA

BEULAH

* MERCER COUNTY WOMEN'S
   RESOURCE CENTER
HILLSIDE OFFICE COMPLEX
HIGHWAY 49 NW
BEULAH, ND 58523
Crisis Phone 1:(701)748-2274
Business Phone:(701)873-2274
HRS AVAIL:24

BISMARK

CRISIS AND EMERGENCY SERVICES
WEST CENTRAL HUMAN SERVICE
   CENTER
600 S. 2ND STREET
BISMARK, ND 58501
Crisis Phone 1:(701)255-3090
Business Phone:(701)255-3090
HRS AVAIL:24

FARGO

* UNITED WAY'S HOT LINE
UNITED WAY OF CASS CLAY, INC.
P.O. Box 447
FARGO, ND 58107
Crisis Phone 1:(701)235-7335
Crisis Phone 2:(701)232-4357
Business Phone:(701)293-6462
HRS AVAIL:24/7 DAYS

GRAND FORKS

NORTHEAST HUMAN SERVICE
   CENTER
1407 24TH AVE. S.
GRAND FORKS, ND 58201
Crisis Phone 1:(701)775-0525
Business Phone:(701)746-9411
HRS AVAIL:24

MINOT

MINOT SUICIDE PREVENTION
   SERVICE
ST. JOSEPH'S HOSPITAL
MINOT, ND 58701
Crisis Phone 1:(701)839-2222
Business Phone:(701)857-2000
HRS AVAIL:24

NEBRASKA

LINCOLN

PERSONAL CRISIS SERVICE
P.O. Box 80083
LINCOLN, NE 68506
Crisis Phone 1:(402)475-5171
Business Phone:(402)475-5171
HRS AVAIL:24

LINCOLN

CONTACT, INC.
P.O. Box 81826
LINCOLN, NE 68501
Crisis Phone 1:(402)464-0602
Business Phone:(402)464-0602
HRS AVAIL:24

NORFOLK

24 HOUR HOTLINE
NORTHERN NEBRASKA COMP. MHC
201 MILLER AVE
NORFOLK, NE 68701
Crisis Phone 1:(800)672-8323
Business Phone:(402)371-7530
HRS AVAIL:24

NORTH PLATTE

RICHARD YOUNG FAMILY LIFE
   CENTER
P.O. Box 1209
NORTH PLATTE, NE 69103-1209
Crisis Phone 1:(308)532-9332
Business Phone:(308)532-4050
HRS AVAIL:24

OMAHA

THE CRISIS LINE, INC
P.O. Box 4581
OMAHA, NE 68104
Crisis Phone 1:(402)341-9111
Crisis Phone 2:(402)341-9112
Business Phone:(402)341-9111
HRS AVAIL:24

NEW HAMPSHIRE

BERLIN

BERLIN EMERGENCY SERVICES
ANDROSCOGGIN VALLEY MH CLINIC
PAGEVILLE RD
BERLIN, NH 03570
Crisis Phone 1:(603)752-7404
Business Phone:(603)752-7404
HRS AVAIL:24

CLAREMONT

* INTAKE/CRISIS/EVALUATION UNIT
COUNSELING CENTER OF SULLIVAN
   CO.
18 BAILEY AVE
CLAREMONT, NH 03743
Crisis Phone 1:(603)542-2578
Business Phone:(603)542-2578
HRS AVAIL:24

CONCORD

*#EMERGENCY SERVICES/
   CONCORD
CNHCMS, INC.
P.O. Box 2032
CONCORD, NH 03301
Crisis Phone 1:(603)228-1551
Business Phone:(603)228-1551
HRS AVAIL:24

DOVER

* STRAFFORD GUIDANCE CENTER,
   INC.
EMERGENCY CRISIS TEAM
130 CENTRAL AVE
DOVER, NH 03820
Crisis Phone 1:(603)742-0630
Crisis Phone 2:(603)332-8090
Business Phone:(603)742-0630
HRS AVAIL:24

KEENE

* THE SAMARITANS OF KEENE
25 LAMSON ST
KEENE, NH 03431
Crisis Phone 1:(603)357-5505
Crisis Phone 2:(603)357-5506
Business Phone:(603)357-5505
HRS AVAIL:24/7 DAYS

LEBANON

* HEADREST INC
14 CHURCH ST.
P.O. Box 221
LEBANON, NH 03766
Crisis Phone 1:(603)448-4400
Business Phone:(603)448-4872
HRS AVAIL:24

MANCHESTER

*#GREATER MANCHESTER MHC
401 CYPRESS ST.
MANCHESTER, NH 03103
Crisis Phone 1:(603)668-4111
Business Phone:(603)668-4111
HRS AVAIL:24

PORTSMOUTH

* SEACOAST MENTAL HEALTH
CENTER
1145 SAGAMORE AVE.
PORTSMOUTH, NH 03801
Crisis Phone 1:(603)431-6703
Business Phone:(603)431-6703
HRS AVAIL:24

SALEM

*#CENTER FOR LIFE MANAGEMENT
SALEM PROF PARK
44 STILES RD
SALEM, NH 03079
Crisis Phone 1:(603)432-2253
Business Phone:(603)893-3548
HRS AVAIL:24

NEW JERSEY

ATLANTIC CITY

CRISIS INTERVENTION PROGRAM/AC
ATLANTIC CITY MEDICAL CENTER
1925 PACIFIC AVE
ATLANTIC CITY, NJ 08401
Crisis Phone 1:(609)344-1118
Business Phone:(609)334-1118
HRS AVAIL:24

FLEMINGTON

HUNTERDON HELPLINE
RT. #31, BOX 36
FLEMINGTON, NJ 08822
Crisis Phone 1:(201)782-4357
Business Phone:(201)782-4357
HRS AVAIL:24

BRIDGEWATER

GUIDELINE
500 N. BRIDGE
BRIDGEWATER, NJ 08807
Crisis Phone 1:(201)526-4100
Business Phone:(201)725-2800
HRS AVAIL:24

GLASSBORO

TOGETHER, INC.
7 STATE ST
GLASSBORO, NJ 08028
Crisis Phone 1:(609)881-4040
Business Phone:(609)881-7045
HRS AVAIL:24

CHERRY HILL

CONTACT "609"
1050 N. KINGS HIGHWAY
CHERRY HILL, NJ 08034
Crisis Phone 1:(609)667-3000
Crisis Phone 2:(609)428-2900
Business Phone:(609)667-0285
HRS AVAIL:24

HOBOKEN

ST. MARY'S COMMUNITY MH
314 CLINTON ST.
HOBOKEN, NJ 07030
Crisis Phone 1:(201)795-5505
Business Phone:(201)792-8200
HRS AVAIL:24

CHERRY HILL

STEININGER CENTER
19 E. ORMAND AVE.
CHERRY HILL, NJ 08034
Crisis Phone 1:(609)428-4357
Crisis Phone 2:(609)541-2222
Business Phone:(609)428-1300
HRS AVAIL:24

LINWOOD

CONTACT ATLANTIC COUNTY
P.O. Box 181
LINWOOD, NJ 08221
Crisis Phone 1:(609)646-6616
Business Phone:(609)653-4613
HRS AVAIL:24

LYNDHURST

* SO BERGEN MENTAL HEALTH
  CENTER
BERGEN REGIONAL COUNS.
  CENTER
516 VALLEY BROOK AVE
LYNDHURST, NJ 07071
Crisis Phone 1:(201)935-3322
Crisis Phone 2:(201)646-0333
Business Phone:(201)460-3510
HRS AVAIL:24

MANCHESTER

THE MHC OF GREATER
  MANCHESTER
401 CYPRESS ST
MANCHESTER, NJ 03103
Crisis Phone 1:(603)688-4111
Business Phone:(603)688-4111
HRS AVAIL:24

MILLVILLE

MILLVILLE HOTLINE
CUMBERLAND CO. GUIDANCE
  CENTER
RD 1, CARMEL RD.
P.O. Box 808
MILLVILLE, NJ 08332
Crisis Phone 1:(609)327-2222
Business Phone:(609)825-6810
HRS AVAIL:24

MONTCLAIR

NORTH ESSEX HELP LINE
MENTAL HEALTH RESOURCE
  CENTER
60 S. FULLERTON AVE
MONTCLAIR, NJ 07042
Crisis Phone 1:(201)744-1954
Business Phone:(201)744-6522
HRS AVAIL:24

MOORESTOWN

CONTACT BURLINGTON CO.
P.O. Box 333
MOORESTOWN, NJ 08057
Crisis Phone 1:(609)234-8888
Business Phone:(609)234-5484
HRS AVAIL:24

MORRISTOWN

MEMO HELPLINE
100 MADISON AVE
MORRISTOWN, NJ 07960
Crisis Phone 1:(201)540-5045
Business Phone:(201)540-5168
HRS AVAIL:24

MT. HOLLY

SCREENING AND CRISIS INTERV.
  PRG.
MEMORIAL HOSP. OF BURLINGTON
  CO
175 MADISON AVE
MT. HOLLY, NJ 08060
Crisis Phone 1:(609)261-8000
Business Phone:(609)261-8000
HRS AVAIL:24

NEWARK

NEWARK EMERGENCY SERVICES
MT. CARMEL GUILD COMMUNITY
  MHC
17 MULBERRY ST
NEWARK, NJ 07102
Crisis Phone 1:(201)596-4100
Business Phone:(201)596-4100
HRS AVAIL:24

NEWARK

EMERGENCY PSYCHIATRIC
  SERVICES
100 BOURBON ST
NEWARK, NJ 07103
Crisis Phone 1:(201)456-6134
Crisis Phone 2:(201)623-2323
Crisis Phone 3:(201)623-2344
Crisis Phone 4:(201)623-2345
Business Phone:(201)456-6134
HRS AVAIL:24

NEW JERSEY (Con't)

PEQUANNOCK
CONTACT MORRIS-PASSAIC
P.O. Box 219
PEQUANNOCK, NJ 07440
Crisis Phone 1:(201)831-1870
Business Phone:(201)831-1870
HRS AVAIL:24

RED BANK
HELPLINE—CRISIS UNIT
RIVERVIEW MEDICAL CENTER/
CHILDREN'S PSYCH. CENTER MH
  SERVICES
1 RIVERVIEW PLAZA
RED BANK, NJ 07701
Crisis Phone 1:(201)671-5250
Business Phone:(201)530-2438
HRS AVAIL:24

RICHWOOD
CONTACT GLOUCESTER CO
P.O. Box 222
RICHWOOD, NJ 08074
Crisis Phone 1:(609)881-6200
Business Phone:(609)881-6200
HRS AVAIL:24

SALEM
CONTACT HELP OF SALEM CO.
P.O. Box 36
SALEM, NJ 08079
Crisis Phone 1:(609)935-4357
Business Phone:(609)935-4484
HRS AVAIL:24

TOMS RIVER
CONTACT OF OCEAN COUNTY
P.O. Box 1121
TOMS RIVER, NJ 08753
Crisis Phone 1:(201)240-6100
Crisis Phone 2:(609)693-5834
Business Phone:(201)240-6104
HRS AVAIL:24

UNION
COMMUNICATION—HELP CENTER
KEAN COLLEGE OF NEW JERSEY
MORRIS AVENUE
UNION, NJ 07083
Crisis Phone 1:(201)527-2360
Crisis Phone 2:(201)527-2330
Crisis Phone 3:(201)289-2101
Business Phone:(201)289-2100
HRS AVAIL:M-F 9AM-1AM,
  SA,SU 2PM-1AM

W. TRENTON
CONTACT OF MERCER COUNTY, NJ,
  INC
KATZENBACH SCHOOL FOR THE
  DEAF
320 SULLIVAN WAY
W. TRENTON, NJ 08628
Crisis Phone 1:(609)896-2120
Crisis Phone 2:(609)585-2244
TTY (609)587-3050
TTY (609)452-1919
HRS AVAIL:24

WESTFIELD
CONTACT—WE CARE
P.O. Box 37
WESTFIELD, NJ 07090
Crisis Phone 1:(201)232-2880
TTY/TDD ONLY (201)232-2444
Business Phone:(201)232-2936
HRS AVAIL:24

NEW MEXICO

ALBUQUERQUE

CRISIS UNIT
BERNALILLO CO. MENTAL HEALTH
  CENTER
2600 MARBLE N.E.
ALBUQUERQUE, NM 87106
Crisis Phone 1:(505)843-2800
Business Phone:(505)843-2800
HRS AVAIL:24

ALBUQUERQUE

AGORA
THE UNIV OF NEW MEXICO CRISIS
  CTR
STUDENT UNION
P.O. Box 29
ALBUQUERQUE, NM 87131
Crisis Phone 1:(505)277-3013
Business Phone:(505)277-3013
HRS AVAIL:24

ALBUQUERQUE

CONTACT LIFELINE
STATION D
P.O. Box 36184
ALBUQUERQUE, NM 87176-6184
Crisis Phone 1:(505)293-1888
Crisis Phone 2:(505)293-1889
Business Phone:(505)293-1888
HRS AVAIL:1PM-11PM M,T,W,TH
  24HR F,S,SU

PORTALES

MENTAL HEALTH RESOURCES, INC.
300 E. 1ST ST
PORTALES, NM 88130
Crisis Phone 1:(800)432-2159
Business Phone:(505)359-1221
HRS AVAIL:24

NEVADA

LAS VEGAS

SUICIDE PREVENTION CENTER OF
  CLARK CO.
3067 GREENBRIER ST.
LASS VEGAS, NV 89121
Crisis Phone 1:(702)731-2990
Business Phone:(702)731-2990
HRS AVAIL:24

RENO

*#SUICIDE PREV. & CRISIS CALL
  CENTER
P.O. Box 8016
RENO, NV 89507
Crisis Phone 1:(702)323-6111
Business Phone:(702)323-4533
HRS AVAIL:24

NEW YORK

ALBANY

HELPLINE C/O EQUINOX COUNSEL.
  CENTER
214 LARK STREET
ALBANY, NY 12210
Crisis Phone 1:(518)436-6000
Business Phone:(518)436-0491
HRS AVAIL:24

ALBANY

CAPITOL DIST. PSYCHIATRIC
  CENTER
75 NEW SCOTLAND AVE
ALBANY, NY 12208
Crisis Phone 1:(518)447-9650
Business Phone:(518)844-79650
HRS AVAIL:24

ALBANY

SAMARITANS OF CAPITOL DIST.
200 CENTRAL AVE.
ALBANY, NY 12206
Crisis Phone 1:(518)463-2323
Business Phone:(518)463-0861
HRS AVAIL:24

BELLMORE

* MIDDLE EARTH CRISIS
  COUNSELING & REFERRAL
  CENTER
2740 MARTIN AVE
BELLMORE, NY 11710
Crisis Phone 1:(516)679-1111
Business Phone:(516)826-0244
HRS AVAIL:24

BUFFALO

BUFFALO SUICIDE PREV. & CRISIS
  SERV
3258 MAIN ST
BUFFALO, NY 14214
Crisis Phone 1:(716)834-3131
Business Phone:(716)834-3131
HRS AVAIL:24

ELLENVILLE

FAMILY OF ELLENVILLE
14 CHURCH ST
ELLENVILLE, NY 12428
Crisis Phone 1:(914)626-8109
Business Phone:(924)626-8109
HRS AVAIL:24

GOSHEN

ORANGE COUNTY HELP LINE
MENTAL HEALTH ASSOCIATION
255 GREENWICH AVE.
GOSHEN, NY 10924
Crisis Phone 1:(914)343-6906
Crisis Phone 2:(914)294-9355
Crisis Phone 3:(914)294-9445
Crisis Phone 4:(914)342-5871
Crisis Phone 5:(914)565-6381
Business Phone:(914)294-7411
HRS AVAIL:24

ISLIP

ISLIP HOTLINE
TOWN HALL
ISLIP, NY 11751
Crisis Phone 1:(516)277-4700
Business Phone:(516)277-4700
HRS AVAIL:9:00AM-12:00AM

ITHACA

* #SUICIDE PREVENTION & CRISIS
  SERVICE OF TOMPKINS CO.
P.O., Box 312
ITHACA, NY 14850
Crisis Phone 1:(607)272-1616
Business Phone:(607)272-1505
HRS AVAIL:24

JAMESTOWN

JAMESTOWN CRISIS LINE
JAMESTOWN GENERAL HOSPITAL
JAMESTOWN, NY 14701
Crisis Phone 1:(716)484-1314
Business Phone:(716)484-1161 x321
HRS AVAIL:24

KEENE

FAMILY COUNS. CENT. OF KEENE,
  NY
P.O. Box 48
KEENE, NY 12942
Crisis Phone 1:(518)523-9720
Business Phone:(518)576-4557
HRS AVAIL:24

LINCROFT

CONTACT MONMOUTH COUNTY
P.O. Box 137
LINCROFT, NY 07738
Crisis Phone 1:(201)544-1444
Business Phone:(201)544-1444
HRS AVAIL:24

NEW PALTZ

OASIS
COUNSELING CENTER
STATE UNIV. COLLEGE
NEW PALTZ, NY 12561
Crisis Phone 1:(914)257-2141
Business Phone:(914)257-2250
HRS AVAIL:24

NEW PALTZ

FAMILY OF NEW PALTZ
2 CHURCH ST.
NEW PALTZ, NY 12561
Crisis Phone 1:(914)255-8801
Business Phone:(914)255-8801
HRS AVAIL:24

NEW YORK

HELP-LINE TELEPHONE SERVICES
3 W. 19TH STREET, SUITE #1010
NEW YORK, NY 10001
Crisis Phone 1:(212)532-2400
TTY (212)532-0942
Business Phone:(212)684-4480
HRS AVAIL:24

NEW YORK CITY

* THE SAMARITANS OF NEW YORK
  CITY
MADISON SQUARE STATION
P.O. Box 1259
NEW YORK, NY 10159
Crisis Phone 1:(212)673-3000
Business Phone:(212)673-8180
HRS AVAIL:24

NIAGARA FALLS

NIAGARA HOTLINE/CRISIS INTERV.
  SERV.
775 3RD ST.
NIAGARA FALLS NY 14302
Crisis Phone 1:(716)285-3515
Business Phone:(716)285-9636
HRS AVAIL:24

PEEKSKILL

PEEKSKILL CRISIS INTERVENTION
1137 MAIN ST.
PEEKSKILL, NY 10566
Crisis Phone 1:(914)739-6403
Business Phone:(914)739-6403
HRS AVAIL:24

PLATTSBURGH

PLATTSBURGH COMM. CRISIS
  CENTER
29 PROTECTION AVE.
PLATTSBURGH, NY 12901
Crisis Phone 1:(518)561-2330
Business Phone:(518)561-2331
HRS AVAIL:24

QUEENS VILLAGE

DIAL-FOR-HELP
CREEDMOR PSYCHIATRIC CENTER
80-45 WINCHESTER BLVD.
QUEENS VILLAGE, NY 11427
Crisis Phone 1:(212)464-7515
Business Phone:
    (212)464-7500 x3111
HRS AVAIL:24

ROCHESTER

* LIFE LINE/HEALTH ASSN. OF
  ROCHESTER
1 MOUNT HOPE AVE.
ROCHESTER, NY 14620
Crisis Phone 1:(716)275-5151
TDD (716)275-2700
Business Phone:(716)423-9490
HRS AVAIL:24

STONY BROOK

* RESPONSE OF SUFFOLK CO. INC.
P.O. Box 300
STONY BROOK, NY 11790
Crisis Phone 1:(516)751-7500
Business Phone:(516)751-7620
HRS AVAIL:24

SYRACUSE

CONTACT SYRACUSE
958 SALT SPRINGS RD.
SYRACUSE, NY 13224
Crisis Phone 1:(315)445-1500
Business Phone:(315)446-2610
HRS AVAIL:24

SYRACUSE

* SUICIDE PREV. SERV/CRISIS
  COUNS. CNTR
ST. FRANCIS HALL
301 PROSPECT AVENUE
SYRACUSE, NY 13203
Crisis Phone 1:(315)474-1333
Business Phone:(315)424-5000
HRS AVAIL:24/7 DAYS

UTICA

UTICA CRISIS INTERVENTION
1213 COURT ST., COTTAGE 46
UTICA, NY 13502
Crisis Phone 1:(315)736-0883
ROME (315)337-7299
HERKIMER (315)866-0123
Business Phone:
    (315)797-6800 x4210
HRS AVAIL:24

VALHALLA

CRISIS INTERVENTION UNIT
WESTCHESTER COUNTY MEDICAL
CENTER
GRASSLANDS ROADS
VALHALLA, NY 10595
Crisis Phone 1:(914)347-7075
Business Phone:(914)347-7075
HRS AVAIL:24

WHITE PLAINS

STERLING MH CLINIC/SPCI
    SERVICE
MHA OF WESTCHESTER CO., INC
29 STERLING AVE
WHITE PLAINS, NY 10606
SUICIDE PREV. SERV. (914)946-0121
CRISIS INTERV. SERV.(914)949-6741
Business Phone:(914)949-6741
HRS AVAIL:24

WOODSTOCK

FAMILY OF WOODSTOCK
16 ROCK CITY RD.
WOODSTOCK, NY 12498
Crisis Phone 1:(914)338-2370
Business Phone:(914)338-2370
HRS AVAIL:24

OHIO

AKRON

*#SUPPORT, INC.
513 W. MARKET ST.
AKRON, OH 44303
Crisis Phone 1:(216)434-9144
TELETEEN (216)434-9143
TTY/TDD (216)434-1706
Business Phone:(216)434-1214
HRS AVAIL:24

ASHTABULA

CONTACT ASTABULA
P.O. Box 674
ASHTABULA, OH 44004
Crisis Phone 1:(216)998-2607
Business Phone:(216)998-2609
HRS AVAIL:24

ATHENS

CARELINE
28 W. STIMSON
ATHENS, OH 45701
Crisis Phone 1:(614)593-3344
Business Phone:(614)593-3346
HRS AVAIL:24

BOWLING GREEN

THE LINK OF BOWLING GREEN
525 PIKE ST.
BOWLING GREEN, OH 43402
Crisis Phone 1:(419)352-1545
Business Phone:(419)352-5387
HRS AVAIL:24

BUCYRUS

CONTACT CRAWFORD CO.
P.O. Box 631
BUCYRUS, OH 44820
Crisis Phone 1:(419)562-9010
ENTERPRISE (419)468-9081
Business Phone:(419)562-9099
HRS AVAIL:24

CANTON

*#CRISIS INTERV. CENTER OF
   STARK CO.
2421 13TH ST., N.W.
CANTON, OH 44708
Crisis Phone 1:(216)452-6000
Business Phone:(216)452-9812
HRS AVAIL:24

CHILLICOTHE

CHILLICOTHE CRISIS CENTER
SCIOTO-PAINT VALLEY MH CENTER
4449 STATE ROUTE 159
CHILLICOTHE, OH 45601
Crisis Phone 1:(614)773-4357
Business Phone:(614)773-0760
HRS AVAIL:24

CINCINNATI

*281-CARE/TALBERT HOUSE
3891 READING RD
CINCINNATI, OH 45229
Crisis Phone 1:(513)281-2273
Business Phone:(513)281-2866
HRS AVAIL:24

CINCINNATI

CONTACT QUEEN CITY
P.O. Box 42071
CINCINNATI, OH 45242
Crisis Phone 1:(513)791-4673
Business Phone:(513)791-5734
HRS AVAIL:24

CLEVELAND

*ST. VINCENT CHARITY HOSPITAL
PSYCHIATRIC EMERGENCY
   SERVICE
2351 EAST 22ND STREET
CLEVELAND, OH 44115
Crisis Phone 1:(216)229-2211
Business Phone:
      (216)861-6200 x2000
HRS AVAIL:24/7 DAYS

COLUMBUS

*SUICIDE PREVENTION SERVICES
1301 HIGH
COLUMBUS, OH 43201
Crisis Phone 1:(614)221-5445
TEEN SUICIDE HOTLINE
      (614)294-3300
Business Phone:(614)299-6600
HRS AVAIL:24

DAYTON

*#SUICIDE PREVENTION CENTER,
   INC.
P.O. Box 1393
DAYTON, OH 45401-1393
Crisis Phone 1:(513)223-4777
Business Phone:(513)223-9096
HRS AVAIL:24

DAYTON

CONTACT DAYTON
P.O. Box 125
DAYTON, OH 45459
Crisis Phone 1:(513)434-6684
Business Phone:(513)434-1798
HRS AVAIL:24

DELAWARE

*HELP ANONYMOUS, INC.
11 E. CENTRAL AVE
DELAWARE, OH 43015
Crisis Phone 1:(614)369-3316
Crisis Phone 2:(614)548-7324
Business Phone:(614)363-1835
HRS AVAIL:24

OHIO (Con't)

DOVER
CRISIS HELP LINE
201 HOSPITAL DR.
DOVER, OH 44622
Crisis Phone 1:(216)343-1811
Business Phone:(216)343-6631
HRS AVAIL:24

EATON
PREBLE COUNSELING CENTER
  HOTLINE
101 NORTH BARRON ST.
EATON, OH 45320
Crisis Phone 1:(513)456-1166
Business Phone:(513)456-6201
HRS AVAIL:24

GREENVILLE
CRISIS HOTLINE
DARKE COUNTY MENTAL HEALTH
  CLINIC
212 E MAIN
GREENVILLE, OH 45331
Crisis Phone 1:(513)548-1635
Business Phone:(513)548-1635
HRS AVAIL:24

KENT
TOWNHALL II HELPLINE
225 E. COLLEGE ST
KENT, OH 44240
Crisis Phone 1:(216)678-4357
PORTAGE CO. ONLY (800)533-4357
Business Phone:(216)678-3006
HRS AVAIL:24

LANCASTER
INFO. & CRISIS SERV./FAIRFIELD
  CO.
P.O. Box 1054
LANCASTER, OH 43130
Crisis Phone 1:(614)687-0500
Business Phone:(614)687-0500
HRS AVAIL:24

MANSFIELD
HELP LINE/ADAPT
741 SHOLL RD.
MANSFIELD, OH 44907
Crisis Phone 1:(419)522-4357
Business Phone:(419)526-4332
HRS AVAIL:24

MARION
CARE LINE
320 EXECUTIVE DR
MARION, OH 43302
Crisis Phone 1:(614)387-7200
Business Phone:(614)387-7200
HRS AVAIL:24

MARYSVILLE
UNION CO. CRISIS HOTLINE
CHARLES B. MILLS CENTER
715 PLUM ST.
MARYSVILLE, OH 43040
Crisis Phone 1:(513)644-6363
PLAIN CITY (614)873-8610
RICHWOOD (614)943-2916
Business Phone:(513)644-9192
HRS AVAIL:24

MEDINA
MEDINA CRISIS INTERVENTION
  HELP LINE
CATHOLIC SOCIAL SERVICES
246 NORTHLAND DR.
MEDINA, OH 44256
Crisis Phone 1:(216)725-4357
Crisis Phone 2:(216)225-4357
Crisis Phone 3:(216)336-4357
Business Phone:(216)725-4923
HRS AVAIL:24

MT. GILEAD
* HOPE LINE, INC.
P.O. Box 142
MT. GILEAD, OH 43338
Crisis Phone 1:(419)947-2520
Business Phone:(419)947-2520
HRS AVAIL:24

OXFORD
OXFORD CRISIS & REFERRAL
  CENTER
111 E. WALNUT ST.
OXFORD, OH 45056
Crisis Phone 1:(513)523-4146
Business Phone:(513)523-4149
HRS AVAIL:24

PORTSMOUTH
SCIOTO CO. DRUG ABUSE COUNCIL
  INC.
1930 ARGONNE ROAD
PORTSMOUTH, OH 45662
Crisis Phone 1:(614)354-1010
SCIOTO, ADAMS CO (800)448-2273
LAWRENCE CO. (800)448-2273
Business Phone:(614)354-2001
HRS AVAIL:24

TOLEDO
*THE NEW RESCUE CRISIS SERVICE
3314 COLLINGWOOD AVE.
TOLEDO, OH 43610
Crisis Phone 1:(419)255-5500
Business Phone:(419)255-9585
HRS AVAIL:24

TOLEDO
TOLEDO FIRST CALL FOR HELP
1 STRANAHAN SQ. #141
TOLEDO, OH 43604
Crisis Phone 1:(419)244-3728
Business Phone:(419)244-3728
HRS AVAIL:24

WOOSTER
DIAL A FRIEND
P.O. Box 303
WOOSTER, OH 44691
Crisis Phone 1:(216)262-9999
Business Phone:(216)262-9499
HRS AVAIL:2PM to 12PM

XENIA
GREENE COUNTY CRISIS CENTER
452 W. MARKET
XENIA, OH 45385
Crisis Phone 1:(513)429-0679
Crisis Phone 2:(513)429-0933
Business Phone:(513)376-8700
HRS AVAIL:24

YOUNGSTOWN
*#HELP HOTLINE, INC.
P.O. Box 46
YOUNGSTOWN, OH 44501
Crisis Phone 1:(216)747-2696
Crisis Phone 2:(216)424-7767
Crisis Phone 1:(216)426-9355
TTY (216)744-0579
Business Phone:(216)747-5111
HRS AVAIL:24

ZANESVILLE
* SIX COUNTY, INC. CRISIS HOTLINE
2845 BELL STREET
ZANESVILLE, OH 43701
Crisis Phone 1:(614)452-8403
Business Phone:(614)454-9766
HRS AVAIL:24

OKLAHOMA

CLINTON
CONTACT WESTERN OKLAHOMA
P.O. Box 572
CLINTON, OK 73601
Crisis Phone 1:(405)323-1064
Business Phone:(405)323-1064
HRS AVAIL:24

ENID
CONTACT NORTHWEST OKLAHOMA
P.O. Box 3165
ENID, OK 73702
Crisis Phone 1:(405)234-1111
Business Phone:(405)237-8400
HRS AVAIL:11:00AM—11:00PM

OKLAHOMA (Con't)

LAWTON
CRISIS TELEPHONE SERVICE
P.O. Box 2011
LAWTON OK 73502
Crisis Phone 1:(405)355-7575
Business Phone:(405)355-7575
Hrs Avail:24

OKLAHOMA CITY
* CONTACT OF METRO. OKLAHOMA
   CITY
P.O. Box 12832
OKLAHOMA CITY OK 73157
Crisis Phone 1:(405)848-2273
Business Phone:(405)840-9396
Hrs Avail:24

OKLAHOMA CITY
* OKLAHOMA ADOLESCENT CRISIS
   TELEPHONE
P.O. Box 26901
OKLAHOMA CITY OK 73190
Crisis Phone 1:(405)271-TEEN
Crisis Phone 2:(800)522-TEEN
Business Phone:(405)217-3539
Hrs Avail:4-10PM 7DAY/WK

PONCA CITY
HELPLINE/PONCA CITY
P.O. Box 375
PONCO CITY OK 74602
Crisis Phone 1:(405)765-5551
Business Phone:(405)765-5551
Hrs Avail:24

TULSA
TULSA HELPLINE
P.O. Box 52847
TULSA OK 74152
Crisis Phone:(918)583-4357
Business Phone:(918)585-1144
Hrs Avail:24

OREGON

ALBANY
LINN COUNTY MENTAL HEALTH
P.O. Box 100
ALBANY OR 97321
Crisis Phone 1:(503)757-2299
Business Phone:(503)967-3866
Hrs Avail:24

CORVALLIS
BENTON COUNTY MENTAL HEALTH
530 N.W. 27TH
CORVALLIS OR 97330
Crisis Phone 1:(503)757-2299
Business Phone:(503)757-6846
Hrs Avail:24

EUGENE
MENTAL HEALTH EMERGENCY
   CENTER/CIRT
1901 GARDEN AVE.
EUGENE OR 97403
Crisis Phone 1:(503)687-4000
Business Phone:(503)687-4085
Hrs Avail:24

EUGENE
WHITE BIRD CLINIC
341 E. 12TH AVENUE
EUGENE OR 97401
Crisis Phone 1:(503)342-8255
Crisis Phone 2:(503)687-4000
Business Phone:(503)342-8255
Hrs Avail:24

OREGON (Con't)

GRANTS PASS
HELPLINE REFERRAL SERVICES
P.O. Box 670
GRANTS PASS OR 97526
Crisis Phone 1:(503)479-4357
Business Phone:(503)479-2349
Hrs Avail:24

KLAMATH FALLS
KLAMATH CRISIS CENTER
1014 MAIN STREET
KLAMATH FALLS OR 97601
Crisis Phone 1:(503)884-0636
Crisis Phone 2:(503)884-0390
Business Phone:(503)884-0636
Hrs Avail:24

MEDFORD
CRISIS INTERVENTION SERVICES
HELP LINE
P.O. Box 819
MEDFORD OR 97501
Crisis Phone 1:(503)779-4357
Business Phone:(503)779-4490
Hrs Avail:24

PORTLAND
* METRO CRISIS INTERVENTION
  SERVICE
P.O. Box 637
PORTLAND OR 97207
Crisis Phone 1:(503)223-6161
Business Phone:(503)226-3099
Hrs Avail:24

SALEM
NORTHWEST HUMAN SERVICES,
  INC.
674 CHURCH ST.N.
SALEM OR 97303
Crisis Phone 1:(503)581-5535
Business Phone:(503)588-5828
Hrs Avail:24

PENNSYLVANIA

ABINGTON
TELEHELP OF MONTGOMERY
  COUNTY
C/O MENTAL HEALTH CENTER
ABINGTON MEMORIAL HOSPITAL
ABINGTON PA 19001
Crisis Phone 1:(215)884-2220
Business Phone:(215)884-2220
Hrs Avail:24

ALLENTOWN
CRISIS INTERVENTION TEAM
LEHIGH COUNTY
512 HAMILTON ST., SUITE #300
ALLENTOWN PA 18101
Crisis Phone 1:(215)820-3127
Business Phone:(215)820-3127
Hrs Avail:24

ALTOONA
* CONTACT ALTOONA
P.O. Box 11
ALTOONA PA 16603
Crisis Phone 1:(814)946-9050
Business Phone:(814)946-0531
Hrs Avail:24 HRS, 7 DAYS/WK

BETHLEHEM
CRISIS INTERVENTION TEAM
  (MH/MR)
NORTHAMPTON COUNTY
BROAD & NEW STREETS
BETHLEHEM PA 18018
Crisis Phone 1:(215)865-0944
Business Phone:(215)865-0944
Hrs Avail:24

PENNSYLVANIA (Con't)

CAMP HILL
TEENLINE
HOLY SPIRIT HOSPITAL, CMHC
N.21 ST. STREET
CAMP HILL PA 17011
Crisis Phone 1:(800)722-5385
Crisis Phone 2:(717)763-2345
Business Phone:(717)763-2239
Hrs Avail:24 HRS., 7 DAYS/WK

CHAMBERSBURG
CONTACT CHAMBERSBURG
221 N. MAIN ST
CHAMBERSBURG PA 17201
Crisis Phone 1:(717)264-7799
Business Phone:(717)263-8007
Hrs Avail:24

DARBY
* PSYCH CRISIS CENTER
FITZGERALD MERCY HOSPITAL
DARBY PA 19023
Crisis Phone 1:(215)237-4210
Business Phone:(215)237-4210
Hrs Avail:24

DOWNINGTON
CHESTER CO. CRISIS
   INTERVENTION CENT.
520 E. LANCASTER AVE
DOWNINGTON PA 19335
Crisis Phone 1:(215)873-1000
Business Phone:(215)873-1000
Hrs Avail:24

ERIE
INFO. & REFERRAL DIVISION
UNITED WAY OF ERIE COUNTY
100 W 10TH ST.
ERIE PA 16501-1466
ERIE HOTLINE (814)453-5656
Business Phone:(814)456-2937
Hrs Avail:24

GETTYSBURG
ADAMS/HANOVER COUNSELING
   SERVICE
37 WEST ST.
GETTYSBURG PA 17325
Crisis Phone 1:(717)334-9111
Business Phone:(717)334-9111
Hrs Avail:24

HARRISBURG
CONTACT HARRISBURG
P.O. Box 6270
HARRISBURG PA 17112
Crisis Phone 1:(717)652-4400
Business Phone:(717)652-4987
Hrs Avail:24

HARRISBURG
DAUPHIN CO. CRISIS
   INTERVENTION
25 S FRONT ST
HARRISBURG PA 17101
Crisis Phone 1:(717)232-7511
Business Phone:(717)255-2705
Hrs Avail:24

INDIANA
THE OPEN DOOR
1008 PHILADELPHIA ST.
INDIANA PA 15701
Crisis Phone 1:(412)465-2605
Business Phone:(412)465-2605
Hrs Avail:24

LANCASTER
CONTACT LANCASTER
447 E. KING ST.
LANCASTER PA 17602
Crisis Phone 1:(717)299-4855
Business Phone:(717)291-2261
Hrs Avail:24

MEDIA
DELAWARE CO. CRISIS
  INTERVENTION/SPS
600 N. OLIVE ST.
MEDIA PA 19063
Crisis Phone 1:(215)565-4300
Business Phone:(215)565-2041
Hrs Avail:24

NANTICOKE
HAZELTON-NANTICOKE CRISIS
  SERVICES
HAZELTON-NANTICOKE MHC
W. WASHINGTON ST.
NANTICOKE PA 18634
Crisis Phone 1:(717)735-7590
Business Phone:(717)735-7590
Hrs Avail:24

NEW BLOOMFIELD
PERRY COUNTY HOTLINE
PERRY HUMAN SERVICES
COURTHOUSE ANNEX
NEW BLOOMFIELD PA 17068
Crisis Phone 1:(717)582-8052
Business Phone:(717)582-8703
Hrs Avail:24

NEW BRIGHTON
CONTACT BEAVER VALLEY
P.O. Box 75
NEW BRIGHTON PA 15066
Crisis Phone 1:(412)728-3650
Business Phone:(412)728-3650
Hrs Avail:24

NEW CASTLE
CONTACT E.A.R.S.
P.O. Box 7804
NEW CASTLE PA 16107
Crisis Phone 1:(412)658-5529
Business Phone:(412)652-0333
Hrs Avail:24

NEWTOWN
CONTACT LOWER BUCKS
P.O. Box 376
NEWTON PA 18940
Crisis Phone 1:(215)752-1850
Business Phone:(215)860-1803
Hrs Avail:24

NORRISTOWN
MONTGOMERY CO. EMERGENCY
  SERV., INC.
CALLER BOX 3005
NORRISTOWN PA 19404-3005
Crisis Phone 1:(215)279-6100
Hrs Avail:24

PHILADELPHIA
PHILADELPHIA SUICIDE & C.I.
  CENTER
1 READING CENTER
1101 MARKET 7TH FLOOR
PHILADELPHIA PA 19107
Crisis Phone 1:(215)686-4420
Business Phone:(215)592-5563
Hrs Avail:24

PHILADELPHIA
CONTACT PHILADELPHIA
P.O. Box 12586
PHILADELPHIA PA 19151
Crisis Phone 1:(215)879-4402
Business Phone:(215)877-9099
Hrs Avail:24

PHILADELPHIA
*TEEN SUICIDE TREATMENT &
  PREV PRG.
HAHNEMANN UNIVERSITY
  HOSPITAL
230 N. BROAD STREET
PHILADELPHIA PA 19102
Crisis Phone 1:(215)977-TEEN
Business Phone:(215)448-7255
Hrs Avail:24 HRS, 7 DAYS/WK

PHILADELPHIA
SUICIDE & CRISIS INTERVENTION
 CENTER
1101 MARKET ST.   7TH FLOOR
PHILADELPHIA PA 19107
Crisis Phone 1:(215)686-4420
Business Phone:(215)686-4420
Hrs Avail:24

PITTSBURGH
*#CONTACT PITTSBURGH, INC.
P.O. Box 111294
PITTSBURGH PA 15238
Crisis Phone 1:(412)782-4023
Business Phone:(412)963-6416
Hrs Avail:24

PITTSBURGH
* HELPLINE/PITTSBURGH
200 ROSS ST.
PITTSBURGH PA 15219
Crisis Phone 1:(412)255-1155
Business Phone:(412)255-1133
Hrs Avail:24/7 DAYS

SCRANTON
FREE INFO & REFERRAL SYSTEM
 TELEPH.FIRST
225 N. WASHINGTON AVENUE
SCRANTON PA 18503
Crisis Phone 1:(717)961-1234
Business Phone:(717)961-1234
Hrs. Avail:24

SHARPSVILLE
CONTACT PENN-OHIO
P.O. Box 91
SHARPSVILLE PA 16150
Crisis Phone 1:(412)962-5777
Business Phone:(412)962-5777
Hrs Avail:4 P.M. -MIDNIGHT

WILKES BARRE
COMM. COUNSELING SERVICES OF
 N.E. PA
110 S. PENNSYLVANIA AVE
WILKES BARRE PA 18702
Crisis Phone 1:(717)823-2155
Business Phone:(717)823-2155
Hrs Avail:24 HRS, 7 DAYS/WK

WILLIAMSPORT
WILLIAMSPORT HELPLINE
815 W. 4TH ST.
WILLIAMSPORT PA 17701
Crisis Phone 1:(717)323-8555
Crisis Phone 2:(800)624-4636
Business Phone:(717)323-8555
Hrs Avail:24

YORK
CONTACT YORK
145 S. DUKE ST.
YORK PA 17403
Crisis Phone 1:(717)845-3656
Business Phone:(717)845-9125
Hrs Avail:24

YORK
CRISIS INTERVENTION SERVICES
 OF YORK
C/O YORK HOSPITAL MH SERVICES
1001 S. GEORGE STREET
YORK PA 17403
Crisis Phone 1:(717)845-2718
Business Phone:(717)845-8655
Hrs Avail:24

RHODE ISLAND

PROVIDENCE
* THE SAMARITANS OF
   PROVIDENCE
33 CHESTNUT ST
PROVIDENCE RI 02903
Crisis Phone 1:(401)272-4044
Business Phone:(401)272-4044
Hrs Avail:24

WAKEFIELD
SYMPATICO
29 COLUMBIA ST
WAKEFIELD RI 02879
Crisis Phone 1:(401)783-0650
Business Phone:(401)783-0782
Hrs Avail:24

S. CAROLINA

AIKEN
* AIKEN COUNTY HELP LINE, INC
P.O. Box 2712
AIKEN SC 29801
Crisis Phone 1:(803)648-9900
Business Phone:(803)648-0000
Hrs Avail:24

COLUMBIA
* HELPLINE OF THE MIDLANDS, INC.
P.O. Box 6336
COLUMBIA SC 29260
Crisis Phone 1:(803)771-4357
Crisis Phone 1:(803)771-6310
Business Phone:(803)799-6329
Hrs Avail:24

CHARLESTON HTS.
* CHARLESTON HOTLINE
P.O. Box 71583
CHARLESTON HTS SC 29415-1583
Crisis Phone 1:(803)744-4357
Business Phone:(803)747-3007
Hrs Avail:24

GAFFNEY
CHEROKEE SUICIDE
   INTERVENTION CENTER, INC
P.O. Box 1231
GAFFNEY SC 29342
Crisis Phone 1:(803)487-HELP
Business Phone:(803)487-3387
Hrs Avail:7PM-1AM

GREENVILLE
HELP-LINE/GREENVILLE
P.O. Box 1085
GREENVILLE SC 29602
Crisis Phone 1:(803)233-HELP
Business Phone:(803)242-0955
Hrs Avail:24

S. DAKOTA

ABERDEEN
NEW BEGINNINGS CENTER
1206 NORTH THIRD
ABERDEEN SD 57401
Crisis Phone 1:(605)229-1239
Business Phone:(605)229-1239
Hrs Avail:24

HURON
OUR HOME, INC.
510 NEBRASKA
HURON SD 57350
Crisis Phone 1:(605)352-9449
Business Phone:(605)352-9098
Hrs Avail:24

SIOUX FALLS

CRISIS LINE/SIOUX FALLS
VOLUNTEER & INFO. CENTER
304 S. PHILLIPS #310
SIOUX FALLS SD 57102
Crisis Phone 1:(605)339-4357
Business Phone:(605)334-7022
Hrs Avail:24

SIOUX FALLS

HELPLINE OF SIOUX FALLS
304 S. PHILLIPS
SIOUX FALLS SD 57102
Crisis Phone 1:(605)339-4357
Business Phone:(605)339-4357
Hrs Avail:24

TENNESSEE

ATHENS

MC MINN/MEIGS CONTACT
P.O. Box 69
ATHENS TN 37303
Crisis Phone 1:(615)745-9111
Business Phone:(615)745-1042
Hrs Avail:24

CHATTANOOGA

CONTACT OF CHATTANOOGA
1202 DUNCAN
CHATTANOOGA TN 37404
Crisis Phone 1:(615)266-8228
Crisis Phone 2:(615)622-5193
Business Phone:(615)629-0039
Hrs Avail:24

CLEVELAND

CONTACT OF CLEVELAND
P.O. Box 962
CLEVELAND TN 37311
Crisis Phone 1:(615)479-9666
Business Phone:(615)472-1916
Hrs Avail:24

JOHNSON CITY

CONTACT MINISTRIES
P.O. Box 1403
JOHNSON CITY TN 37605
Crisis Phone 1:(615)926-0144
DEAF CONTACT (615)926-7423
Business Phone:(615)926-0140
Hrs Avail:24

KINGSPORT

CONTACT—CONCERN
P.O. Box 798
KINGSPORT TN 37662
Crisis Phone 1:(615)246-2273
Business Phone:(615)247-7761
Hrs Avail:24

KNOXVILLE

HELEN ROSS MC NABB CENTER
1520 CHEROKEE TRAIL
KNOXVILLE TN 37920
Crisis Phone 1:(615)637-9711
Business Phone:(615)637-9711
Hrs Avail:24

KNOXVILLE

CONTACT TELE. OF KNOXVILLE
P.O. Box 11234
KNOXVILLE TN 37939-1234
Crisis Phone 1:(615)523-9124
Business Phone:(615)523-9108
Hrs Avail:24

MARYVILLE

CONTACT OF BLOUNT COUNTY
P.O. Box 0382
MARYVILLE TN 37803
Crisis Phone 1:(615)984-7689
Business Phone:(615)984-7690
HRS AVAIL:24

TENNESSEE (Con't)

MEMPHIS
* SUICIDE/CRISIS INTERV.
  SERV./MEMPHIS
P.O. Box 40068
MEMPHIS TN 38104
Crisis Phone 1:(901)274-7477
Business Phone:(901)276-1111
Hrs Avail:24

MEMPHIS
* CHARTER LAKESIDE HOSPITAL
2911 BRUNSWICK ROAD
MEMPHIS TN 38134
Crisis Phone 1:(901)377-4733
Business Phone:(901)377-4700
Hrs Avail:24/7 DAYS

NASHVILLE
*#CRISIS INTERVENTION CENTER,
  INC.
P.O. Box 40752
NASHVILLE TN 37204-0752
Crisis Phone 1:(615)244-7444
Business Phone:(615)298-3359
HRS AVAIL:24

OAK RIDGE
CONTACT OF OAK RIDGE
P.O. Box 641
OAK RIDGE TN 37830
Crisis Phone 1:(615)482-4949
Business Phone:(615)482-5040
Hrs Avail:24

TULLAHOMA
TULLAHOMA CONTACT—LIFE LINE
P.O. Box 1614
TULLAHOMA TN 37388
COFFEE COUNTY (615)455-7133
FRANKLIN CO. (615)967-7133
BEDFORD CO. (615)684-7133
MOORE CO. (615)759-7133
Business Phone:(615)967-7133
Hrs Avail:24

TEXAS

AMARILLO
*#SUICIDE & CRISIS CENTER,
  AMARILLO
P.O. Box 3250
AMARILLO TX 79106
Crisis Phone 1:(806)359-6699
TOLL FREE IN-STATE (800)692-4039
Business Phone:(806)353-7235
Hrs Avail:24

ARLINGTON
CONTACT TARRANT COUNTY
P.O. Box 1431
ARLINGTON TX 76010
Crisis Phone 1:(817)277-2233
Business Phone:(817)277-0071
Hrs Avail:24

AUSTIN
INFORMATION HOTLINE & CRISIS
  CENTER
NECHES CROSS. 20006 GASTON PL.
AUSTIN TX 78723
Crisis Phone 1:(512) 472-HELP
Hrs Avail:24

BEAUMONT
SUICIDE RESCUE, INC.
2750 I 10-E
BEAUMONT TX 77703
Crisis Phone 1:(713)833-2311
Business Phone:(713)833-2311
HRS AVAIL:24

BEAUMONT

* RAPE & SUICIDE CRISIS
  OF SE TEXAS
P.O. Box 5011
BEAUMONT TX 77706
Crisis Phone 1:(409)835-3355
Business Phone:(409)832-6530
Hrs Avail:24

CORPUS CHRISTI

* CRISIS SERVICES/
  CORPUS CHRISTI
4906-B EVERHART
CORPUS CHRISTI TX 78411
Crisis Phone 1:(512)993-7410
Business Phone:(512)993-7416
Hrs Avail:24

DALLAS

*# SUICIDE & CRISIS CENTER
2808 SWISS AVE
DALLAS TX 75204
Crisis Phone 1:(214)828-1000
Business Phone:(214)824-7020
Hrs Avail:24

DALLAS

* CONTACT-DALLAS/TELEPH.
  COUNSEL.
P.O. Box 742224
DALLAS TX 75374
Crisis Phone 1:(214)233-2233
TEEN-CONTACT (214)233-TEEN
Business Phone:(214)233-0866
Hrs Avail:24

DEL RIO

DEL RIO CRISIS LINE
YOUTH COUNSELING CENTER
1401 LAS VACAS RD
DEL RIO TX 78840
Crisis Phone 1:(512)775-0571
Business Phone:(512)774-2585
Hrs Avail:24

EDINBURGH

EDINBURGH HELP LINE
P.O. Box 1108
EDINBURGH TX 78539
Crisis Phone 1:(512)383-0121
Business Phone:(512)383-5341
Hrs Avail:24

EL PASO

EL PASO CRISIS INTERVENTION
  SERVICES
5250 EL PASO DR
EL PASO TX 79905
Crisis Phone 1:(915)779-1800
Business Phone:(915)779-7130
Hrs Avail:24

FT WORTH

*#CRISIS INTERVENTION
C/O FAMILY SERVICE, INC.
1424 HEMPHILL
FT. WORTH TX 76104
Crisis Phone 1:(817)927-5544
Business Phone:(817)927-8884
Hrs Avail:24

HOUSTON

HOUSTON-BAY AREA CRISIS
  HELPLINE
18301-A EGRET BAY
HOUSTON TX 77058
Crisis Phone 1:(713)333-5111
Business Phone:(713)333-3580
Hrs Avail:24

HOUSTON

*#CRISIS INTERVENTION OF
  HOUSTON, INC.
P.O. Box 13066
HOUSTON TX 77219
CENTRAL (713)228-1505
BAY AREA (713)333-5111
Business Phone:(713)527-9426
Hrs Avail:24

LAREDO

* LIFELINE OF LAREDO, INC.
P.O. Box 2703
LAREDO TX 78044-2703
Crisis Phone 1:(512)722-5433
Business Phone:(512)722-7885
Hrs Avail:6PM-6AM, 7 DAYS

LUBBOCK

CONTACT LUBBOCK
P.O. Box 6477
LUBBOCK TX 79493-6477
Crisis Phone 1:(806)765-8393
TEEN LINE (806)765-7272
Business Phone:(806)765-7272
Hrs Avail:24/7DAYS
TEENLINE 6-10PM

ORANGE

SUICIDE RESCUE
P.O. Box 891
ORANGE TX 77630
Crisis Phone 1:(713)883-5521
Business Phone:(713)883-5521
Hrs Avail:24

PLANO

CRISIS CENTER OF COLLIN COUNTY
P.O. Box 1808
PLANO TX 75074
Crisis Phone 1:(214)881-0088
Business Phone:(214)881-0081
Hrs Avail:24/7 DAYS

RICHARDSON

RICHARDSON CRISIS CENTER
P.O. Box 877
RICHARDSON TX 75080
Crisis Phone 1:(214)783-0008
Business Phone:(214)783-0008
Hrs Avail:24

SAN ANGELO

* CONCHO VALLEY CTR. FOR HUMAN
ADVANCE
244 N. MAGDALEN
SAN ANGELO TX 76903
Crisis Phone 1:(915)653-5933
Business Phone:(915)655-8965
Hrs Avail:24

SAN ANTONIO

CONTACT SAN ANTONIO
P.O. Box 5217
SAN ANTONIO TX 78201
Crisis Phone 1:(512)733-1111
Business Phone:(512)732-2216
Hrs Avail:2PM-10PM

SAN ANTONIO

* UNITED WAY HELP LINE
P.O. Box 898
SAN ANTONIO TX 78293-0898
Crisis Phone 1:(512)227-4357
Business Phone:(512)224-5000
Hrs Avail:24

WICHITA FALLS

CONCERN, INC.
P.O. Box 1945
WICHITA FALLS TX 76307
Crisis Phone 1:(817)723-0821
Business Phone:(817)723-8231
Hrs Avail:24

UTAH

LOGAN

LOGAN HELPLINE
121 A UMC UTAH STATE UNIV
LOGAN UT 84322
Crisis Phone 1:(801)752-3964
Business Phone:(801)752-1702
Hrs Avail:24

MIDVALE

SALT LAKE CO. DIV. OF MH
6856 SOUTH 700 EAST
MIDVALE UT 84047
Crisis Phone 1:(801)566-2455
Business Phone:(801)566-2455
Hrs Avail:24

OGDEN

OGDEN EMERGENCY SERVICES
WEBER CO. MHC
2510 WASHINGTON BLVD 5TH FL.
OGDEN UT 84401
Crisis Phone 1:(801)626-9270
Business Phone:(801)626-9100
Hrs Avail:24

PROVO

* UTAH COUNTY CRISIS LINE
P.O. Box 1375
PROVO UT 84603
Crisis Phone 1:(801)377-8255
Business Phone:(801)377-8255
Hrs Avail:24

SALT LAKE CITY

SALT LAKE CITY CRISIS
  INTERVENTION
#50 N. MEDICAL DR.
SALT LAKE CITY UT 84132
Crisis Phone 1:(801)581-2296
Business Phone:(801)581-2296
Hrs Avail:24

SALT LAKE CITY

SALT LAKE VALLEY MENTAL
  HEALTH
1228 S. 900E
SALT LAKE CITY UT 84105
Crisis Phone 1:(801)483-5444
Business Phone:(801)483-5444
Hrs Avail:24

VIRGINIA

ALEXANDRIA

ALEXANDRIA COMM MH CENTER
206 N. WASHINGTON ST. 5TH FL
ALEXANDRIA VA 22314
Crisis Phone 1:(703)836-5751
Business Phone:(703)836-5751
Hrs Avail:24

ALEXANDRIA

ALEXANDRIA C.A.I.R. HOTLINE
418 S. WASHINGTON ST. SUITE 101
ALEXANDRIA VA 22314
Crisis Phone 1:(703)548-3810
Business Phone:(703)548-0010
Hrs Avail: NOON TO MIDNIGHT

ARLINGTON

*#NORTHERN VIRGINIA HOTLINE
P.O. Box 187
ARLINGTON VA 22210
Crisis Phone 1:(703)527-4077
Business Phone:(703)522-4460
Hrs Avail:24

BLACKSBURG

RAFT
201 MAIN ST.
BLACKSBURG VA 24060
Crisis Phone 1:(703)951-3434
Business Phone:(703)951-4283
Hrs Avail:24

VIRGINIA (Con't)

BRISTOL
BRISTOL CRISIS CENTER
P.O. Box 642
BRISTOL VA 24203
Crisis Phone 1:(703)466-2312
Crisis Phone 2:(703)628-7731
Business Phone:(703)466-2218
Hrs Avail:24

FREDERICKSBURG
FREDERICKSBURG HOTLINE
P.O. Box 7132
FREDERICKSBURG VA 22404
Crisis Phone 1:(703)321-1212
Business Phone:(703)373-6608
Hrs Avail:24

HARRISONBURG
LISTENING EAR SERVICES
MASSANUTTEN MENTAL HEALTH
  CENTER
1241 N. MAIN ST
HARRISONBURG VA 22801
Crisis Phone 1:(703)434-2538
Business Phone:(703)434-2539
Hrs Avail:24

LYNCHBURG
THE CRISIS LINE OF CENTRAL VA
P.O. Box 2376
LYNCHBURG VA 24501
Crisis Phone 1:(804)528-HELP
Business Phone:(804)384-0231
Hrs Avail:6:00PM-12:00AM

MARTINSVILLE
CONTACT MARTINSVILLE-HENRY
  CO.
P.O. Box 1287
MARTINSVILLE VA 24112
Crisis Phone 1:(703)632-7295
Business Phone:(703)638-8980
Hrs Avail:24

PETERSBURG
CONTACT OLD DOMINION, INC.
P.O. Box 942
PETERSBURG VA 23804
Crisis Phone 1:(804)733-1100
Crisis Phone 2:(804)733-1101
Business Phone:(804)861-0330
Hrs Avail:24

PORTSMOUTH
** SUICIDE-CRISIS CENTER, INC
P.O. Box 1493
PORTSMOUTH VA 23705
Crisis Phone 1:(804)399-6393
Business Phone:(804)393-0502
Hrs Avail:24

RICHMOND
CONTACT OLD DOMINION—
  RICHMOND
1919 HUGENOT ROAD
RICHMOND VA 23235
Crisis Phone 1:(804)226-4357
Business Phone:(804)379-9065
Hrs Avail:24

RICHMOND
EMERGENCY SERVICE/RICHMOND
  CO. MHC
501 N. 9TH ST., RM. #205
RICHMOND VA 23218
Crisis Phone 1:(804)780-8003
Crisis Phone 2:(804)648-9224
Business Phone:(804)643-5301
Hrs Avail:24

ROANOKE
* TRUST: ROANOKE VALLEY
  TROUBLE CENTER
360 WASHINGTON AVE.
ROANOKE VA 24016
Crisis Phone 1:(703)344-1978
Crisis Phone 2:(703)344-1948
Business Phone:(703)345-8859
Hrs Avail:24/7 DAYS

VIRGINIA (Con't)

ROANOKE
SANCTUARY
836 CAMPBELL AVENUE S.W.
ROANOKE VA 24016
Crisis Phone 1:(703)981-2776
Business Phone:(703)981-2776
Hrs Avail:24

VIRGINIA BEACH
CONTACT TIDEWATER
P.O. Box 23
VIRGINIA BEACH VA 23458
Crisis Phone 1:(804)428-2211
Hrs Avail:24

WINCHESTER
CONCERN HOTLINE, INC.
P.O. Box 2032
WINCHESTER VA 22601
WINCHESTER (703)667-0145
FRONT ROYAL (703)635-4357
WOODSTOCK (703)459-4742
Business Phone:(703)667-8208
Hrs Avail:24

VERMONT

BRATTLEBORO
HOTLINE FOR HELP, INC.
17 ELLIOT ST.
BRATTLEBORO VT 05301
Crisis Phone 1:(802)257-7989
Business Phone:(802)257-7980
Hrs Avail:24

RANDOLPH
ORANGE CO. MH SERVICE EMER
    SERVICE
P.O. Box G
RANDOLPH VT 05060
Crisis Phone 1:(800)622-4244
Business Phone:(802)728-4466
Hrs Avail:24

BURLINGTON
THE CRISIS SERVICES OF
    CHITTENDEN CO.
MED. CENTER HOSPITAL OF
    VERMONT
BURGESS BUILDING
BURLINGTON VT 05401
Crisis Phone 1:(802)656-3587
Business Phone:(802)656-3587
Hrs Avail:24

ST. ALBANS
ST. ALBANS EMER. & CRISIS
    SERVICE
FRANKLIN GRAND ISLE MH
    SERVICE, INC.
8 FERRIS STREET
ST. ALBANS VT 05478
Crisis Phone 1:(802)524-6554
Business Phone:(802)524-6554
Hrs Avail:24

B'BRIDGE ISLAND

HELPLINE HOUSE
282 KNECHTEL WAY NE
B'BRIDGE ISLAND WA 98110
Crisis Phone 1:(206)842-HELP
Business Phone:(206)842-7621
Hrs Avail:24

BELLINGHAM

THE CRISIS LINE
WHATCOM CO. CRISIS SERVICES
124 E. HOLLY ST #201
BELLINGHAM WA 98225
Crisis Phone 1:(206)734-7271
WHATCOM CO. (206)384-1485
Business Phone:(206)671-5754
Hrs Avail:24

BREMERTON

BREMERTON CRISIS CLINIC
500 UNION
BREMERTON WA 98312
Crisis Phone 1:(206)479-3033
Business Phone:(206)373-5031
Hrs Avail:24

CHEHALIS

LEWIS CO. INFO. & REFERRAL/
 HOTLINE
P.O. Box 337
CHEHALIS WA 98532
Crisis Phone 1:(206)748-6601
IN WASHINGTON (800)562-6160
Business Phone:(206)748-6601
Hrs Avail:24

ELLENSBURG

ELLENSBURG CRISIS LINE
507 NANUM
ELLENSBURG WA 98926
Crisis Phone 1:(509)925-4168
Business Phone:(509)925-2166
Hrs Avail:24

EVERETT

* CARE CRISIS LINE
2801 LOMBARD AVE
EVERETT WA 98201
Crisis Phone 1:(206)258-4357
Business Phone:(206)259-3191
Hrs Avail:24

MOSES LAKE

GRANT COUNTY CRISIS LINE
MENTAL HEALTH & FAMILY
 SERVICE
P.O. Box 1057
MOSES LAKE WA 98837
Crisis Phone 1:(509)765-1717
Business Phone:(509)765-9239
Hrs Avail:24

OLYMPIA

CRISIS CLINIC/THURSTON &
 MACON CO.
P.O. Box 2463
OLYMPIA WA 98507
Crisis Phone 1:(206)352-2211
Business Phone:(206)754-3888
Hrs Avail:24

PULLMAN

WHITMAN COUNTY CRISIS LINE/
 LATAH
COUNTY NIGHTLINE
P.O. Box 2615 CS
PULLMAN WA 99163
Crisis Phone 1:(509)332-1505
Business Phone:(509)332-1505
Hrs Avail:24

RICHLAND

CONTACT TRI-CITIES AREA
P.O. Box 684
RICHLAND WA 99352
Crisis Phone 1:(509)943-6606
Business Phone:(509)943-9017
Hrs Avail:24

SEATTLE

*#CRISIS CLINIC
1530 EASTLAKE EAST
SEATTLE WA 98102
Crisis Phone 1:(206)461-3222
Business Phone:(206)461-3210
Hrs Avail:24

SPOKANE

SPOKANE CRISIS SERVICES
SPOKANE CITY COMM MH
S. 107 DIVISION
SPOKANE WA 99202
Crisis Phone 1:(509)838-4428
Business Phone:(509)838-4651
Hrs Avail:24

TACOMA

TACOMA CRISIS LINE
P.O. Box 5007
TACOMA WA 98405
Crisis Phone 1:(206)759-6700
Business Phone:(206)756-5250
Hrs Avail:24

YAKIMA

OPEN LINE/YAKIMA
CENTRAL WASHINGTON
    COMPREHENSIVE MH
P.O. Box 959
YAKIMA WA 98907
Crisis Phone 1:(509)575-4200
STATEWIDE TOLL FREE
    (800)572-8122
Business Phone:(509)575-4084
Hrs Avail:24

WISCONSIN

APPLETON

APPLETON CRISIS INTERVENTION
    CENTER
3365 WEST BREWSTER
APPLETON WI 54914
Crisis Phone 1:(414)731-3211
Business Phone:(414)735-5354
Hrs Avail:24

APPLETON

*LIFE LINE/APPLETON
408½ COLLEGE AVE.
P.O. Box 2474
APPLETON WI 54913
Crisis Phone 1:(414)734-2323
Business Phone:(414)738-5588
Hrs Avail:24

BELOIT

BELOIT HOTLINE
P.O. Box 1293
BELOIT WI 53511
Crisis Phone 1:(608)365-4436
Business Phone:(608)365-4436
Hrs Avail:24

BOSCOBEL

SUICIDE PREVENTION GROUP
401 E. BLUFF ST.
BOSCOBEL WI 53805
Crisis Phone 1:(608)365-4436
Business Phone:(608)365-4436
Hrs Avail:24

CEDARBURG

COPE
OZAUKEE COUNTY HOTLINE
P.O. Box 723
CEDARBURG WI 53012
Crisis Phone 1:(414)377-2673
Business Phone:(414)377-1477
Hrs Avail:24

EAU CLAIRE

* SUICIDE PREVENTION CENTER
1221 WHIPPLE ST.
EAU CLAIRE WI 54701
Crisis Phone 1:(715)834-6040
Business Phone:(715)839-3274
Hrs Avail:24

ELKHORN

* LAKELAND COUNSELING CENTER
HWY NN
P.O. Box 1005
ELKHORN WI 53121
Crisis Phone 1:(414)741-3200
Business Phone:(414)741-3200
Hrs Avail:24

FOND DU LAC

CIC/FOND DU LAC
459 E 1ST ST
FOND DU LAC WI 54935
Crisis Phone 1:(414)929-3535
Business Phone:(414)929-3500
Hrs Avail:24

GREEN BAY

* CRISIS INTERVENTION CENTER/
  GREEN BAY
131 S. MADISON STREET
GREEN BAY WI 54301
Crisis Phone 1:(414)432-8832
Business Phone:(414)432-7855
HRS AVAIL:24/7 DAYS

LA CROSSE

HARBOR HOUSE
1608 MARKET ST.
LA CROSSE WI 54601
Crisis Phone 1:(608)785-0530
Business Phone:
    (608)785-0530 x3516
Hrs Avail:24

LA CROSSE

FIRST CALL FOR HELP
P.O. Box 2373
LA CROSSE WI 54602-2373
FIRST CALL FOR HELP
    (608)782-8010
FIRST CALL WI (800)362-8255
FIRST CALL MN & IA (800)356-9588
Business Phone:(608)782-8010
Hrs Avail:24

MADISON

* EMERGENCY SERVICES MHC OF
  DANE COUNTY, INC.
31 S. HENRY
MADISON WI 53703
Crisis Phone 1:(608)251-2345
Business Phone:(608)251-2341
Hrs Avail:24

MILWAUKEE

UNDERGROUND SWITCHBOARD
P.O. Box 92455
MILWAUKEE WI 53202
Crisis Phone 1:(414)271-3123
Business Phone:(414)271-2810
Hrs Avail:24

OSHKOSH

* CRISIS INTERN. SERV.-HELPLINE,
  INC
471 HIGH AVENUE
OSHKOSH WI 54902
Crisis Phone 1:(414)233-7707
Crisis Phone 2:(414)722-7707
Business Phone:(414)233-7709
Hrs Avail:24

STURGEON BAY

HELPLINE-HELP OF DOOR CO., INC.
P.O. Box 319
STURGEON BAY WI 54235
Crisis Phone 1:(414)743-8818
Business Phone:(414)743-8818
Hrs Avail:24

WISC. RAPIDS

WOO CO. UNIFIED SERVICES
CRISIS INTERV. & REFERRAL
310 DEWEY ST.
WISC. RAPIDS WI 54494
WISCONSIN RAPIDS (715)421-2345
MARSHFIELD (715)384-5555
Business Phone:(715)421-2345
Hrs Avail:24

W. VIRGINIA

CHARLESTON
CONTACT KANAWHA VALLEY
CHRIST CHURCH UNITED
  METHODIST
QUARRIER & MORRIS STS.
CHARLESTON WV 25301
Crisis Phone 1:(304)346-0826
Business Phone:(304)346-0828
Hrs Avail:24

HUNTINGTON
CONTACT HUNTINGTON
520 11TH ST
HUNTINGTON WV 25701
Crisis Phone 1:(304)523-3448
Business Phone:(304)523-3447
Hrs Avail:24

HUNTINGTON
PRESTERA CENTER FOR MH
  SERVICES
3375 U.S. RT. 60 EAST
P.O. Box 8069
HUNTINGTON WV 25705
Crisis Phone 1:(304)525-7851
Business Phone:(304)525-7851
Hrs Avail:24

LEWISBURG
GREENBRIAR VALLEY MH CLINIC
100 CHURCH ST.
LEWISBURG WV 24901
Crisis Phone 1:(304)647-5587
Business Phone:(304)645-3319
Hrs Avail:24

PRINCETON
SOUTHERN HIGHLANDS COMM
  MHC
12TH ST. EXTENSION
PRINCETON WV 24740
Crisis Phone 1:(304)425-9541
Business Phone:(304)425-9541
Hrs Avail:24

WHEELING
UPPER OHIO VALLEY CRISIS
  HOTLINE
P.O. Box 653
WHEELING WV 26003
Crisis Phone 1:(304)234-8161
Business Phone:(304)234-1848
Hrs Avail:24

WYOMING

CHEYENNE
CHEYENNE HELPLINE
P.O. Box 404
CHEYENNE WY 82001
Crisis Phone 1:(307)634-4469
Business Phone:(307)632-4132
Hrs Avail:6 PM TO 7 AM

WORLAND
COMMUNITY CRISIS SERVICE, INC.
P.O. Box 872
WORLAND WY 82401
Crisis Phone 1:(307)347-4991
Business Phone:(307)347-4992
Hrs Avail:24

TELEPHONE NUMBERS FOR CONTACTING MAJOR SURVIVORS OF SUICIDE SUPPORT GROUPS

Alabama

Birmingham	Mental Health Association of Jefferson County	(205)322-0445
Mobile	Survivors of Suicide	(205)343-3781 or 342-0616

Alaska

Anchorage	Survivors of Suicide	(907)276-1600

Arizona

Mesa	Survivors of Suicide	(602)844-7320
Tucson	Survivors of Suicide	(602)323-9373

California

Burlingame	Suicide Prevention & Crisis Center of San Mateo County	(415)877-5604
Los Angeles	Survivors Support Group	(213)657-6014 or 386-5111
Napa	North Bay Suicide Prevention	(707)257-3470
Pacific Grove	Survivors of Suicide	(408)375-6966
Sacramento	Friends for Survival	(916)392-0664
San Anselmo	Marin County Grief Counseling Program	(415)454-4566
San Diego	Survivors of Suicide Survivors of Suicide	(619)295-7661 (619)232-2753 or 422-4867
San Francisco	Self-Help Grief Group	(415)752-4866
San Jose	Suicide Support Group	(408)299-6250
Walnut Creek	Survivors of Suicide Support Group	(415)944-0645

Colorado

Boulder	Boulder Resources for SOS	(303)440-0907
Colorado Springs	Heartbeat/Colorado Springs	(303)633-4601 or 596-2575
Denver	American Association of Suicidology Heartbeat/Metro Denver	(303) 692-0985 (303) 777-9234

Colorado (Con't)

Grand Junction	Seasons	(303)245-6039
Pueblo	Heartbeat/Pueblo	(303)545-2477

Connecticut

Middletown	Survivors of Suicide	(203)344-3043
Newington	Safe Place/Samaritans	(203)249-0582
Wethersfield	Jo Ann Mecca and Priscilla Vasalla	(203)563-3035

Florida

Bradenton	Living Afterwards	(813)753-1247
Jacksonville	Survivors Group	(904)387-5641
Jupiter	The Courage to Survive	(305)747-3165
Orlando	Survivors of Suicide	(305)425-2624
Pinellas Park	Pinellas Emergency Mental Health Services, Inc.	(813) 545-5636 or 545-5637
Tampa	Supportive Services for Survivors of Suicide	(813)238-8411 or 238-8821

Georgia

Albany	Suicide Survivors	(912)888-4047
Atlanta	Survivors of Suicide	(404)256-9797

Illinois

Aurora	Survivors of Suicide	(312)897-5531
Belleville	Survivors of Suicide	(618)397-0963
Chicago	L.O.S.S.	(312)236-5172
Geneseo	Transition	(309)944-4435
Oak Brook	The Compassionate Friends	(312)323-5010

Indiana

Fort Wayne	We the Living	(219)432-6293
Hammond	STRESS (Striving to Reach Every Survivor of Suicide	(219)845-2720
Indianapolis	Survivors of Suicide	(317)353-4743
South Bend	Survivors of Suicide	(219)287-0363

Iowa

Cedar Rapids	Foundation II Suicide Survivors Group	(319)362-2174
Iowa City	Ray of Hope, Inc.	(319)337-9890
Waterloo	Suicide Grief Support Group	(319)234-1724 or 233-5538

Kansas

Bird City	Heartbeat/Northwest Kansas	(913)734-2626 or 734-2502
Parsons	Parsons Ray of Hope	(316)421-3254
Topeka	Survivors of Suicide	(913)357-5119 or 232-5086

Kentucky

| Louisville | Survivors of Suicide | (502)895-9122 |

Louisiana

Metairie	Survivors of Suicide	(504)529-3415 or 834-7589
Monroe	Support after Suicide	(318)323-9479
New Orleans	Coping with Suicide	(504)866-3792

Maine

| Biddeford | Biddeford Ray of Hope | (207)284-4360 |

Maryland

Baltimore	Seasons: Suicide Bereavement, Inc.	(301)321-4539
Bethesda	Seasons: Suicide Bereavement, Inc.	(301)951-3665
Mechanicsville	Survivors of Suicide	(301)884-5503
Riverdale	Surviving Suicide	(301)577-3140
Rockville	Seasons: Suicide Bereavement, Inc.	(301)460-4677

Massachusetts

Falmouth	Safe Place/Samaritans	(617)548-8900 or 771-7770 or 255-1888
Framingham	Safe Place/Samaritans	(617)875-4500
Lawrence	Safe Place	(617)688-0030

Michigan

Alpena	Survivors of Suicide	(517)354-2781
Ann Arbor	Survivors of Suicide	(313)966-4747
Detroit	Survivors of Suicide	(313)224-7000
Edwardsburg	Michiana S.O.S. Support Group	(616)699-7472
Flint	Catholic Social Services	(313)232-9950
Grand Ledge	Survivors of Suicide of East Lansing	(517)626-6317
Grand Rapids	West Michigan Survivors of Suicide	(616)455-0372
Mattowan	Survivors of Suicide	(616)624-6755
Port Huron	Center for Human Resources	(313)985-5168

Missouri

Crestwood	Survivors after Suicide	(314)961-0608
Joplin	Joplin Ray of Hope	(417)782-1443
St. Louis	Life Crisis Services, Inc., SOS	(314)647-3100

New Hampshire

Concord	Central New Hampshire Community Mental Health Services, Inc.	(603)228-1511, ext. 278

New Jersey

New Brunswick	Survivors of Suicide Team	(201)249-8500

New Mexico

Albuquerque	Survivors of Suicide	(505)844-9273 or 298-4295

New York

Albany	Safe Place	(518)463-2323
Brooklyn	Friends & Relatives	(718)643-1946
Ithaca	After Suicide	(607)272-1505

North Carolina

Charlotte	To Life	(704)332-LIFE
Raleigh	Hopeline, Inc.	(919)755-6588

North Dakota

Fargo	Suicide Bereavement Support Group	(701)232-6471

Ohio

Akron	Survivors	(216)864-7743
Canton	Crisis Center, Survivors	(216)452-6000
Cleveland	Survivors, Inc.	(216)252-5800
Columbus	Survivors of Suicide	(614)457-7876
	Survivors of Suicide	(614)464-2646 or 279-9382
	Survivors of Suicide	(614)444-0800
Dayton	Survivors of Suicide	(513)223-9096 or 223-4777
Mount Gilead	Hopeline, Inc.	(419)947-2520
Owensville	Cincinnati Survivors of Suicide	(513)732-1697
Springfield	Survivors of Suicide	(513)399-9500
Urbana	Survivors of Suicide	(513)788-2575
Westerville	Survivors of Suicide	(614)882-9339
Youngstown	Survivors of Suicide	(216)747-5111

Pennsylvania

Monroeville	Survivors of Suicide, Allegheny East	(412)371-6606
Philadelphia	Survivors of Suicide	(215)545-2242
Quakertown	Survivors Support	(215)538-2686

Rhode Island

Providence	Samaritans (Safe Place)	(401)272-4044

Tennessee

Memphis	Survivors of Suicide	(901)274-7477
South Fulton	Survivors of Suicide	(901)479-2688

Texas

Amarillo	Survivors Group	(806)376-4251
Corpus Christi	Survivors after Suicide	(512)993-7416
Dallas	Dallas Suicide and Crisis Center	(214)824-7020
Fort Worth	Survivors of Suicide	(817)924-9201
Houston	Crisis Intervention of Houston	(713)527-9864
Plano	Plano Crisis Center	(214)881-0081

Vermont

Brattleboro	Survivors of Suicide	(802)254-5593
Rutland	Survivors of Suicide	(802)775-5595

Virginia

Alexandria	Suicide Survivor Support Group	(703)273-3454 or 360-6910
Charlottesville	Seasons: Suicide Bereavement	(804)971-5745
Portsmouth	Survivors of Suicide Support Group	(804)399-6393
Virginia Beach	Survivors of Suicide	(804)481-1211

Washington

Kennewick	Survivors of Suicide	(509)783-7416
Seattle	Crisis Clinic	(206)447-3210
Vancouver	Surviving Suicide Trauma	(206)694-7468

West Virginia

West Liberty	Suicide Survivors Support Group	(304)336-7863

Wisconsin

Eau Claire	Suicide Support Survivors Group	(715)839-4121 or 834-3176
Madison	Survivors of Suicide	(608)251-2345
Milwaukee	Survivors Helping Survivors	(414)649-6000
Milwaukee	Survivors of Suicide	(414)442-4638

CANADA
Alberta

Edmonton	Aid Service of Edmonton/Suicide Bereavement Program L.O.S.S.	(403)426-3242 (403)476-7035
Lethbridge	The Samaritans	(403)320-9334
Red Deer	Bereavment Support Services Program	(403)342-2266

British Columbia

Vancouver	S.A.F.E.R.	(604)879-9251

Ontario

Hamilton	Council on Suicide Prevention	(416)549-8076 or 523-6611
London	Canadian Mental Health Assn./Survivors of Suicide	(519)434-9178
Toronto	Survivor Support Program	(416)595-1716
Windsor	Bereavement Services	(519)255-7440

Saskatchewan

Saskatoon	St. Patrick's Survivors of Suicide	(309)384-2504

MENTAL HEALTH ORGANIZATIONS

For information concerning psychiatrists write:

American Psychiatric Association
1400 K Street N.W.
Washington, DC 20005

For information concerning psychoanalysts write:

American Psychoanalytic Association
309 E. 49th Street
New York, NY 10022

For information concerning psychologists write:

American Psychological Association
1200 17th Street N.W.
Washington, DC 20036

For information concerning professional counselors write:

National Board Certified Counselors
5999 Stevenson Avenue
Alexandria, VA 22304

For information concerning social workers write:

National Association of Social Workers
7981 Eastern Avenue
Silver Spring, MD 20910

For information concerning marriage and family therapists write:

American Association for Marriage and Family Therapy
1717 K Street N.W. #407
Washington, DC 20006

For a referral list of active members of the Academy of Ortho-molecular Psychiatry write:

> David Hawkins, M.D.
> 1691 Northern Boulevard
> Manhasset, Long Island, NY 11030

> Alan Cott, M.D.
> 303 Lexington Avenue
> New York, NY 10016

For a referral list of nutritionally oriented doctors write:

> Linus Pauling Institute of Science and Medicine
> 2700 Sand Hill Road
> Menlo Park, CA 94025

For additional information and resources on Behavior Therapy write:

> Association for Advancement of Behavior Therapy
> 420 Lexington Avenue
> New York, NY 10017

For additional information and resources on Rational-Emotive Therapy write:

> Institute for Rational-Emotive Therapy
> 45 East 65th Street
> New York, NY 10021

For additional information and resources on Reality Therapy write:

> Institute for Reality Therapy
> 7301 Medical Center Drive
> Suite 202
> Canoga Park, CA 91307

Additional recommended readings for helping yourself or helping others who are suicidal:

Gordon, S. *When Living Hurts.* New York: United Hebrew Congregation, 1986.

Kiev, A. *The Courage to Live.* New York: Thomas Y Crowell, 1979.

FILM AND VIDEO RESOURCES
ON SUICIDE PREVENTION

1. *Amy and the Angel* (Film)

A terrific movie for abetting discussion after reading the "It's a Wonderful Life" chapter in this book. This 16mm, 30-minute movie shows a 17-year-old youngster what life would have been like if she had never been born. I've utilized this movie with junior high, high school, and professional groups, and one thing I can promise you is that the happy ending never fails to bring tears from the audience, so bring a generous supply of Kleenex! Order from Coronet/MTI Teleprogram, 108 Wilmot Road, Deerfield, IL 60015 (1-800-621-7870).

2. *A Tribute to Tim* (Video)

I once showed a group of teachers and counselors all the audo-visual resources I routinely utilize during my suicide prevention lectures, and they unanimously chose this one as the best. This VHS production is short and moves at a very fast pace. The video shows a suicidal student being saved by his friend even when the first teacher they seek out is too busy to help. If you believe kids model the behavior of others (and by now you should), then this is the video you will want to show. The fact that the music is intense, the plot races along, and the saga is complete with a trick ending ensures that no one will fall asleep while viewing this cliff hanger. Contact the Suicide Prevention & Education Center, 982 Eastern Parkway, Louisville, KY 40217 (502-635-5924).

3. *But Jack Was a Good Driver* (Film)

Though bell bottom pants and outdated clothing from 1974 generally produce a few chuckles from the audience, this movie does a fairly good job of familiarizing young teens and adults with the warning signs of suicide. As Bob and his classmate Ed stroll through the cemetery they begin to wonder whether Bob's death was really a suicide rather than an accident. The fact that Bob is portrayed by young Larry Wilcox (remember Eric Estrada's blond-haired partner from the TV show "Chips Patrol") certainly gives this 16mm, 15-minute movie a shot in the arm for success. If you're interested, write McGraw-Hill Films, Box 641, Del Mar, CA 92014 (1-800-421-0833).

4. *Help Me! The Story of Teenage Suicide* (Film)

   This 25-minute movie is unique in that it not only shows you how people reacted inappropriately to the suicidal individual, but how they might have responded to her in a more productive and helpful manner. A good all-around learning tool for teens and adults. Available from SL Productions, Box 41108, Los Angeles, CA   90014   (213-254-8528).

5. *In Loveland: Study of Teen-age Suicide* (Film)

   This is an excellent 16mm, 28-minute movie for professional counselors, teachers, nurses, and hotline voluteers. I would not, however, recommend it as a tool for youth groups or for suicide prevention in the classroom. Produced by ABC news, this movie tries to trace the events which led 15-year-old Mark Cada of Loveland, Colorado, to take his own life. Mark's sister, parents, friends, and his family's pastor do an amateur psychological autopsy of sorts to see what went wrong. If you want mixed audience reactions to produce discussion from a professional group, then this is the medium for which you are looking. Coronet/MTI Teleprogram, 108 Wilmot Road, Deerfield, IL 60015 (1-800-621-7870).

6. *Suicide: The Warning Signs* (Film)

   If your agency, school, or institution is on a budget and you would like just one good all-around suicide prevention tool, I would suggest this 16mm, color, 24-minute film. I have shown this movie to over 16,000 individuals of all ages and from nearly every walk of life without a single complaint. Three dramatized vignettes (a 14-year-old class clown who is accident prone, a young woman dissatisfied with her self-image who is depressed, and a college student upset over the loss of his girlfriend and poor academic performance) illuminate the danger signals of suicide as well as the steps needed to give psychological first aid. This film has my seal of approval and soon will have yours too. Coronet/MTI Teleprogram, 108 Wilmot Road,   Deerfield, IL 60015   (1-800-621-7870).

7. *The Inner Voice in Suicide* (Video)

This hard-hitting video cassette runs 32 minutes and is available in both ¾" and ½" sizes. Every clinician who plans to do therapy with suicidal individuals should see this tape. Dr. Robert Firestone, clinical psychologist, provides an in-depth interview with a 38-year-old woman who attempted suicide a number of years before the video was produced. Her self-critical thought patterns, ambivalence, and intense self-hatred are clearly illuminated. This movie is not intended—nor should it ever be utilized—for teen or general public suicide prevention seminars. It is, however, the finest audio-visual aid I've seen for helping counselors to dissect the complex ideology under-lying the ultimate act of self-destruction. Direct all inquiries and orders to The Glendon Association, 2049 Century Park East, Suite 3000, Los Angeles, CA 90067 (213-552-0431).

SOURCES OF SUICIDE INFORMATION, BROCHURES, AND PAMPHLETS

American Association of Suicidology
2459 S. Ash
Denver, CO 80222
(303)692-0985

Youth Suicide National Center
1825 Eye St. NW, Suite 400
Washington, DC 20006
(202) 429-2016

National Committee for Youth Suicide Prevention
1811 Trousdale Drive
Burlingame, CA 94010
(415)877-5604

BOOKS FOR SURVIVORS OF SUICIDE

Hewett, J. *After Suicide.* Philadelphia: Westminster Press, 1980.

Bolton, I. *My Son, My Son. . . A Guide to Healing After a Suicide in the Family.* Available by writing Link Counseling Center, 218 Hilderbrand Ave., Atlanta, GA 30328—$10.95 plus $2.00 postage.

Rosenfeld, L., and Prupas, M. *Left Alive: After a Suicide Death in the Family.* Springfield: Charles C. Thomas, 1984.

NEWSLETTERS FOR SURVIVORS

Survivors of Suicide Quarterly
Suicide Prevention Center
184 Salem Avenue
Dayton, OH 45406
First issue free, $8.00 per year

Afterwords
Adina Wrobleski
5124 Grove Street
Minneapolis, MN 55436-2481
$10.00 per year

PAMPHLETS FOR SURVIVORS

Grief after Suicide pamphlet
Mental Health Association
414 West Moreland Blvd., Room 101
Waukesha, WI 53186
$.50

After Suicide: A Unique Grief Process brochure
Eleanora "Betsy" Ross
Ray of Hope, Inc.
Box 2323
Iowa City, IA 52244

Care of the Suicide Survivor pamphlets
Suicide Prevention Center, Inc.
184 Salem Avenue
Dayton, OH 45406
single copies free

SOURCE OF GENERAL COUNSELING AND THERAPY MATERIALS FOR PROFESSIONALS AND PEER COUNSELORS

Accelerated Publishers
3400 Kilgore Avenue
Muncie, IN 47304
(317)284-7511

SOURCE OF SUICIDE PREVENTION LECTURES AND SUICIDE SURVIVORS EXCHANGE INFORMATION

Howard Rosenthal, Ed.D., NCC
7548 Parkdale 3D
Clayton, MO 63105

ABOUT THE AUTHOR

ABOUT THE AUTHOR

Dr. Howard Rosenthal is one of the most popular behavioral science lecturers in the Midwest. In the past three years alone, over 30,000 individuals have heard his suicide prevention presentations. He has been chosen as the keynote speaker for a number of large workshops, and his articles on mental health have been published in the U.S. and overseas.

Dr. Rosenthal has over thirteen years of clinical experience including three years in which he served as the program director for Life Crisis Services, Inc., a suicide-crisis intervention center in St. Louis, MO, where he ran one of the largest suicide survivors groups in the country.

He has been a guest on major radio and television shows and has been quoted in numerous newspaper articles. In addition, he has appeared and consulted in suicide prevention films and videos.

He received his doctorate in counseling psychology from St. Louis University, is a national certified counselor, and a licensed professional counselor in the state of Missouri. He currently has a private practice in St. Louis, MO, is a therapist at the Stress Center of St. Charles County, and teaches courses for Maryville College and the St. Louis Community College District.